D1243659

THE ESSENTIAL GUIDE FOR PARENTS

Family Finance

ANN DOUGLAS
ELIZABETH LEWIN

Dearborn™
Trade Publishing
A **Kaplan Professional** Company

WINNETKA-NORTHFIELD
PUBLIC LIBRARY DISTRICT
WINNETKA, IL
446-7220

This publication is designed to provide accurate and authoritative information in regard to the subject matter covered. It is sold with the understanding that the publisher is not engaged in rendering legal, accounting, or other professional service. If legal advice or other expert assistance is required, the services of a competent professional should be sought.

Vice President and Publisher: Cynthia A. Zigmund
Editorial Director: Donald J. Hull
Senior Project Editor: Trey Thoelcke
Interior Design: Lucy Jenkins
Cover Design: Design Solutions
Typesetting: Elizabeth Pitts

© 2001 by Ann Douglas and Elizabeth Lewin

Published by Dearborn Trade, a Kaplan Professional Company

All rights reserved. The text of this publication, or any part thereof, may not be reproduced in any manner whatsoever without written permission from the publisher.

Printed in the United States of America

01 02 03 10 9 8 7 6 5 4 3 2 1

Library of Congress Cataloging-in-Publication Data

Douglas, Ann, 1963-
   Family finance : the essential guide for parents / Ann Douglas, Elizabeth Lewin.
     p.   cm.
Includes index.
   ISBN 0-7931-4356-X (7.25 × 9 pbk)
   1. Finance, Personal. 2. Parents—Finance, Personal.   I. Lewin,
Elizabeth. II. Title.
   HG179 .D675 2001
   332.024′0431—dc21

                                          2001000681

Dearborn Trade books are available at special quantity discounts to use as premiums and sales promotions, or for use in corporate training programs. For more information, please call the special sales department at 800-621-9621, ext. 4364, or write to Dearborn Financial Publishing, Inc., 155 N. Wacker Drive, Chicago, IL 60606-1719.

DEDICATION

To Julie, Scott, Erik, and Ian, my four little tax deductions.
—A.D.

To Taylor, Matthew, and Sarah, my three March grandchildren.
—E.L.

CONTENTS

Why a Book about Family Finances?

· ·

While the bookstore shelves are overflowing with books on personal finance, what's been missing up until now is a book that's written specifically for the people who need it most: parents with young children. Some skeptics might argue that there's no need for a financial planning book for parents. After all, why should the rules of the financial planning game change just because you've got a baby drooling on your shoulder?

A WHOLE NEW BALL GAME

Like it or not, the rules of the game do change significantly the moment you become a parent. That eight-pound bundle of joy alters everything about your life, including your financial situation.

You already know how much having a baby has changed your eating and sleeping patterns. (Remember that there was a time in the not-so-distant past when you could sleep in as late as you wanted on weekends, and when your idea of eating out meant sitting down in a restaurant rather than hitting the local fast food restaurant drive through!) What you might not have stopped to consider, however, is just how much becoming a parent has changed your financial habits as well.

If you're like most new parents, you have probably experienced a fair bit of turbulence on the financial front since your baby first arrived on the scene.

- Your household income may have been through a roller coaster ride since junior made his grand entrance. You may have seen your household income shrink significantly while you or your partner were on maternity leave, or disappear altogether if you decided to take an extended, unpaid leave or quit your job to stay at home with your baby.

- You may have seen your personal debt levels skyrocket if your income dropped but you failed to adjust your spending habits. You don't have to be a rocket scientist to figure out that you need to cut back on your expenditures when your income takes a hit, but a surprising number of couples fall into this trap after baby arrives. We happen to think this problem arises because the majority of new parents are too sleep-deprived to worry about financial matters. After all, given the choice between sitting down and setting a budget or flopping out on the couch while their colicky baby snatches a catnap in the baby swing, most parents will hit the couch in a second.

- Instead of spending your paychecks on clothes and entertainment as you no doubt did in your prebaby days, now you're more likely to spend your hard-earned cash on stuff for the baby: diapers, clothes, toys, baby equipment, and so on. In fact, we'll hazard a guess that your baby is the best-dressed member of the family. Kind of makes you wonder why she's willing to spend so much time slumming with adults who spend their non-working hours living in sweatshirts covered in every conceivable baby-related stain, now doesn't it!

- You may find it increasingly hard to relate to the financial planning advertisements you see on TV. After all, how can you dutifully max out your 401(k) contributions if you're scrambling to find enough cash to buy a new car seat for your toddler? Similarly, all the hype about mutual funds may leave you scratching your head and wondering if you're doing something wrong. Do other families with young children actually have money to invest in anything other than diapers?

- You may recently have become a homeowner for the very first time, urged to take the plunge by that classic prebaby nesting urge that makes real estate agents rub their hands in glee. If you've been renting up until now, you could find yourself in for a bit of a rough ride financially if you drained your checking account to pay for the lawyer's fees, the land transfer tax, and so on and find yourself hit with one of the unpleasant surprises of home ownership. If, for example, the furnace packs it in on the coldest night of the year or a pipe bursts and sends water pouring through your kitchen ceiling, there's no landlord to call to make the problem go away. Like it or not, the buck stops with you and your checkbook.

- You may find yourself thinking about life insurance, wills, powers of attorney, and other heavy-duty financial issues for the very first time. Now that you're responsible for a child, you may feel a pressing need to create a safety net for your growing family by putting your affairs in order—something that may take you by surprise if you've always taken a fly-by-the-seat-of-your-pants approach to life.

INFORMATION OVERLOAD

It's not difficult to see why many parents with young children find themselves feeling overwhelmed by the amount of financial information they need to master to make the best possible choices for their families. You need to consider so many complex—and conflicting—issues before you can map out a financial game plan for your family, it's easier to ignore the whole subject entirely.

Then too, most families with young children face a time crunch. Who has the time or the inclination to pour through financial planning books, wade through the mountains of content on the growing number of personal finance Web sites, or make sense of those mind-numbing annual reports that the mutual fund companies love to send out?

That's why this book has been organized in bite-sized chunks—so that you can read it as your schedule and to-do list allow. You can either read the book from front to back, or hop from chapter to chapter, zeroing in on the topics that are of greatest interest at a particular time. Either way, you'll find that the book is packed with practical, no-nonsense tips on dealing with the key financial challenges faced by couples with young children, including:

- Keeping your debt level under control when there are a million and one demands on your paycheck

- Avoiding the money-related conflicts that cause problems for so many couples

- Deciding whether it makes financial sense for you (or your partner) to continue working after you start your family

- Identifying your financial goals and coming up with a game plan that will allow you to achieve them

- Determining whether you should focus your efforts on paying down your credit card balances, starting an educational savings plan for your child, or contributing to a 401(k)

- Finding ways to save money on as many items in your family's budget as possible—from food to clothing to utilities to automotive expenses to bank charges

- Starting a nest egg so that you'll have funds available in the event that life tosses an unexpected curve ball your way

- Making sure that you're taking advantage of the tax breaks that are available to families with young children

- Raising money-smart kids

WHAT YOU WON'T FIND IN THIS BOOK

What you won't find in this book is preachy advice from a so-called expert who makes you feel like some kind of financial incompetent because you didn't start contributing to an IRA when you landed your first job flipping hamburgers, or who shakes her head in disgust when she learns that you waste money on donut shop coffee even though there's a perfectly good coffeemaker wasting away on your kitchen counter. We understand the financial challenges faced by parents with young children because we've lived through the "diaper and debt" years ourselves!

You won't benefit from just our experience as you read this book, of course. You'll also hear first-hand accounts of the financial challenges faced by other families. More than 75 parents agreed to share the most intimate details of their financial lives with us as we researched this book—the good, the bad, and the ugly. They told us about the mistakes they made that took them to the brink of bankruptcy and how they managed to get themselves back on solid financial ground. They also offered practical tips on saving money on mortgages, car loans, groceries, and more. Because of their input, *Family Finance* is packed with gems of wisdom that you won't find in any other financial planning book: first-hand advice from real parents who've been there, done that—and lived to tell!

We hope you enjoy the book.

ACKNOWLEDGMENTS

• •

We would like to take this opportunity to thank the members of the *Family Finance* book panel, who shared intimate details of their families' financial affairs with us during the months we researched this book: Leigh Abthorpe, Kim Adam, Beth Ali, Heidi Anderson, John Baker, Misty Baker, Ken Barker, Nicole Barker, Angel Blake, Melissa Blount, Jennifer Blowers, Laurie Caloren, Rose Carré, Anne Cavicchi, Sandra Cloud, Maureen Corbett-Gentile, Cindy Dawson, Sheryl Donnelly, Samantha Downing, Diane Dronyk, Stephanie Estabrook, Elyse Ferguson, Troy Ferguson, Paul Forget, Jane Garver, Laura Gazley, LaRee Goddu, Lori Harasem-Mitchell, Greg Horn, Johnna Horn, Anne Hoover, Toni Howard, Lisa Irvin, Amber Jackson, Debra Young Krizman, Andy Lawler, Michele Lawler, Lisa Levine, Fiona Lozinski, Louise Chatterton Luchuk, Jackie McEachern, Heather McKinnon, Laura & Christopher Molinar, Cindy Mount, Kathie O'Gorman, Lori Peters, Maria Phillips, Jennifer Pitoniak, Kristin Reynolds, Karen Rolfe, Allen Rosen, Jan Rosen, Carol Scott, Jason Scott, David Smith, Sharon Smythe, Mary Spicer, Victoria Stegall, Laura Ann Tripp, Melinda Tuck, Jackie Walti, Dulcie White, Susan Overs Wilson, Pilaar Yule, Susan Yusishen, and Ann K. Zadeh, as well as those panel members who chose to share their experiences anonymously.

We would also like to thank the following people who helped us out behind the scenes while we were researching this book: Julie Riberio, National City Mortgage, Trumbull, Connecticut; Ross Galloway, PaineWebber, New Haven, Connecticut; and Bernadine DiVecchio, Country Living Associates, Westport, Connecticut. Last but not least, we would like to thank our agent, Ed Knappman of New England Publishing Associates, and our editor, Cynthia Zigmund, for their ongoing enthusiasm about and commitment to this project, and the book's technical reviewer, Allyson Lewis, for her helpful comments on the manuscript.

CHAPTER 1

That Was Then, This Is Now

· ·

Prenatal classes don't cover the topic and financial planning books generally choose to ignore it: just how dramatically your financial priorities can change once you decide to take the plunge and become a parent.

It's not difficult to see why your priorities tend to evolve once you start having children. For the first time in your life, you need to consider more than how much money you have to spend on eating out or sprucing up your wardrobe. Suddenly, you have to start thinking about heavy-duty financial issues like life insurance, 401(k)s, and mortgages.

> ## " Money Talk
> · · · · · ·
> "We went from two incomes supporting two people to one income supporting three people!"
> —*Leigh, 31, mother of two*

Cindy, 40, who gave birth to twins five years ago, found that the financial changes brought on by parenthood were huge. "We went from buying grownup toys to children's toys, from planning exotic vacations to planning for family fun time, and from buying leather pants to buying plastic pants! Did starting our family require a big financial adjustment on our part? In a major way!"

THE FINANCIAL HEEBIE-JEEBIES

Some couples find that they start rethinking their financial habits the moment the pregnancy test comes back positive.

"One night, our priority became the children," recalls Diane, a 29-year-old mother of two. "All our money was spent on things for the baby and what the baby might need in the future."

"Before becoming pregnant, I was quite relaxed about money and only had myself to worry about," adds Stephanie, a 26-year-old mother of one. "Starting a family made me want to have an emergency fund—to start putting money away as savings, something I had never done before."

"Having a child changed how I thought about financial matters," notes Christine, 24. "Before that, I was in a university, having fun and living life to its fullest, but with the birth of my daughter, I realized that I had to start saving money, spending less on myself and spending everything on her. Mutual funds, education plans, life insurance—these became my priorities."

Your financial habits are likely to undergo a more dramatic transformation if you and your partner decide to go from two incomes to one after your children arrive.

Kate and David, 40-year-old parents of two young children, made debt reduction a priority once they knew a baby was on the way. "We really focussed on paying off my husband's student loan prior to my leaving my employment in order to eliminate the burden of that debt," Kate recalls.

For Melinda, a 33-year-old mother of three, the emphasis was on reducing household expenses. "After our first child was born, we sold my car. We had to relearn our spending habits and figure out how to cut corners everywhere." (If, like Melinda, you could use a crash course in the art of trimming your budget, you might want to take a sneak peek at Chapter 4. The chapter is filled with practical, nitty-gritty strategies for reducing your family's day-to-day expenditures.)

Show Me the Money!

Start setting aside some money each week from the moment you find out that you're pregnant. If you get in the saving habit early in your pregnancy, you should have a nice nest egg to rely on when you start shopping for baby. Pregnancy is also a great time to focus on paying off any personal debt you've acquired over the years. Who knows? If you're lucky, you might even manage to get rid of your own student loan before you have to start saving for junior's education!

Money Talk

"I always worked a lot and we always had extra money to spend. Money worries have been the most stressful thing about parenting so far!"
—Lori, 27, mother of one

Of course, not everyone has the luxury of getting their financial house in order prior to starting a family. If, as is the case with many couples, your pregnancy is unplanned, the financial fallout can be considerable. "My family was started by accident," says Heidi, a 23-year-old single parent. "It was a totally major adjustment for me. I was living with my mother, making $12 an hour, and spending every cent I earned on whatever. I didn't have a car or any real bills. I had no concept of rent, daycare fees, groceries, and so on. I did not budget for anything. It was only after my son was a year old that I finally managed to be self-reliant and move out of my mother's house."

On the other hand, not every parent-to-be finds it necessary to undergo a total financial transformation the moment the pregnancy test comes back positive. Many are surprised by how little their financial situation changes when they start their families. "I have always lived on a budget, saved for rainy days, and looked to the future," explains Krista, a 32-year-old mother of one. "So when Ryan was born, I didn't find it hard to make the budget continue to work. Ryan's needs came first and I made sure he didn't go without. We would just go without somewhere else. This wasn't hard for us because we lived like this even before he was born."

More often than not, however, there are some lifestyle changes involved—a fact that leaves parents like 24-year-old Christine feeling grateful that expectant parents have nine months to get their financial act together. "Pregnancy gives you time to prepare for the changes that having a baby bring, even financial ones. When you look at diapers, formula, food, clothes, you realize how quickly money is spent. Having a baby was a major financial adjustment, but not one that happened overnight. My situation changed rather gradually, along with my belly."

Paul and Cyndie, both 34, decided to postpone starting their family until they were in their late 20s. That gave them the opportunity to establish their careers and sow their financial wild oats before they became parents. Paul explains: "One of the main reasons that held me back from having kids earlier in life was my worry that it would have a major impact on our finances . . . However, the very fact that we were ready for a family reshaped our financial priorities. We were ready to settle down. We had done some travelling and led a pretty full social life. Once Nicolas came along, outings, events, and trips were no longer important."

WHAT IT REALLY COSTS TO HAVE CHILDREN

The latest statistics about the cost of raising children are enough to scare you into refilling that birth control pill prescription. According to the U.S. Department of Agriculture, a middle-income family can expect to spend more than $160,000 to raise a child from birth to age 18 (see Figure 1.1). For higher-income families, the total is closer to $234,000. (Clearly, those designer togs and high-priced educational toys really add up over time!)

FIGURE 1.1

Annual Expenditure Per Child by Husband-Wife Families by Family Income and Expenditure Type: 1999

Age of Child	Total	Housing	Food	Transpor-tation	Clothing	Health Care	Child care/ Education	Misc.[1]
Income: less than $36,800								
Less than 2 years old	6080	2320	860	730	380	430	760	600
3 to 5 years old	6210	2290	960	700	370	410	860	620
6 to 8 years old	6310	2210	1240	820	410	470	510	650
9 to 11 years old	6330	2000	1480	890	460	510	310	680
12 to 14 years old	7150	2230	1560	1000	770	510	220	860
15 to 17 years old	7050	1800	1680	1350	680	550	360	630
Income: $36,800-61,900								
Less than 2 years old	8450	3140	1030	1090	450	560	1250	930
3 to 5 years old	8660	3110	1190	1060	440	530	1380	950
6 to 8 years old	8700	3030	1520	1180	480	610	890	990
9 to 11 years old	8650	2820	1790	1250	530	660	580	1020
12 to 14 years old	9390	3050	1800	1360	900	670	420	1190
15 to 17 years old	9530	2620	2000	1720	800	700	730	960
Income: more than $61,900								
Less than 2 years old	12500	4990	1370	1520	590	640	1880	1560
3 to 5 years old	12840	4960	1550	1500	580	620	2050	1580
6 to 8 years old	12710	4880	1870	1610	630	700	1410	1610
9 to 11 years old	12600	4670	2170	1680	690	760	980	1650
12 to 14 years old	13450	4900	2280	1800	1140	760	750	1820
15 to 17 years old	13800	4470	2400	2180	1030	800	1330	1590

[1]Expenses include personal care items, entertainment, and reading material.

Source: Department of Agriculture, Center for Nutrition Policy, and Promotion, *Expenditures for Children by Families 1998 Annual Report*

Think that's scary? Here's an even more frightening statistic! *U.S. News and World Report* estimates that it can cost as much as $1.4 million to raise a child to age 18. Of course, you have to take these particular figures with a grain of salt: the journalist who wrote the article in question factored in "acquisition costs" of up to $50,000 to cover the costs of infertility treatments for couples who are having difficulty conceiving and $1 million in forgone wages for time that one or both parents missed from work for family-related reasons!

Does this mean that only the wealthiest of couples can afford to have children? Should you be prepared to slap your paystub on the table when you go to see your doctor for a preconception checkup to prove to the world that you've got the financial resources to raise a child?

Hardly.

What the statistics fail to point out is that it is possible to juggle your budget and lifestyle to provide for the needs of your growing family. If, for example, you or your partner decides to stay at home to raise your children for at least the first few years, you can chalk up some significant savings in the child care column. Similarly, if you borrow baby items or shop second-hand, you can bring that first-year clothing figure down considerably.

The statistics also fail to tell you how to adjust for the costs associated with second and subsequent children. While you may spend a small fortune on baby gear for your first-born, any other children you have will be able to reuse much of that equipment. Unless you're blessed with triplets who each require their own car seat and high chair at the same time, you can figure that second and subsequent

Facts and Figures
• • • • • •

According to the Census Bureau, children under the age of 19 currently make up 29 percent of the total U.S. population.

children aren't going to cost you quite as much as their older brother or sister. These economies of scale carry over to other budget lines as well. Certain costs, like shelter, are unlikely to double if you have two children as opposed to just one—unless, of course, you decide to move out of your tiny bachelor apartment and into a 3,000-square-foot monster home!

Finally, you aren't expected to cough up the entire $160,000 at once. If you were, the birthrate would be next to zero! Even if you take the figures at face value and assume that you are going to spend $160,000 on each child over the next 18 years, keep in mind that you're only talking about an extra $170 per week—a much less frightening figure.

The moral of the story? There's enough to worry about when you're a parent. Don't let statistics like this make you crazy! Instead, read this book, arm yourself with the facts, and stop panicking about where the $160,000 is going to come from.

CHAPTER 2

Till Debt Do Us Part

Why So Many Families End Up Hitting the Debt Wall

• •

Despite what many people believe, it's not those late third-trimester shopping trips that do in the budgets of many new parents (although, frankly, those weekly trips to Toys-R-Us don't exactly help!). It's the fact that many parents—particularly first-time parents—forget to adjust their spending habits to reflect the fact that their financial situation has changed.

As we noted in the previous chapter, new parents often find themselves faced with a double-edged sword. At the very time when their expenses are skyrocketing, one partner or the other ends up sacrificing a paycheck to take some time off work to care for the new arrival. In some cases, the decision to stay home with baby is temporary; in others, it's permanent. Either way, the family budget can take a significant hit.

That's something that Melinda and Robert, both 33, discovered for themselves when he switched jobs while she was pregnant with their second child. "There was a large adjustment in salary, and gone were any bonuses and benefits such as drug and dental plans," she recalls. "We found that we had to use credit cards to pay for anything other than mortgages, utilities, and groceries. Diapers, shampoo, and similar items were all purchased with a credit card. Needless to say, we found ourselves with a large credit card debt. We solved our problem, not overnight, but by gradually learning how to trim our expenses and by putting any lump sum of money that we received against our credit card balance."

Cindy, 40, and John, 42, experienced similar financial difficulties after Cindy changed careers following the birth of their twins five years ago. Faced with the choice of commuting two hours each way or setting up her own business so that she could spend more time with her young family, Cindy decided to leave her high-paying job in the big city to take a shot at entrepreneurship.

Like most entrepreneurs, Cindy found that it took a while for her business to start turning a profit—something that led to a major financial crunch for her and John. Because Cindy was and still is the sole breadwinner for the household—John is unable to work because of a disability—the family's lifestyle took a major hit. They began relying on credit to get by. The result? An extraordinary amount of debt. Cindy and John have spent the past few years trying to get back on their feet financially. "We have lost almost everything we worked for in the past," Cindy admits. "But budgeting, changing our lifestyle, and really coming to terms with how we spend our money has helped us to solve our financial problems. More planning and less spending have been the keys to turning things around."

> ## Money Talk
> • • • • • • •
> "Communicate. Make sure your partner understands where you're coming from and has a good idea of your comfort zone when it comes to financial matters."
> —*Kristin, 30, mother of one*

FOR RICHER AND FOR POORER

While Cindy and John experienced tremendous stress as a result of their financial difficulties, unlike many couples, they managed to refrain from blaming one another for the mess they found themselves in, choosing to focus instead on finding shared solutions to their money woes. "You can't take it out on each other: you need to just work at making it better," Cindy insists. "Our attitude was, 'We made the decision to spend the money as we did, so now we both have to be responsible for regaining lost ground.'" In the end, they both agreed that extra frills like eating out would have to be put on hold until the family was back on more solid ground financially.

A lot of couples could learn a lesson or two from Cindy and John. According to a recent study, seven out of ten couples fight about money on a regular basis.

The problem, according to University of Denver psychology professor Howard Markham, who was interviewed in a recent article in *Money,* is that arguments about money frequently mask deeper problems in the relationship. "Too often, talk about money turns into a test of wills rather than a rational discussion about goals."

The financial tug of war is more likely to be a problem for couples in which the partners have radically different

> ## Facts and Figures
> • • • • • • •
> According to a recent study conducted by *Working Mother* magazine, the female partner assumes responsibility for managing the family's finances in two-thirds of dual-income households.

spending styles. If, for example, one partner is a natural-born saver while the other considers credit cards to be the eighth wonder of the world.

Are You and Your Partner Financial Soulmates?

Money tends to be one of those issues that is seldom discussed until after the honeymoon is over, and for good reason: it's a lot easier to ignore many of the less-than-flattering characteristics of your beloved before you're living under the same roof!

You might, of course, get a few hints about your partner's financial style while you're dating. Perhaps her idea of a hot date involves cruising the thrift shops looking for some second-hand treasures. Or maybe his idea of fun is spending the night on the town, buying rounds of drinks for all his friends so that he can impress everyone with his generosity.

While you might find yourself feeling mildly annoyed by your partner's spending habits before you start living under the same roof, for the most part, the rose-colored glasses don't come off until after the honeymoon is long behind you—typically when you and your partner are faced with your first major financial decision, like buying a house or having a baby. That's when it becomes obvious for the very first time to what extent your financial styles are compatible. (See quiz in Figure 2.1.)

So what do you do if you discover that you and your partner have radically different spending styles? Part ways? Agree to disagree? Try to find some financial middle ground?

It depends.

If the rest of your relationship is solid, you've got a strong incentive to try to find ways to repair the financial trouble spots. If, on the other hand, you're fighting about sex, conflicting career goals, and everything else under the sun, perhaps there isn't much of a relationship left to save.

This was certainly the case for Christine, 24, a single mother of one, and her former partner. "Nine months after the birth of our child, my partner and I separated. One of the reasons was finances. My partner still lived life to the fullest. He was a waiter who did not save money, still bought luxury items without thought to the future, and never gave thought to future expenses that would overwhelm us. I tried to save money, but did not have any control over him. Controlling someone else's spending habits is next to impossible because you can't have the money police follow them around all the time."

Other couples go through an initial period of adjustment when they first set up house together.

FIGURE 2.1
Quiz: Are You Financially Compatible?

Wondering if you and your partner are financial soulmates, or whether your financial styles are about as compatible as oil and water? Here's a quick way to find out. Place a check mark under the "Me" column for a particular statement if you agree with it. Place a check mark under the "My Partner" column if you think your partner would agree with it. (Better yet, let him or her answer this part of the quiz!) When you're finished responding to all of the statements, you'll have an idea how closely your financial styles match up.

	Me	My Partner
I spend a lot of time worrying about money.	❑	❑
I have a pretty good idea of our net worth at any given time.	❑	❑
I hate owing money to anyone, including the bank. I wish we were debt free.	❑	❑
A penny spent on interest payments is a penny wasted.	❑	❑
I don't like to carry an outstanding balance on my credit card.	❑	❑
One of my goals is to be mortgage-free as soon as possible.	❑	❑
I don't mind doing without certain things if it means we can save some money.	❑	❑
I think through my purchases carefully. I'm not an impulse buyer.	❑	❑
Setting aside a nest egg makes me feel secure.	❑	❑
I typically use my income tax refund to get ahead financially (e.g., paying off debts).	❑	❑
Money isn't much of a worry to me.	❑	❑
I have no idea what my net worth is, nor do I particularly care.	❑	❑
Debt doesn't bother me all that much. Money is a tool to get the things you want in life.	❑	❑
I'd rather spend money on interest charges than postpone a purchase indefinitely.	❑	❑
I don't mind owing money on my credit card if it means I'm able to purchase the things I want.	❑	❑
I'm not in any particular rush to pay off my mortgage. I'd rather use the money for other things.	❑	❑
I hate depriving myself of things I want in order to save money.	❑	❑
If I see a great deal on something, I want to buy it right then and there. Why wait?	❑	❑
Knowing that I can borrow money if I need it makes me feel secure.	❑	❑
I typically use my income tax refund to purchase things I want.	❑	❑

The first ten statements are the types of things a saver would say. The next ten are the kinds of statements that a spender would make. Are you and your partner savers, spenders, or are you each a little of both? (Hint: Some people act like savers in some situations and spenders in other situations.) How compatible are your financial styles?

"My husband and I were young when we got married and we had very different spending habits," admits Kathleen, a 32-year-old mother of one. "I must say I nagged him constantly and I would get very angry, but with time I just gave up. He eventually learned how his free-spending habits were hurting us and he slowly changed his ways by himself. In the beginning, he made me carry all the money and he only used his credit card for gas. Today, he is very careful of his spending. My husband and I are now a great financial team, but it took us a long time to get to this point."

"It was hard for a couple of years," adds Carolyn, a 35-year-old mother of three, whose partner, Doug, had a tendency to overspend during the early years of their marriage. "I would have to be the 'enforcer,' which is not a fun role. I would get completely exasperated when I was trying to save 25 cents on something and he would be spending constantly."

"This has been, and to a degree still is, a major issue for us," says Fiona, a 32-year-old mother of six. "We have had many disagreements and hard times in our marriage because of our initially opposing views on money and its purpose. By setting goals together while keeping each person's individual needs in mind, we were able to come up with a strategy that has allowed us to have some freedom in spending, while at the same time pursuing our dreams."

The fact that you have different spending habits doesn't have to spell doomsday for your relationship. Many couples find ways to work around the problem.

"We are definitely different in our spending habits," explains Laura, a 22-year-old mother of one. "My husband likes to spend his money, and I like to make sure our bills get paid before anything else! In order to help him stop spending, I control the money. If he would like money to spend on the extras, he asks if we have enough money and I answer him honestly."

"Jeff and I have different spending habits," adds Kristin, a 30-year-old mother of one. "He tends to be more of a free spender and is more optimistic about

---

Money Talk
• • • • • • •

"Set up three different bank accounts—one for each partner and one for the household."
—Cindy, 40, mother of two

Show Me the Money!
• • • • • • •

"Allow the one who is the stronger saver to handle the finances, and have the spender try to put some control on their urges, even if that means going on a weekly allowance. In the end, it all comes down to how badly you both want financial success. If it's important, sacrifices have to be made in the short term. You can't just live for today, paycheck to paycheck."
—Paul, 34, currently awaiting the birth of his second child

our financial situation. He's also a lot more comfortable with debt than I am. While I'm not a big saver, I tend to be more conservative and prefer to incur as little debt as possible. It's a struggle, but by talking things through we can usually come to a compromise we both can live with."

"My husband loves to spend money on his hobby, sports card collecting, and I do not have a hobby that is expensive, so I sometimes resent the fact that he takes a fair bit of our money and puts it toward buying sports cards," admits Stephanie, a 26-year-old mother of one. "We've learned to compromise about this issue. We ensure that all of the bills are taken care of and that we've contributed to our savings and spent some money on the family before he can spend any money on his hobby."

"My husband and I have very different spending habits," notes Diane, a 29-year-old mother of two. "I am the spender and he is the saver. This does tend to be an issue because I like to 'get my money's worth.' I believe you get what you pay for, which means I don't always buy the cheapest item available. He likes to buy the cheapest one no matter what. We haven't come to a magic solution yet. We just try to compromise as much as possible."

Couples in which both partners have a tendency to overspend often find it difficult to discipline themselves to make the best financial choices. "My husband and I are both spenders," admits Jackie, a 31-year-old mother of two. "We do save—we make 401(k) contributions and we're saving for our children's education, etc.—but not nearly as much as we could and should. I am responsible for the finances in our house, and I tend to get stressed when I pay the bills each month. I will rant for a few days about how we must do this and that better with our money, but it never seems to happen." So even though there may be some occasional sparring involved, if you and your partner don't see eye to eye on financial matters, the fact that one of you is a saver could be a blessing in disguise.

> **" Money Talk**
> • • • • • • •
>
> "We are fortunate in that we have very similar approaches to money. We've also always earned very similar wages, so that creates a sense of equality."
> —Louise, 28, mother of one

THE DIRTY LITTLE SECRET

Contrary to popular belief, overspenders aren't the only ones who can find themselves experiencing serious money problems. If you're in the habit of living from paycheck to paycheck—and frankly a lot of Americans are!—you could find yourself being blown out of the water financially by one of life's little curve balls, such as a job loss or an unplanned pregnancy.

Kathleen, 32, and Victor, 34, found themselves facing a financial crisis shortly before their son was born. Kathleen explains, "When my husband and I lost our jobs due to downsizing and a plant closing only a couple of months before Tyler was due, I really didn't know what we were going to do. Fortunately, we lived in a small house, we had been saving our money, we already knew how to live on a budget, and we had a loving, supportive family who were there when we needed their help. We made it through a lot better than some others at my husband's plant. Many people lost their homes and eventually their marriages. They just couldn't hold it together financially or emotionally."

Darla, 38, and Marvin, 40—the parents of five children—found themselves faced with a similar crisis when they were hit with two real estate losses over a short period of time. Darla explains, "It started when my husband took a job in another city 250 miles away. We had to sell our home and ended up taking a loss of $35,000. Then we sold a piece of land that we owned and took another loss of $55,000. I started using credit cards to get over some humps, and one thing led to another and we ended up in a snowball situation. We eventually had to take a second mortgage out on our home because I was having some serious medical problems like panic attacks and migraine headaches due to the stress of the financial situation. We are now on the right track again, and I am happy to say that we no longer have any credit cards to get us in trouble. We pay cash for everything so our spending is mostly under control."

The Bottom Line
• • • • • •

When Carolyn, 35, and Doug, 35, hit the debt wall a few years ago, they were forced to change their spending habits overnight. "We cut back on everything," recalls Carolyn, a mother of three. "No meals or coffees out, no magazines, no cable, using the library instead of buying books, and my husband started bringing his lunch to work. I always had plenty of groceries in the house, so we couldn't use the excuse that there was nothing to make for dinner and decide to eat out instead. The most effective way for us to cut our expenses was to simply not carry much money."

Money problems like these couples faced are more common than you might think. In 1998, 1.4 million Americans filed for bankruptcy. The problem is that no one wants to talk about it. Sex may be a perfectly acceptable topic for conversation, but money problems continue to be treated like every family's dirty little secret.

How Financially Fit Is Your Family?

While the majority of us seem satisfied to let our finances take care of themselves, most experts recommend that we put a lot more time and effort into coming up with a financial game plan.

FIGURE 2.2
Net Worth

ASSETS
    Possessions _____
        House _____
        Other real estate _____
        Car _____
        Household furnishings _____
        Electronic and computer equipment _____
        Jewelry _____
        Other _____

    Savings and investments
        Bank accounts _____
        Certificates of deposit _____
        Employee savings plans _____
        Life insurance cash value _____
        Stocks _____
        Bonds _____
        Mutual funds _____
        Educational savings plans _____
        Other _____

        Retirement savings _____
        Pension plan value _____
        Roth IRAs _____
        401(k)s _____
        Other _____

LIABILITIES
    Personal debts _____
    (Be sure to note the balance owing and fhe interest rate charged for any loans or credit cards)
    Mortgage _____
    Car loan _____
    Credit card balances _____
    Personal loans _____
    Lines of credit _____
    Unpaid bills (e.g., utility or phone bills) _____
    Income tax owing _____
    Money owed to relatives _____
    Other debts _____

FIGURE 2.2
Net Worth (Continued)

Investment debts _____

Investment loans _____

Business loans _____

Other debts _____

Total debts _____

NET WORTH

What you own _____

Less what you owe _____

Your net worth _____

Of course, figuring out where you're headed and how you're going to get there is hard if you don't have an idea where you are right now. If you've never sat down and taken a financial snapshot of your family, there's no time like the present to do so! You can use the tools on these pages to calculate your *Net Worth* (Figure 2.2) and to analyze your *Income versus Expenses* (Figure 2.4)—two important indicators of your family's overall financial well-being.

Note: if you prefer a high-tech approach to number crunching, you can either use one of the many excellent personal finance software packages available for this purpose or use one of the online financial calculators available at <www.quicken.com>, <www.money.com>, the Web sites of most major mutual fund companies, and at the various financial Web sites you'll find listed in Resources at the end of this book.

Analyzing Your Net Worth Statement

While the bottom-line figure on your net worth statement is important—it tells you whether you own more than you owe or vice versa—you can learn even more from it. Figure 2.3 shows you what to look for and how you might want to respond.

Wondering how your income stacks up to that of other American families? Here's what you need to know, based on 1999 statistics.

- The top 5 percent of American families earned more than $155,040.

FIGURE 2.3
Making Sense of Your Net Worth Statement

If your net worth statement shows that . . .	You might want to . . .
You have an excessive amount of debt.	Focus on debt reduction.
You have a large outstanding balance on your credit cards.	Consider applying for a lower-interest debt consolidation loan and cutting up your credit cards.
You're paying a high rate of interest on your credit card.	Consider paying for a "no frills" credit card with a lower interest rate.
You're paying a high rate of interest on your mortgage or other loans.	Consider refinancing your mortgage and other loans at a lower rate—unless, of course, your financial institution charges a huge penalty for doing so.
You have money sitting in your savings account or in U.S. savings bonds as well as a large amount of debt.	Use as much of your savings as possible to pay down your debts.
You have a large amount of money sitting in a checking account that is earning little or no interest.	Find a checking or savings account that pays a higher rate of interest on your money.
You don't have an emergency fund that equals three to six months worth of net income.	Make it a priority to start building up a nest egg so you won't be caught off guard if you lose your job or find yourself faced by some other financial curve ball.

- The next wealthiest 20 percent of American families earned between $59,400 and $88,082.

- The next 40 percent of American families earned between $39,600 and 59,400.

- The lowest 20 percent of American families have incomes below $22,826.

Now that you've had the chance to size up your financial net worth at this point, you should take a moment to consider how you're doing on a month-to-month basis by analyzing your cash flow. In other words, is your income greater than your expenses, or vice versa?

FIGURE 2.4
Income versus Expenses

INCOME

Your salary _____

Your partner's salary _____

Bonuses _____

Investment income _____

Rental income _____

Spousal support _____

Child support _____

Other sources of income _____

EXPENSES

Taxes and other income deductions

Federal income tax _____

State income tax _____

401(k) contributions _____

Social Security _____

Medicare _____

Federal/state unemployment tax _____

Union dues _____

Other deductions _____

Household expenses

Rent or mortgage _____

Property taxes _____

Homeowners insurance _____

Utilities (heat, electricity, water) _____

Service contracts (cleaning, lawn care, snow removal, etc.) _____

Telephone _____

Cable TV _____

Household equipment _____

Household repair _____

Other _____

Food

Groceries _____

Restaurant meals and takeout food _____

Other _____

FIGURE 2.4
Income versus Expenses (Continued)

Transportation
Car loan payments _____
Gasoline _____
Maintenance/repairs _____
License fees (vehicle and driver's license) _____
Tolls and parking fees _____
Bus, subway, or commuter train fares _____
Taxis _____
Other _____

Personal care
Medical insurance premiums _____
Clothing _____
Dry cleaning _____
Hair salon _____
Health club membership _____
Other _____

Debt repayment
Credit cards _____
Line of credit _____
Student loans _____
Other debts _____

Entertainment
Movies _____
Concerts _____
Vacations _____
Gifts _____
Books _____
Video rentals _____
Hobbies _____
Wine, beer, and other alcoholic beverages _____
Other _____

Professional services
Accountant _____
Lawyer _____
Financial advisor _____

FIGURE 2.4
Income versus Expenses (Continued)

Health care
Unreimbursed medical expenses _____
Drugs _____
Dental care _____
Eye care _____
Other _____

Educational expenses
Tuition _____
Books _____
Other _____

Insurance
Life insurance _____
Disability insurance _____
Medical insurance _____

Other expenses
Child Care _____
Charitable donations _____
Other _____

Analyzing Your Income and Expenses

The purpose of an income and expenses statement is to take a snapshot of your financial situation by figuring out how much money is coming in and how much money is going out. This task will be a lot easier if you're the kind of person who keeps detailed financial records. If you're not, you'll have your work cut out for you as you try your hand at forensic accounting, providing a "postmortem" on your past financial affairs!

You don't have to be a rocket scientist to interpret an income and expenses statement. It's pretty obvious whether you're dealing with good news or bad. Here's what you might discover as you work through this particular exercise— and how you might want to change your financial strategies, depending on what you find.

Now that you've had a chance to engage in some heavy-duty financial navel-gazing, you might be interested to find out how your family's financial situation measures up to that of the "average" American household—whatever that means! The most recent figures from the Bureau of Labor Statistics are summarized in Figure 2.6.

FIGURE 2.5
Making Sense of Your Income and Expenses Statement

If your cash flow statement shows . . .	You might want to . . .
You are spending more money than you are bringing in.	Look for ways to boost your income and/or to cut your spending so that you end up with at least a small surplus at the end of each month.
You are spending an excessive amount of money on certain types of expenditures (e.g., entertainment, dining out, clothing) than your income allows.	Look for ways to cut back your spending in these areas without sacrificing your lifestyle altogether. (You'll find plenty of ideas in Chapter 3.)
You are spending a significant amount of money simply servicing your debts.	Start working on paying off your credit cards, line of credits, car loans, mortgage, and other loans.

If your spending on one of these budget lines seems to be way out of whack—if, for example, your household income is around $35,000, but you're spending more than $5,000 on entertainment—you might want to look for some ways to reduce your expenses. The logical first step is to put your family on a budget.

Now before you run screaming from the room, allow us to have our say about budgets. We agree that there are a lot more fun things to do with your time than camping out at the kitchen table and trying to come up with a game plan for your spending, and that it can be a little tedious to try to track your spending day after day. Unfortunately, budgets are a necessary evil—an unavoidable aspect of money management, like paying your bills and filing your tax return.

Don't get us wrong, writing a budget doesn't have to be a test of endurance, nor does sticking to it have to be an exercise in deprivation. Not if you're smart about it, anyway. Here are some tips on writing a budget that you can actually live with.

- *Decide what you hope to achieve by following a budget.* Are you hoping to eliminate your credit card debts? Save for a vacation? Or build up your emergency savings account? You're more likely to stick with your budget if you've got some concrete goals in mind.

- *Reach for your calculator.* Pull out your income and expenses statement and rework it so that it will help you to achieve your financial goals. Want to take the kids on a trip to Disney World next winter? Better start setting aside some money every week so you'll be able to afford that rendezvous with Mickey. Hoping to pay off your car loan this year? Look for other areas of your budget where you can cut back a little, and then apply this "found money" against the balance of your car loan each month.

- *Look at the big picture.* Going on a crash weight-loss diet doesn't work. Neither does going on a crash money diet. Rather than going for the "quick fix" in an effort to eliminate your debt or build up your savings overnight, come up with a budget that you can stick with over the long run.

- *Get other family members to buy into the plan.* There's no point coming up with a budget if you're the only one who's prepared to stick to it. That's why it's important to get your partner and your children involved in setting the budget. Obviously, you won't be lecturing your one year old about the evils of spending more than you earn, but older children can certainly learn this all-important lesson. You'll find lots of tips on teaching kids about money elsewhere in this book.

FIGURE 2.6
Average Annual Income and Expenditures, 1999

		% of after-tax income
Income before taxes	$43,952	
Food	5,031	13.6%
Housing	12,057	32.6
Apparel and Services	1,743	4.8
Transportation	7,011	19.0
Health Care	1,959	5.2
Entertainment	1,891	5.1
Personal Insurance and Insurance	3,436	9.2
Other	3,899	10.5
Total	$37,027	100.0

Source: Bureau of Labor Statistics. Consumer Expenditures, 1999.
<www.stats.bla.gov/news.release/cesan.nws.htm>

- *Keep it simple.* Rather than spending hours trying to account for every nickel and dime, settle for keeping track of the big chunks of money. Does it really matter whether the $20 you had in your pocket was spent on five magazines or fifteen takeout coffees? Not unless you've got a Type A++ personality or you're someone with a lot of time on your hands! Just log the expense as $20 for "spending money" and you'll save yourself and those around you a lot of grief.

- *Realize that you're going to fall off the wagon from time to time.* Everyone does. The secret is to get back on as soon as possible—not to abandon your budget entirely and go on the ultimate spending spree, figuring that because you've already blown it, you might as well shop till you drop. Remember, it's a lot less painful to cope with a $200 financial faux pas than a $5000 budgetary blow out.

Up until now, we've been focusing on big-picture budget issues—how to come up with a money plan for your family and how to get your spending habits back on track if you momentarily become derailed. Now let's talk about one of the biggest causes of money-related woes for families with young children—credit card debt.

CHAPTER 3

The Perils of Plastic

• •

You no doubt noticed a recurring theme in the last chapter: the evils of credit cards. Despite what you might think, we're not trying to convince you that credit cards are without their merits. They are, after all, an excellent source of free credit (provided you pay off your balance in full each month, and you aren't tempted to take a cash advance) and they offer a safe and convenient alternative to carrying large amounts of cash. It's just that, like almost everything else in life, credit cards have their dark side. While we all like to think that we do a good job of handling our

Show Me the Money!
• • • • • • •
Most financial planners recommend that you limit yourself to two cards: a "convenience card" you use to make day-to-day purchases that you would otherwise buy with cash or by check, and a second card that you only use for big-ticket items (a stereo or computer, for example).

credit cards, financial industry figures show that, at any given time, 60 percent of us have outstanding balances on our credit cards that are costing us a small fortune in interest.

Here are some other rather damning facts about credit cards.

- More than 1 billion credit cards are in circulation in the United States—four credit cards for every man, woman, and child.

- The amount of consumer debt in the United States has skyrocketed from $21.5 billion in 1950 (the year the Diner's Club card—American's first credit card—was invented) to more than $1 trillion today. The total amount of debt carried on MasterCard and Visa cards alone is a mind-boggling $455 billion dollars, up from $350 billion in 1994.

- Americans charged more than $400 billion on their credit cards in 1998, according to RAM Research, a credit card tracker. That $50 billion in finance charges could have bought the inventory of 5,000 Jaguar dealerships or paid for the lifetime services of Michael Jordan many times over!

- Five percent of Americans admit being more than 30 days behind on their credit card bills.

There's no denying it, we're a credit-driven society. Through both good times and bad, we've learned to live beyond our means—financing today's dreams with tomorrow's paychecks.

HOW TO AVOID GETTING IN TROUBLE WITH CREDIT CARDS

What the numbers don't tell you, of course, is how incredibly seductive credit cards can be. It's easy to forget that you're spending "real" money when no bills and coins change hands. It's also easy to lose track of how many $40 purchases you've made over the course of a month—until a $1,000 credit card bill shows up on your doorstep.

As with anything else in life, when it comes to managing your credit cards, an ounce of prevention is worth a pound of cure. Here are some tips on avoiding credit card problems.

- *Limit the number of credit cards you use.* The more cards you have, the more likely you'll be tempted to use them. Rather than carrying around a wallet full of department store and gas company credit cards, stick with one or two major credit cards.

Facts and Figures
• • • • • •

Think you've got too many credit cards? Imagine what it would be like to be Walter Cavanagh, a financial planner in Santa Clara, California, who turned up in the 1998 Guinness Book of Records with 1,397 credit cards and a total credit limit of $1.65 million. You've got to wonder what Walter's clients have to say about that.

- *Ask your bank to chop your credit limit.* Credit card companies love nothing more than to "reward" good customers by raising their credit limits. (Why not? They're in the business of making money! If you've got a couple of thousand dollars worth of room on your credit card, you might be tempted to dash out and buy that home theater system you've been drooling over for years.) More often than not, you don't even have to request a credit limit increase. It just happens. You get a congratulatory letter from your credit card company, letting you know that they've topped up your credit limit with an extra couple of thousand dollars, or you're glancing at your credit card statement and notice that the credit limit has doubled or tripled since the last time you checked. If you don't want to be tempted to overspend just because the credit card company is willing to lend you more money, then pick up that phone and decline this "opportunity" to dig yourself into a financial hole.

- *Switch from a credit card to a charge card.* Visa and MasterCard are credit cards. You're only required to make a token payment each month to keep your account in good standing. American Express and Diner's Club, on the other hand, are charge cards and you're expected to pay off the balance in full each month. While you're not guaranteed to stick to the financial high road just because you're carrying an American Express or Diner's Club card in your wallet, you'll be less likely to overspend if you know you're supposed to write a check for the total owing at the end of the month.

Show Me the Money!
• • • • • •

Keep track of your credit card slips so that you can compare them against your monthly statement. If you notice any errors, contact your credit card company immediately and ask them to investigate.

- *Think about what you're buying on credit.* It's one thing to buy a fax machine for your small business on credit. With any luck, that purchase will help to put money back in your pocket. It's quite another to borrow money so that you can live beyond your means—and, whether you're prepared to admit it to yourself or not, that's exactly what you're doing if you carry an unpaid credit card balance that is largely made up of restaurant meals, purchases at the liquor store, and other goods that have long since been consumed. (Besides, who wants to be paying interest on a night on the town six months after the fact!)

- *Don't allow yourself to be sweet-talked into signing up for more cards than you need.* The credit card companies are masters when it comes to wooing customers. They will throw in all kinds of bells and whistles to win your business. These companies may offer you cards that waive your annual fee, offer you discounted interest rates on any outstanding credit card balance, allow you to participate in affinity programs (e.g., programs that support your favorite charity or nonprofit organization by passing along a percentage of your annual or transaction fees), or allow you to accumulate frequent-flyer points or to receive credits toward the purchases of automobiles or other big-ticket items. Don't make the mistake of signing up for more credit cards than you can reasonably manage just because they're making you an attractive offer that might—we repeat, *might*—save you money down the road.

FINANCE CHARGES: DO YOU NEED AN INTERPRETER?

Not quite sure when you are—and aren't—being charged interest on your credit card balance? Join the club! Most Americans have difficulty understanding how—and when—interest is charged on their credit cards.

Here's what you need to know about the weird and not-so-wonderful world of finance charges.

First, let's start with the awful truth: the only way to avoid paying any interest at all is to pay your credit card balance in full as soon as it is due. If you do not pay this amount in full, your credit "revolves" (i.e., your outstanding balance is carried over to the next statement) and finance charges are tacked on.

These charges will be calculated using one of the following methods:

- *Average daily balance method, excluding newly billed purchases.* The finance charge that appears on your bill is only calculated on your outstanding balance from the previous month. You aren't charged interest on any new purchases that you make this month. Unfortunately for consumers, this method of calculating interest is

Show Me the Money!
• • • • • • •

Credit cards aren't the only form of credit that can get you into trouble. Those "buy now, pay later" promotions are another all-too-common trap. The only time you should take advantage of these programs is if the store in question is offering interest-free loans and you have the necessary funds sitting in your bank account right now. As long as you still have the money to pay off the loan when it eventually comes due, you can take advantage of this opportunity to earn interest on your money in the meantime. The best way to ensure that the funds are still available when you need them is either to throw them into a term deposit or to write them out of your check register so that you forget that they're still sitting in your bank account.

quickly going the way of the dinosaur. Guess it doesn't allow the credit card companies to add to their record profits quickly enough!

- *Average daily balance method, including newly billed purchases.* With this method, there isn't any grace period for newly purchased items. You start paying interest on those new purchases from the moment that they're made. (Technically speaking, these charges cause your average daily balance to increase, so you pay more interest.) If your creditor uses this method to calculate your finance charges, you should pay off your balance as soon as possible. Don't wait for your bill's due date to roll around, or you'll simply end up paying more interest.

- *Two-cycle method.* A few credit card issuers are now relying on the two-cycle method of calculating interest. If you fail to pay your balance off in full during one of the two billing cycles, you end up paying interest on both billing cycles.

If you aren't able to pay off your credit card debt in full each month, you end up spending a lot of money on finance charges. The reason is obvious: no matter how much money you pay off each month, the creditor takes its full finance charge out of your payment before it deducts anything from the balance you owe. At the same time, the company continues to compound the interest on your outstanding balance.

Here's something else you need to know about to avoid credit card disasters. In recent years, many credit card issuers have started lowering the percentage of the minimum payment required to keep an account in good standing. Instead of having to pay off 4 percent of your credit card debt each month—the norm just a few years ago—some cards only require you to pay off 2 percent of your debt. If you have a large outstanding balance on your account and you only make these 2 per-

Show Me the Money!
• • • • • • •

Some credit card issuers are now charging higher interest rates to cardholders who exceed their credit limits, pay late, or skip a payment. In some cases, one slip-up on your part can result in a doubling of your finance charges!

cent minimum payments, you will find yourself paying off little more than the interest each month.

Here's a rather hair-raising example of how bad things can get if you fall into the 2 percent trap. If you pay $50 on a credit card debt of $2,500 the first month and then make your 2 percent minimum monthly payments each month after that, you will take 28 years to pay off the balance, and you will pay a total of $5,896 in interest. Let's look at it another way: if you spend $2,500 on baby equipment and other baby-related expenses during your child's first year of life, and are only able to make minimum payments on your credit card thereafter, you won't manage to pay off the balance on your credit card until long after Junior has graduated from college!

FINDING A CREDIT CARD YOU CAN LIVE WITH

Wondering how to go about deciding which credit card is right for you? It's not an easy task. After all, with 20,000 United States companies lining up for your credit card business, the task of evaluating your options can be nothing short of overwhelming. It's particularly important to be on the lookout for the following bank credit card traps that can end up costing you a lot of money:

- *The no-fee card with ultra-low interest.* You've no doubt received letters in the mail advising you that you've been preapproved for a no-fee credit card that boasts an unbelievably low rate of interest. What you might not notice about the solicitation, however, is the fact that the interest rate may skyrocket after the initial six-month honeymoon period, and that an annual fee may kick in later on.

- *The reduced rate credit card.* Some credit card companies will encourage you to switch your credit card business to them by offering to charge you a reduced rate of interest on the balance that you transfer. Unfortunately, this reduced rate often doesn't apply to additional purchases that you make on the card: it only applies to the balance you're transferring from your old credit card company. Make sure you know what the credit card rate will be down the road before you decide to change cards.

- *Tier system.* Certain credit cards reward you for carrying a larger balance. You may be offered a reduced rate of interest once your balance exceeds $2,500, for example. As attractive as this offer may sound, it's no bargain; while you're paying a reduced interest rate of interest on all or a portion of the balance, you're borrowing a larger amount of money.

- *The spending requirement.* Most of us don't need any encouragement to give our credit cards a workout, but some credit cards encourage you to do exactly that. In exchange for a very low rate of interest, these cards may require that you charge a certain amount of money each year. If you're not quite as charge-happy as your credit card company might like, you'll lose your preferential interest rate on any unpaid balance.

- *The finance charge requirement.* Believe it or not, some credit card companies charge you a penalty for paying off your bill in full each month. If they can't make money off you one way, they simply change the rules of the game! The GE Rewards card began this practice a few years back, charging a $25 annual fee to cardholders who didn't manage to ring up at least $25 in financing charges over the course of the year. Other issuers are shortening or eliminating the grace period (i.e., the number of days you have to pay your bill before interest is applied to your outstanding balance).

Show Me the Money!
• • • • • •

Credit card rebate offers aren't what they used to be. Most airlines now require 25,000 frequent flyer miles in order to issue you a free airline ticket, up from 20,000 previously. GM cardholders, who were once able to accumulate a credit toward a new car purchase of up to $1,000 annually, or $7,000 over a seven-year period, are now only allowed to earn credits of half that amount.

- *The bait and switch tactic.* It's one of the sleaziest tactics used by the credit card companies, but it's also one of the most effective. You're invited to apply for a "preapproved" gold card with no annual fee—but then, despite the promise of pre-approval, you are turned down. The issuer then sends you the standard credit card instead, one that features a higher interest rate than what you were promised, a lower spending limit, and an annual fee. While you don't have to take the card—you're free to cut it into a million pieces and send it back—the account may still show up on your credit history, leading other potential lenders to wrongly assume that you're overextended in the credit department.

If you aren't able to obtain approval for a regular credit card, perhaps because your credit rating is less than healthy, you can still get a special type of credit card: a secured card. With a secured credit card, you deposit a certain amount of money in a savings account, and the bank gives you a credit card for a certain amount— usually the amount that's sitting in this savings account. If you prove your credit- worthiness by paying on time, you may eventually be allowed to switch to a regular credit card. If you end up defaulting on your payments, however, your cash deposit may be seized to cover your outstanding debts.

BEATING THE CREDIT CARD COMPANIES AT THEIR OWN GAME

One of the best ways to reduce the amount of money you spend on credit card charges is to apply for a card that features a low interest rate. Of course, the very best way to save money on credit card charges is to avoid carrying any balance at all—something that's obviously much easier said than done!

If you decide to apply for a low-interest rate credit card, you could be in for a shock. Getting approved isn't as easy as most people assume. You see, credit card companies that issue low-interest credit cards are working on a tight profit margin. This means that they have to be very careful about who they take on as customers. The last thing they want is to have to absorb losses incurred by customers who default on their payments or declare bankruptcy.

That's why credit card companies offering these attractive interest rates typically ask you to fill out a far lengthier and more detailed credit card application than what you'd normally need to fill out. They'll delve into every conceivable area of your financial life so that they can make an informed decision about whether or not you "deserve" one of their cards. We kid you not! About the only thing they won't ask you is how much of your allowance you managed to sock away when you were a kid!

You can increase your odds of being approved for a low-interest rate credit card by:

- Catching up on any unpaid bills before you apply for the low-interest rate credit card.

- Not doing anything that may make you appear like a high risk. For example, if you have four or more credit cards with outstanding balances, pay off one or more of them by transferring the unpaid balance to one of your other credit cards—preferably one that offers the lowest interest rate of the bunch.

Show Me the Money!

The bank that issued your credit card has just announced that it is slashing interest rates on its credit cards. This is good news for you, right? Not necessarily. Believe it or not, your bank may limit this new rate to new customers, or it may insist that you pay off your outstanding credit card balance in order to qualify for the new rate. Sometimes you have to threaten to take your credit card balance elsewhere in order to get them to give you the preferred interest rate.

- Making sure that you aren't using any more than 75 percent of your approved credit limit, if you're using more than that, the credit card company may assume that you're already financially overextended.

- Reducing the total amount of credit that is available to you by cancel-ing any credit cards that you are no longer using. Believe it or not, lenders view charge accounts or home equity lines of credit that you are not using as a risk. After all, you could go on a spending spree at any time. Don't close these accounts all at once, however, or a lender may assume that you're running into financial troubles. Just close one or two a month and ask each account holder to report this information promptly to all of the credit bureaus that they deal with, and then follow up with the credit bureaus directly to make sure that everything has been handled correctly.

- Resisting the temptation to apply for too many low-interest credit cards at the same time. When your application for a new credit card comes in, the issuing company requests your credit history. All credit requests show up on the credit bureau's computer. Too many inquiries over a short period of time can make you look like a poor risk. Potential lenders may assume that you're desperate for cash or that you've been rejected by a string of other companies.

Show Me the Money!
• • • • • • •
Beware of transfer traps. Fees can be involved in transferring a credit card balance from one company to another. In some cases, these fees can wipe out any savings that you might otherwise enjoy by switching to a lower-interest credit card.

HOW MUCH DEBT IS TOO MUCH DEBT?

Here's a lesson that many families learn the hard way: there's a world of difference between the amount of money that the banks are willing to lend you and the amount of debt that you feel comfortable carrying.

Don't understand what we're talking about? Let us explain.

Financial institutions look at your debt-to-income ratio (the percentage of your take-home pay that is used to service personal debts other than your mortgage) to determine whether or not you can handle any more debt. If your debt-to-income ratio is less than 15 percent, you are managing your credit well. If it is more than 15 to 20 percent, you could be heading for financial trouble.

Financial difficulties can sneak up and catch you unaware. One minute you're on solid financial ground—or at least you think you are! The next, you're dodging phone calls from creditors and wondering how things could go so wrong so quickly.

It's all too easy to ignore the warning signs that you're headed for money trouble. After all, who even wants to consider the possibility that they could be flirting with financial disaster? Often, it's easier to convince yourself that things are going to be all right—"We've got a good income, so there's really no problem"—than it is to face up to the fact that you're overloaded with debts and sinking fast.

That's why it's important to take realistic stock of your financial situation on a regular basis—to take a good hard look at your spending habits, warts and all. If you know that your money management habits place you somewhere between saint and sinner, but you're not quite sure which way you're leaning, try your hand at the quiz listed in Figure 3.1.

How to Dig Yourself Out of a Financial Hole

Show Me the Money!

Find it hard to budget for those large bills that only show up once a year—the property taxes, the car insurance, and so on? Here's a painless way to ensure that you always have the necessary funds on hand. Add up the amount of money you end up spending on these types of bills and then divide the total by 52. This is the amount of money you need to set aside each week to make sure that you've got enough money on hand when the bills come due. If, for example, your car insurance costs $1,200 and your property taxes are $2,500, you need to set aside about $72 dollars each week. If you're extraordinarily disciplined about money, you could allow these extra funds to accumulate in your general household checking account. If, however, you think you might be tempted to use these funds for a less noble purpose, you might be better off transferring these funds into a separate savings account.

If you took the quiz and discovered to your horror that you're in worse financial shape than you realized, you're probably wondering what you can do to turn your situation around. Here are a few ideas.

- *Eliminate all nonessential expenditures.* That means doing without the frills like cable TV, magazine subscriptions, and dinners out until you're back on solid financial ground again.

- *Pay off your most expensive debts first.* Eliminate the balances on your department store cards, gas cards, and credit cards (high-interest rate debt) before you try to finish paying off your line of credit, your car, or your mortgage (low interest-rate debt).

FIGURE 3.1
Quiz: Are You Headed for Financial Trouble?

Do you know how to spot the warning signs that you're headed for financial trouble? The following quiz should help you to decide if it's time to put away your credit cards on ice for a while. Check off as many statements as apply to your situation and then tally up your total to find out how well you're doing in heading off the financial storm clouds.

_____ I frequently end up paying my bills after they are past due.

_____ I am bouncing checks on a regular basis.

_____ I am getting further in debt with each passing month.

_____ I find myself dipping into my savings in order to come up with enough money to pay my bills.

_____ I have used an advance from one credit card to make the minimum payment on another card.

_____ Most months, I am only able to pay the minimum amount on my credit cards.

_____ At least one of my credit cards is over the limit.

_____ I frequently borrow money or use my credit card to pay for items that I previously bought with cash.

_____ I am receiving calls from collection agencies because of my overdue bills.

_____ I have put off spending money on prescription drugs, dental checkups, and car repairs because I can't afford them.

_____ My utilities have been cut off from time to time because I've been unable to pay my bills.

_____ If I lost my job (or my partner lost his/her job), we'd be in serious financial trouble right away.

_____ I have less than a month's income stashed away in my emergency fund.

_____ I've lost track of how much money I actually owe to my creditors.

_____ I have experienced problems with my partner because of my spending habits.

_____ Sometimes I find it hard to concentrate at work because I'm so worried about my debts.

_____ I feel depressed and hopeless when I think about my financial situation.

_____ I have given false information on at least one occasion in order to obtain credit.

_____ My wages have been garnished on at least one occasion to pay some of my outstanding debts.

_____ I am having difficulty sleeping because I'm worried about my financial situation.

If you checked off more than five of these statements, you're clearly headed for financial trouble. Don't think you're in the clear if you only checked off one or two statements, however. Take it as a wake up call that it's time to pull up your financial socks and change the way you manage your money.

- *Consider getting a consolidation loan if it will help to decrease the amount of money you are spending on interest payments.* There's just one catch: this strategy can backfire if you start using your credit cards again. You have to promise yourself that you're going to put your credit cards away until you've finished paying off your consolidation loan—perhaps even cut them up altogether.

- *Look for pockets of cash that you can apply to your debts.* It doesn't make sense to have $2,000 sitting in your checking account if you're paying 20 percent interest on a $2,000 balance on your credit card. While you might feel like you're doing something wrong by spending the small bit of cash you've managed to sock away over the years, in the end, you'll be further ahead if you use it to reduce your debt.

- *Get in the habit of saving before you spend.* While this may almost sound like blasphemy to anyone who has bought into the "buy now, pay later" advertising pitches, you'll save a small fortune in interest if you get in the habit of deferring major purchases until you have the necessary money sitting in your bank account. As an added bonus, you won't find yourself scrambling to find the money when it's finally time to pay the bill— something that could become a major problem if you were to lose your job in the meantime. If you're not a natural-born saver (and frankly, not many people are), you might find it easier to rely on forced savings methods, like signing up for a preauthorized contribution to a mutual fund or a payroll deduction plan for retirement savings. The best savings plan, after all, is the one that you don't have to think about.

- *Learn how to anticipate expenses so that you don't get caught short of funds.* If your car is due for a brake job, set some money aside before you pay a visit to your friendly neighborhood mechanic—not after the credit card bill is past due. Similarly, if your property taxes are due each March, start setting aside funds months in advance so that the money will be there when you need it. Then, instead of writing a check against your line of credit and paying interest on your property taxes, you'll be able to settle the bill with cash.

- *If you like using a credit card because it's more convenient than carrying cash, start using a debit card instead.* It's as convenient as using a credit card, but you aren't left with a massive bill to pay at the end of the month.

- *Don't allow yourself to fall back into the hole again.* Cut up your credit cards so that you won't be tempted to run them up to their limit again. If you don't like the idea of getting rid of your credit cards entirely, store them in your safety deposit box at the bank or wrap them in plastic, drop them into a plastic container filled with water, and store the container in your freezer. Hey, it's one way to put your spending habits on ice!

WHAT YOU DON'T KNOW ABOUT YOUR CREDIT RATING CAN HURT YOU

Here's a statistic that will make your hair stand on end: studies have shown that one in four credit files contains some sort of error. If it's a serious enough error, it could make it impossible for you to obtain credit until the error is corrected—convincing evidence that what you don't know about your credit rating can hurt you.

Your credit rating is established at the moment your first application for credit is approved—perhaps when you obtained your first credit card, arranged your first car loan, or bought some sort of electronic gizmo on the installment plan.

The way to establish a good credit rating is to borrow money and pay it back on time. If you don't, the word will get out that you're not a good credit risk—and bad news travels fast in credit-granting circles.

Here's something else you need to know. The bad news also sticks around for a very long time. If you miss a payment or are late with a payment, this fact will show up on your credit file for the next seven years—ten years if you happen to declare personal bankruptcy. And you thought that breaking mirrors was bad luck!

Big Brother Is Watching You

Each month, your local credit bureau contacts your creditors and asks them to report on your creditworthiness. The credit bureau collects data on all of your credit accounts: what types of loans you have outstanding, how long you've had them, your outstanding balance, whether or not you pay on time, whether or not you've missed any payments, and your current credit rating according to each of your creditors. This information is then recorded in your credit file so that it can be made available to prospective creditors the next time you apply for a loan.

Some people are surprised to learn just how many different types of organizations report credit information to the credit bureau. The list is almost mind-boggling: not only credit card companies report on your creditworthiness—utilities, landlords, hospitals, and banks do as well. What's more, if a civil suit judgment is held against you, that will show up on your credit rating, too.

Time and time again, each of your creditors assigns you a credit rating based on your credit history. Here's what the codes mean.

- *R* refers to your credit rating on revolving credit (credit cards on which you can pay as much or as little as you would like each month, as long as you make at least the minimum payment).

- *I* refers to your credit rating on installment credit (loans on which you make fixed payments on a predetermined schedule).

- *O* refers to your credit rating on open credit (cards such as American Express that require you to pay the balance in full each month).

You are then given a rating from zero to nine that indicates how responsibly you handle credit. Here's what some of those numbers signify.

- *0* means that you have been approved for credit, but you don't have a credit history yet, either because your credit was just approved or because you've never actually used the credit card that you applied for.

- *1* means that you pay your bills within 30 days.

- *2* means that you pay in 30 to 60 days and are a payment behind.

- *5* means that you take 120 days or more to pay and that your account is currently overdue.

- *9* means that a collection agency has been called in to try to obtain payment on your account.

The two components of your credit card rating are then matched up. You are assigned a rating of *R1* if you make your revolving credit payments within 30 days and a rating of *I2* if you pay your installment credit bills in 30 to 60 days and are currently a payment behind.

Not everything shows up on your credit rating, however. Delinquent student loans, unpaid tax bills, and missed rent payments are just a few of the things that don't get picked up by Big Brother.

Credit bureaus do not make judgments about you. They aren't involved in rating your credit or assessing your ability to pay. Their job is simply to collect the relevant information and pass it on to potential lenders. It's your bank, department store, gasoline company, or credit card company that uses this information to decide whether or not you are, in fact, a good credit risk. Some companies take into account as many as 100 different factors in making this judgment—things like the number of times you have paid your bills more than 60 days late; the size of your line of credit; the number of recent inquiries into your credit history; and any liens, foreclosures, and bankruptcies.

How to Check Your Credit Rating

While the whole credit rating process sounds tremendously scientific, errors can and do occur. That's why it's important to get in touch with your local credit bureau to find out how to obtain a copy of your credit report. You will generally be asked to pay a small fee (typically $8 or so) for this report, but you can obtain a copy of your credit report for free if a credit application of yours has been turned down by a potential lender. (You can find out exactly what's involved in getting a copy of your credit report by contacting Equifax, 800-685-1111 <www.equifax .com>; Experian (formerly TRW), 800-397-3742 <www.ex perian.com>; and TransUnion, 800-888-4213 <www.tuc.com>.)

Once your credit report arrives, sit down and review it carefully to make sure that it's free of errors. If you find an error caused by one of your creditors (e.g., your credit card company has reported that you typically pay your bills in 120 days, but you've never been a day late with a payment in your life), you will need to get in touch with the creditor and ask them to contact the credit bureau to have the information corrected. If you find that your credit report contains information about someone else's credit situation—a horrifying but all-too-common occurrence—then you will need to provide whatever written proof you can and ask the credit bureau to investigate. The credit bureau must investigate any errors you discover, delete the data if it is inaccurate, and notify creditors who received your report within the past six months that the original report contained erroneous information.

If the credit bureau's investigation does not resolve the dispute—an unfortunate but all-too-common outcome—the credit bureau will let you tell your side of the story (150 words of it, anyway!) and will add your information to your permanent credit record. This is your chance to explain your side of the story—to present your version of the facts and tell potential creditors what really happened. Believe

> ## Money Talk
> • • • • • • •
>
> "Separating from my partner almost led to my bankruptcy, but I did not give in. After being refused a small loan to help get me back on my feet and being offered the alternative of bankruptcy, I realized that I would have to work some major miracles to pay off credit cards, car loans, and everyday expenses while supplying the little things that my child needed. I became a very frugal person. I also wasn't afraid to ask for help. I went to a friend who had money to spare and asked for just enough to cover my credit card bills and car loan payments for one month. Then I cut up the cards. I frequented used clothing stores and swapped clothes with other families to keep my daughter looking decent. I made her baby food. I started looking for a better job. Now I am doing much better financially. Everything is being paid on time and I no longer need my parents' help."
>
> —Christine, 24, single mother of one

it or not, your statement will be taken seriously by credit grantors and could make the difference between a yes or a no the next time you apply for a loan.

HOW TO TELL WHEN IT'S TIME TO CALL IT QUITS

Each year, more than 1.4 million Americans file for bankruptcy. For many, filing for bankruptcy is the wisest financial move they could make; for others, it's a poor decision that comes with an enormous price tag.

Congress passed the Bankruptcy Act of 1978 to make it easier for individuals to repay a significant portion of their debts and to ease the previous burdens associated with going bankrupt. This has led to a dramatic increase in the number of personal bankruptcies, their fallout costing each U.S. household approximately $400 a year in higher prices and interest charges.

It's hard to think rationally about your bankruptcy options when you're fielding embarrassing phone calls from creditors at home and at work. While you don't want to throw in the towel too easily, it's important to know how to tell when to call it quits.

Before you take the step of declaring personal bankruptcy, you should plan to talk with a lawyer about the various petitions that you must fill out and file under the various chapters of the Bankruptcy Act. Chapter 7 covers a straight bankruptcy (the court collects, sells, and distributes your assets, with certain exceptions), while Chapter 13 (the so-called wage-earner plan) allows you to consolidate your debts and repay a percentage of them as approved by the court over a three- to five-year period. During this period, your creditors must suspend interest and late charges on most of your debts and may not continue any action against you. (Certain types of debts cannot be discharged under bankruptcy proceedings, including recent student loans, alimony, child support, and most taxes. Each state sets its own rules about which types of property are exempt from bankruptcy proceedings.)

Show Me the Money!
• • • • • • •

You've no doubt heard all of the advertisements for companies that promise to repair your credit report. What these ads don't tell you is that a fairly hefty fee is involved—$200 to $1,000 on average—and that the results are anything but guaranteed. All these companies can do to improve your credit report is write to the credit bureau on your behalf to challenge certain items that appear on your report—something you could do for yourself.

What to Do Before You Throw in the Towel

Of course, you can do plenty before you get to that point. If you're lucky and you spot the warning signs early enough, you may be able to head off bankruptcy altogether. Here are some steps you should take if you think you're headed for a financial meltdown.

- *Get in touch with your creditors.* Explain why you aren't able to make your payments right now, and ask them if they'll either give you more time to repay your debts or reduce the amount of your monthly payments. In most cases, they'll agree. They would rather extend your loan term or reduce your payments than receive nothing from you at all.

> **Money Talk**
> • • • • • • •
>
> "I filed for bankruptcy many, many years ago when I was still married to my first husband. It was devastating emotionally. I was ashamed that we couldn't take care of our financial situation. I would advise other couples to exhaust every possible means to pay their bills before they resort to bankruptcy. The blow to your credit and your self-esteem is just not worth it."
> —*Kim, 34, currently pregnant with her second child*

- *Go for credit counseling.* If you want to get out of debt, but you just can't do it on your own, you might want to go for credit counseling. The Consumer Credit Counseling Service (CCCS) is a private, nonprofit organization with offices throughout the country. The goal of the service is to help people to come up with a plan for managing their debt: to work with you to establish a budget, to come up with a debt repayment schedule that you can live with, and to negotiate with your creditors on your behalf. Once your creditors have agreed to your repayment plan, you'll hand over a certain sum of money to your local CCCS office which will, in turn, distribute these funds to your creditors according to the proportion of debt owed to each. (For example, if your deposit is $1,000 per month and your Master-Card debt represents 25 percent of your total debt, then $250 will go to MasterCard.) Going the CCCS route has some definite advantages. Some creditors will actually suspend finance and late payment fees for people using the CCCS repayment program. To find the CCCS office nearest you, call 800-388-2227.

- *Consider getting a debt consolidation loan or home equity loan.* Of course, going this route is only a good idea if you're able to obtain a loan that will bring down your monthly payments and reduce the amount of interest that you're paying—and if you have the self-discipline to cut up your credit cards so that you won't fall into the same trap again. You'll want to be particularly careful if you're putting your home on the line, as would be the case if you were to finance your debts by obtaining a home equity loan or home equity line of credit.

Even though you may be sorely tempted to bury your head in the sand and ignore your debt problems, in these situations, ignorance is definitely not bliss. Bottom line? The sooner you manage to wrestle the debt monster to the ground, the sooner you'll get your life back again.

CHAPTER 4

Will That Be One Income or Two?

• •

No doubt about it: the dual-income family is here to stay. For a variety of complex reasons—not the least of which is economics—the two-parent, one-paycheck family has found its way onto the endangered species list. More often than not, American families are relying on two paychecks just to get by.

Consider the following facts:

- According to the U.S. National Center for Health Statistics, 80 percent of working women will become pregnant at some point during their working lives.

- In 1998, 58 percent of married couples with children under the age of six and 68.1 percent of married couples with children under the age of 18 were both employed outside the home. (See Figure 4.1.)

- Eight out of ten teenagers who participated in the Families and Work Institute's recent Youth and Employment Study reported that their mother was employed outside the home, while nine in ten reported that their father was employed outside the home.

- According to the U.S. Census Bureau, the number of married women in the workforce nearly tripled between 1951 and 1998, jumping from 23 percent to 62 percent. Not surprisingly, families with two wage earners tend to have a higher household income than those with a single wage earner.

In 1997, full-time, year-round female workers earned just 74 percent of what full-time, year-round male workers took home that year—the narrowest gap ever between male and female wage earners, but a significant gap nonetheless.

THE REST OF THE STORY

If the decision about whether to work outside the home or stay at home with your kids were merely a matter of finances, you'd have your answer in a flash. Key some numbers into your calculator, hit the total, and—voilà!—your decision would be made for you.

Unfortunately, complex issues like this one can rarely be boiled down to a simple financial calculation. There are so many other issues to consider, like how you feel about being a working or stay-at-home parent and what the long-term career costs are of dropping out of the workforce to raise a family.

Before we get any further along in this chapter, allow us to insert a brief note about terminology. We both hate the terms *working parent* and *stay-at-home parent,* but we've yet to find any workable alternatives. We know that parents who are at home with their children are working parents, too— and we know that they often do anything but stay-at-home. They're too busy volunteering at their children's schools, taking their kids to the park to play, and sometimes even running part-time businesses on the side. So if you're tempted to throw tomatoes at us because you don't like the fact that we call parents who work outside the home "working parents" and parents who work inside the home "stay-at-home parents," please think about throwing that tomato at the folks who write the dictionary. It's their fault we weren't able to come up with the perfect term!

This chapter of the book was one of the toughest ones for us to write, not just because of the terminology issue, but also because we discovered that there

FIGURE 4.1
Families with Own Children

Employment status of parents by age of youngest child and family type, 1999 annual averages:

Children under 18 years	
Families headed by men with children under 18*	86.3%
Families headed by women with children under 18*	74.7%
Married-couple families with children under 18	
Both employed	64.1
Mother employed, not father	4.2
Father employed, not mother	29.1
Neither parent employed	2.7
Children 6-17 years old	
Families headed by men with children*	84.8%
Families headed by women with children*	79.1%
Married-couple families with children 6-17	
Both employed	69.6
Mother employed, not father	4.9
Father employed, not mother	22.6
Neither parent employed	2.9
Children under 6	
Families headed by men with children*	88.5%
Families headed by women with children*	67.4%
Married-couple families with children under 6	
Both employed	57.4
Mother employed, not father	3.3
Father employed, not mother	36.9
Neither parent employed	2.4

*No spouse present
U.S. Department of Labor, Bureau of Labor Statistics

is no "right answer" that applies to all families—even to families who have virtually identical financial situations, for Pete's sake!

We danced around the chapter for an entire week, trying to figure out how we were going to take a financial approach to an issue that, for many parents, often has very little to do with money. At one point we even tried to convince ourselves that the book didn't really need a chapter on this topic, but that was just the coward in us looking for an easy way to wriggle out of facing that blank computer screen day after day! In the end, we decided that two separate issues were involved—the number crunching and the soul searching—and that we'd have to tackle them both if this chapter was going to have anything valuable to say.

Here goes!

The Hidden Costs of Working

Let's start by tackling the easiest part of the working versus staying-at-home issue first—the dollars and cents part.

If you worked through the budget exercises in the previous chapter, you've already got a good sense of your financial health (whether you're earning more than you spend, or vice versa). Now all you need to do is fiddle with a few of the lines in your budget to assess the financial fall-out of staying at home versus working outside the home. Simply carry forward the numbers that you listed in Figure 2.4 to Figure 4.2 and then start playing with some alternative scenarios—like what would happen if you went from two incomes to one (or even one-and-a-half).

> ## Money Talk
> • • • • • • •
>
> "We have always worked under the assumption that one of us would be staying home part-time. The definition of 'part-time' has changed over the years, but the importance hasn't. At this point, I'm not interested in pursuing a full-time career. I find that working three days per week is ideal."
>
> —Louise, 28, mother of one

You'll want to pay particular attention to the lines of your budget that are most likely to be affected by your decision to work or stay at home.

- *Income.* If you or your partner decide to leave your job, you can expect this figure to drop significantly—unless, of course, you intend to make other changes to offset the income loss. The breadwinner, for example, might decide to look for a better paying job, or the stay-at-home parent

---

FIGURE 4.2
Income versus Expenses

INCOME	DUAL-INCOME	SINGLE-INCOME
Your salary		
Your partner's salary		
Bonuses		
Investment income		
Rental income		
Spousal support		
Child support		
Other sources of income		

EXPENSES	DUAL-INCOME	SINGLE-INCOME
Taxes and other income deductions		
Federal income tax		
State income tax		
401(k) contributions		
Social Security		
Medicare		
Federal/state unemployment tax		
Union dues		
Other deductions		
Household expenses		
Rent or mortgage		
Property taxes		
House insurance		
Utilities (heat, electricity, water)		
Service contracts (cleaning, lawn care, snow removal, etc.)		
Telephone		
Cable TV		
Household equipment		
Household repair		
Other		
Food		
Groceries		
Restaurant meals and takeout food		
Other		
Transportation		
Car loan payments		
Gasoline		

FIGURE 4.2
Income versus Expenses (Continued)

EXPENSES	DUAL-INCOME	SINGLE-INCOME
Transportation (Continued)		
Maintenance/repairs		
License fees (vehicle and driver's license)		
Tolls and parking fees		
Bus, subway, or commuter train fares		
Taxis		
Other		
Personal care		
Medical insurance premiums		
Clothing		
Dry cleaning		
Hair salon		
Health club membership		
Other		
Debt repayment		
Credit cards		
Line of credit		
Student loans		
Other debts		
Entertainment		
Movies		
Concerts		
Vacations		
Gifts		
Books		
Video rentals		
Hobbies		
Wine, beer, and other alcoholic beverages		
Other		
Professional services		
Accountant		
Lawyer		
Financial advisor		
Health care		
Unreimbursed medical expenses		
Drugs		
Dental care		

FIGURE 4.2
Income versus Expenses (Continued)

EXPENSES	DUAL-INCOME	SINGLE-INCOME
Health care (Continued)		
Eye care	_____	_____
Other	_____	_____
Educational expenses		
Tuition	_____	_____
Books	_____	_____
Other	_____	_____
Insurance		
Life insurance	_____	_____
Disability insurance	_____	_____
Medical insurance	_____	_____
Other expenses		
Child care	_____	_____
Charitable donations	_____	_____
Other	_____	_____
Total Expenses	_____	_____

might decide to try to bring in some extra income by running a business from home. (Don't forget to factor in the value of any benefits you or your partner receive through your employers. A dental plan is pure gold to a family with young children!)

- *Child care.* According to the latest figures from the Children's Defense Fund, American parents pay between $4,000 to $10,000 per child per year for full-time child care. You don't have to do much number crunching to see how much money you would save on this line of your budget by staying home as opposed to paying for full-time child care for two or more children.

- *Transportation.* The cost savings on the transportation budget line is a lot less clear cut. Some single-income families consider the second car to be sacred—the only thing that keeps the stay-at-home parent sane. Others view it as an unnecessary frill. Only you can decide how important having a second car is to you. If you're lucky enough to live on a bus route or to live across the street from a recreation center, a park, and a shopping mall, you might decide that you don't need that second vehicle after all. You'll find out about the true cost of running a car in Chapter 7.

- *Food.* While your family still needs to eat whether you work outside the home or stay at home, you may find that the amount of money you spend on groceries and both takeout and restaurant meals changes significantly if one parent is available at home to prepare meals. Part of this adjustment is due to sheer necessity, of course; the same funds aren't available to pick up a pizza every time you're feeling too tired to cook.

- *Clothing.* If you wear your street clothes to work each day, you're not going to see a huge difference in this budget category if you decide to leave your job. If, on the other hand, you are expected to wear suits or dressy clothing to work, you may find yourself spending a significant amount of money on clothing, dry-cleaning bills, and so on. If you left your job, or started working from home as a freelance consultant, you would dramatically reduce your expenditures in this area.

- *Miscellaneous.* Ah, miscellaneous. That mysterious black hole in your budget. You may find that the miscellaneous category goes on a drastic reducing diet if you become a single-income family—again, partially due to necessity, but also because you find fewer places to spend your money. You'll no longer be expected to pitch in $10 to buy a gift for a coworker who just had a baby or to buy $20 of Girl Scout cookies from your boss's daughter. These "little things" can really add up, often to $500 or more per year for someone working outside of the home.

As you can see, working holds a lot of hidden costs. You spend more money on transportation, child care, clothing, and perhaps other types of items than you would if only one of you were working. These costs can sneak up on you, so sometimes it can be a bit of a shock to tally them up and consider the bottom line. Some couples who do this calculation find that they're not taking home much more money with both of them working than they would if just one of them were working. Others find that they're actually further ahead financially if they lose the second paycheck.

Facts and Figures

According to the Children's Defense Fund, approximately 13 million American children require child care each year.

The Hidden Costs of Staying at Home

While most parents find it relatively easy to assess the short-term costs of staying at home to raise a family, what many fail to consider are the long-term financial implications of that choice.

First of all, you'll likely lose ground when it comes to saving for your retirement. While your partner can make Individual Retirement Account (IRA) contributions in your name while you're at home raising a family, in reality, fewer dollars will be available to do so. What this means for most families is that you'll simply end up dividing up the pot of money that your partner might otherwise have contributed to his or her own 401(k) plan, resulting in a lower standard of living come retirement time than you would enjoy if you'd both been working full time and maxing out your 401(k) contributions. Of course, if one of your children grows up to be the next great NHL superstar and decides to provide for you in your old age, you'll be ahead of the game financially. Just be forewarned that it doesn't always work out that way!

Second, there are the career costs associated with deciding to drop out of the workforce for an extended period of time. You're likely to miss out on promotions, and you may quickly lose touch with developments in your industry or profession, something that could necessitate a period of retraining when you decide to go back to work again.

Third, the stay-at-home partner loses his or her financial safety net. If your marriage breaks up or the breadwinner dies suddenly, the stay-at-home partner could find himself or herself thrown back into the workforce with few, if any, marketable skills.

The grass isn't necessarily greener on the stay-at-home side of the fence. A recent study concluded that two-income families are generally happier and healthier than families in which only the male partner works. They have fewer financial worries, and both partners are less likely to suffer from depression than parents who are at home full time raising their children. "The news about the two-career couple today is very good indeed," write Rosalind C. Barnett and Caryl Rivers, authors of *She Works/He Works: How Two-Income Families Are Happier, Healthier, and Better-Off,* a book based on the study.

That's why it's important to look at more than just the bottom line when you're making this all-important decision. Sometimes, it makes sense to continue as a two-paycheck family, even if your childcare costs and other work-related expenses end up wiping out the second income altogether. If, for example, you're in a profession where it's difficult to take a couple of years off (if you're self-employed, the vice-president of a large corporation, or a doctor with a busy medical practice, for example), you might decide that working outside the home is worthwhile, even if you're not making any money over the short run. After all, you'll be forking over major amounts of cash for childcare-related expenses for only a couple of years.

What the Numbers Won't Tell You

Up until now, we've focused on the dollars-and-cents component of the working versus staying-at-home issue. What we haven't tackled yet are all of the non-monetary aspects of this decision, such as how you might feel about leaving the workforce to be at home with your children.

If you get a great deal of satisfaction from working, and you think you'd be completely stir-crazy by the end of your first day as a stay-at-home parent, then keeping your job probably makes sense even if you can afford to stay home. Think about it: how much quality time are you going to manage to spend with your kids if you feel bored or depressed all the time?

The flip side of the coin also applies, of course. If being at home with your children is extremely important to you, you may decide that you're going to stay home with them, whether you and your partner can actually afford to lose that second income or not. That's what Cindy, a 40-year-old mother of two, and her partner, John, decided to do. They've never looked back. "We suffered financially when I quit my full-time job, but I wouldn't change a thing," she explains. "It has given us both a remarkable number of memories with our children that we would have missed if we both kept working in a city two hours away and commuting."

Money Talk

"We were both commuting to work, so the cost of childcare would have been astronomical. We didn't decide that I would stay home until after the baby was born. I never realized the extent of a mother's love until then. I couldn't bear the thought of leaving her every day. We decided then that I was staying home even if we had to start selling furniture."
—*Melinda, 33, mother of three*

Making a Decision You Can Live With

Whether you decide to stay at home with your children or continue working, what's important is how comfortable you and your partner feel about the decision that you have made. That's why the two of you should make this decision together.

Some couples find that there's no decision to be made. They've always known what's right for them. This was certainly the case for Fiona, a 32-year-old mother of six, and her husband Christopher. "My husband's mother stayed home full time until he was 18 years old, so he grew up thinking that's what other moms did. We always knew that when there were kids, I would stay home with them, and he would go to work."

David, 38, and Phyllis, 37, parents of two young children, also found it relatively easy to make their decision. In their case, they decided that it made the most sense for them both to continue working. "We looked both at financials and at the impact on Phyllis's career if she were to stop working," David recalls. "She had recently completed her master's degree and was really just getting started with new responsibilities. We felt that having her return to work was the best decision for our family, provided we could get quality daycare.

Kristin and her husband Jeff, both 30, reached a similar conclusion. "We briefly discussed the issue of one of us staying home, but it was not feasible," she explains. "I am the primary breadwinner in our family and my husband was not interested in staying home. Before returning to work, I did a quick calculation of how much money we would need to meet all of our current financial obligations—no frills, just the basics. With just Jeff's salary, there was a shortfall, so I figured out how many other children I would need to look after to make enough money. It turns out I would need to look after four children in addition to my son Nathan to make staying at home work. I wasn't willing to do that because I didn't feel Nathan would be getting much benefit from my being at home if I had four other children to care for."

> ## Money Talk
> • • • • • •
>
> "This was not a financial decision at all for us. We both felt we needed to work for the mental stimulation."
> —Jackie, 31, mother of two

Other couples find that the decision is a lot less clear cut. They have to do a lot of number crunching and soul searching before they can decide what's best for their family. Kate, a 40-year-old mother of two, and her husband, David, spent a lot of time trying to figure out how they could go from living on two incomes to one after their first child arrived. "We were quite committed to having one of us at home with the children. We worked over our budget many times in advance to ensure that we would know what our budget ceiling would be for such things as vehicle, rent, and so on." In the end, they found a way to trim their budget enough to meet their goal of having Kate stay at home with their children.

HOW CAN YOU QUIT WHEN YOU'RE THE BOSS?

In most cases, the idea of dropping out of the workforce—even temporarily—is nothing more than pie in the sky if you happen to be self-employed. As much as your clients may try to tell you that they'll be banging on your door when you hang out your shingle again in five years' time, the odds of this actually happening are slim to none. The business that you worked so hard to build over a period of time can be reduced to nothing overnight if you have to start handing your valued customers over to your competitors.

A better option for self-employed workers who are eager to be at home with their children is to scale down the business or to reduce their involvement in it for a certain period of time. Some entrepreneurs will cut back on the number of hours they devote to the business each week. Others will hire someone to run the business so they can take some time off. Both of these solutions allow the entrepreneurial parent to buy some time away from work without folding the business entirely.

TRIMMING YOUR BUDGET

If you decide that you or your partner will stay home after Junior arrives, you'll need to go back through your budget line by line and look for areas in which you can boost your income or slash your expenses. If you flip back to Figure 4.2, you'll have all the numbers you need at your fingertips.

Here are the major areas that are worth zeroing in on.

Income

- Look for ways to boost your income without increasing your work-related expenses. The breadwinner might negotiate for a raise or start looking for a better paying job, or the parent who's at home with the children might try to find a part-time job or start a home-based business in order to bring in a little extra income. Despite what you might assume by watching the Bill Gateses of the world in action, being self-employed is anything but a get-rich-quick scheme. Studies have shown that a "typical" small business takes from one to three years to start turning a profit.

> *Money Talk*
> • • • • • • •
>
> "The decision about my staying home was pretty much made for us when the job I was doing ended. I did go to work teaching for a couple of years, but the stress and the aggravation were not worth the money I was making. Because my husband has a very good job, it was easy for us to decide that I would quit working and stay at home. As for being feasible or not, we decided to make it feasible: we decided to continue to be a one-car family, to remain in a smaller house, and so on. And we haven't regretted our decision."
>
> —*Leigh, 31, mother of two*

Household Expenses

- Reduce your rent payments by moving to a smaller apartment or house, or by relocating to a less expensive area.

- Reduce your mortgage payments by moving to a less expensive area, buying a smaller house, or refinancing your existing mortgage if interest rates are lower. (Be sure to read the chapter on mortgages before you refinance so you'll know what types of upfront fees to expect.) If you go the refinancing route, you can reduce your interest rate and increase the amortization period of the new mortgage (the time it takes to pay off your mortgage), and both measures can help to improve your cash flow considerably. While the whole idea of extending the length of your mortgage contradicts everything you ever learned about borrowing money, there are times when such a move is justified. If taking a longer amortization period makes it possible for you to stay at home with your children and that's important to you, you should consider the additional interest costs that you'll incur as part of the cost of staying at home with your kids.

- Obtain quotes from other house insurance companies to ensure that you're getting the best possible value for your insurance dollar. If you find that you're paying too much for insurance, switch to a more cost-effective policy.

- Save money on your utility bills by insulating your home better, replacing any ancient appliances that gobble up energy (e.g., freezers), switching from an electric water heater to a gas water heater, and looking for ways to conserve energy around the house (turning the thermostat down a degree or two, hanging your wet clothes on the clothesline rather than popping them into the dryer, and so on).

Show Me the Money!

Some electric companies are willing to come to your home to suggest ways that you could reduce your energy consumption. In some communities, this type of energy audit is free; in others, you'll have to pay a nominal fee. Either way, the energy audit could put a whole lot of money back in your pocket.

- Cancel as many service contracts as possible (e.g., cleaning, lawn care, snow removal, etc.), get rid of a lot of those gimmicky phone features that cost a couple of dollars apiece, cancel your cable TV altogether or cut back to a no-frills cable TV package, and look for other ways to save money on your household expenses.

- Make sure that you're signed up for the long distance savings package that's best suited to your family. Some are ideal for people who do a lot of phoning during prime time; others are best for people who do all of their calling in the evening and on the weekend. The best way to find out which one would be best for your family is to ask various phone company representatives to recalculate your last phone bill based on their particular long distance savings plan. Hey, if they want your business, they should be prepared to do a little work to earn it!

- Come up with creative ways to negotiate for the best possible deals on home repairs. If your roof needs replacing, chances are the other houses on your street that were built at the same time need replacing, too. Get together with your neighbors and approach area roofing companies to see if they'll give you a group discount on roof repairs.

> ## Money Talk
> • • • • • • •
>
> "We shop around a lot for the best long distance phone rates. Then we give our current long distance carrier the competitor's best rate. If they won't match it, we switch."
> —*Michele, 32, mother of one*

- Buy your furniture from wholesalers and through discount outlets. If you're shopping at a regular retail outlet, be sure to check the scratch and dent room to find any pieces of furniture worth buying. Your furniture is going to take a bit of a beating from dinky cars and hockey sticks anyway; you might as well save some money and buy it pre-scratched!

- Decorate with paint rather than wallpaper, and look for seconds and ends of rolls when you're shopping for carpet or flooring.

Automotive Expenses

- If you're not a good negotiator, the next time you're shopping for a new car, bring along a friend or relative who is. You could save yourself hundreds—even thousands—of dollars as a result. Hint: You'll improve your negotiating position if you know the going price for the vehicle you're considering, so be sure to do some research online before you hit the dealership.

- If you don't need a car on a day-to-day basis because you have access to an excellent public transit system, consider joining a car co-op or car-sharing group. You will have access to a pool of cars that you can book as the need arises, such as when you do your weekly grocery shopping or if you are headed out of town.

Food

- Consider joining—or starting—a food-buying co-op so that you can purchase food directly from wholesalers, cutting your food-buying costs by 25 percent or more.

- Don't go to the same grocery store from week to week. Compare prices by checking out the various grocery store flyers each week and then give that week's business to the store that is offering the best prices on the items you need.

- Don't set foot in a grocery store without a grocery list. It's the impulse buys, not the basic grocery items, that really add to your weekly grocery bill.

- Know your prices. Just because an item is on sale doesn't necessarily mean it's a good buy. Nor are generics always cheaper than name brands.

- Don't forget to check out the top and bottom shelves when you're looking for a particular item; the most expensive items are deliberately placed at eye level, where they're easier to find.

- Don't just wander aimlessly in the grocery store, buying whatever catches your eye. Plan your grocery list ahead of time so that you'll have the ingredients you need on hand to make healthy, low-cost dinners from scratch. If you don't take the time to do this, you'll simply end up ordering pizza because you don't have enough ingredients on hand to make anything!

> **Money Talk**
>
> "Make saving a game. Trick yourself by putting away everything you save with coupons. Or throw all your change in a jar. Then use that money to have some fun you didn't think you could afford."
>
> —*Melodie Moore, publisher of The Skinflint News, quoted in Good Housekeeping*

- Think big. You can usually save about 25 cents per pound on meat by opting for the family-sized packages. Either use the entire package at one time to make a large batch of casseroles, or divide the package into smaller portions that can be popped into the freezer for use at another time. Don't make the same mistake with perishable items, however. Nothing is more discouraging than watching a fridge full of lettuce turn brown because you couldn't get through it all in time.

- Check your cash register tape before you drive out of the parking lot. One moneysaving expert swears that one in ten grocery items are improperly rung through by a cashier—something that could end up costing you a small fortune.

- Make your meals from scratch. It's far less expensive to make your own tuna casserole than to buy one out of the freezer at the grocery store. It's also a whole lot tastier! If you hate spending hours in the kitchen by yourself, consider starting a co-operative kitchen. A co-operative kitchen involves pulling a group of people together and spending an afternoon or an evening cooking in bulk. Everyone pools their money to buy ingredients, pitches in with the preparation, and then takes home a bunch of homemade entrées that they can store in their freezer.

- Find creative alternatives to frozen dinners. If you simply get in the habit of freezing extra portions of your own dinner entrees (think leftovers!) in reheatable plastic serving containers, you'll always have a supply of "frozen dinners" to pull out of the freezer on nights when you don't have the time or the energy to whip something up from scratch. As an added bonus, you'll be able to cater to the whims of the picky eaters in your family by giving them their pick of any of the dinners you've tucked away in the freezer: lasagna, tuna casserole, or your world-famous chicken stew.

- Instead of buying baby food in jars, make your own. Simply purée mashed fruits or vegetables, adding small amounts of water until the baby food has reached the desired consistency. An added bonus to going this route: your baby will become accustomed to the types of food that your family eats on a regular basis before actually starting to eat table food!

- Grow your own vegetables so that you won't spend as much money on produce during the summer months. If you're not much of a gardener, make weekly visits to the local farmers' market or purchase a share in an organic farm. Ann Douglas, one of the authors of this book, purchased a share in a local organic farm a few years ago and had delicious fresh produce show up on her doorstep on a weekly basis. Far more produce showed up than her family could reasonably eat, so she shared the basket full of goodies with her neighbors. Over the course of the growing season, she managed to save a couple of hundred dollars over what she would have paid for the same types of produce in a grocery store.

- Don't get hypnotized by the large warehouse stores. Bigger isn't necessarily better. In fact, you could find yourself paying more for certain types of items than you would at a regular grocery store. You really have to know your prices.

Money Talk
• • • • • • •

"We order out maybe once a year and never eat in restaurants. We prefer to make meals ahead in bulk and freeze them for those nights when we have no desire to cook. We enjoy backyard picnics in the summer and living room picnics in the winter."

—*Fiona, 32, mother of six*

Dining Out

- Figure out how often you can afford to eat out and how much you can afford to spend. You may find that you can afford one $30 dinner out a month—a nice break for the parent who's at home all day with the kids—or you may find that dinners out are one luxury you'll have to do without for at least the foreseeable future. If this is the case, you might want to consider doing some budget-friendly entertaining in your own home: swap invitations with another family with young children so that you can each enjoy occasional dinners out.

- Find out if your favorite restaurant offers a special discount night. Some restaurants, for example, let kids eat for free on Friday nights.

Transportation

- Carpool to work or take public transit so that you can sell the second car and still leave the stay-at-home parent with a set of wheels at least some of the time.

- Swap the gas-guzzler for a more fuel-efficient vehicle.

- Consider sharing a car with another family. Just make sure you resolve the insurance and maintenance issues upfront.

Personal Care

- Unless you're a regular at the gym, consider switching from an annual membership to a pay-as-you-go membership. If your health club doesn't offer this option—and, frankly, some of the big health club chains don't— call your local YMCA/YWCA instead.

Clothing

- Shop at second-hand clothing stores as much as possible when you're buying clothes for both yourself and your children. You can pick up nearly new clothing at a fraction of what you would pay for new. If you've got expensive taste in clothing, don't despair. Some consignment shops even specialize in gently used designer clothing!

- Learn to sew. You can save a tremendous amount of money on clothing—particularly children's clothing—if you sew even a portion of your wardrobe. If the mere word *sew* gives you horrible flashbacks about your eighth grade home economics class, perhaps it would be best to skip this tip entirely. If, however, you were one of those home economics whiz kids who knew intuitively how to set a sleeve in an armhole, it's time to put those long dormant talents to good use.

> **Show Me the Money!**
>
> When you're hitting the second-hand shops, don't forget to bring along some of your own used clothing to sell. While you won't get a huge amount of money for each item, what you do get will help to make any items you purchase that much more affordable.

- Don't purchase any item that needs to be dry cleaned. Those $10 dry cleaning charges quickly add up to more than what you paid for the item. The only exceptions to this hard and fast rule are business clothing and outer wear.

- If you're purchasing new clothing for your children, try to shop at stores that will replace the item if it wears out before your child outgrows it. This can save you a lot of money if you have an eight-year-old boy who's addicted to road hockey!

- Don't just fixate on the price tag. Keep in mind that an expensive pair of overalls that lasts through three kids may be cheaper in the long run than a poor quality pair that doesn't even make it through one kid.

- Join any customer loyalty programs offered by your favorite retail clothing stores. You'll receive coupons and advance notice of sales.

- Watch for end-of-season sales on name-brand merchandise. If you're a Land's End addict, you might want to pay particular attention to the overstocks page on their Web site. The prices that are "On the Counter" are marked down more and more each day until they're sold out. Check it out for yourself by visiting the site at <www.landsend.com>.

- Shop for seconds at manufacturers' retail outlets. Often the flaw is either unnoticeable or something you can repair yourself with a needle and thread.

- Invite a group of friends over for a clothing swap. Ask everyone to bring a half-dozen items of clothing that are in mint condition, but that they are no longer wearing. Take turns choosing from the pile of clothing and—voilà!—you'll each have the makings of a new wardrobe and space for it in your clothes closet to boot.

Bank Charges

- Make sure that the type of bank account you're using is the one that best fits your family's needs. You can get some help in comparing apples to oranges to grapefruits by using the chart in Figure 4.3.

- Think your bank charges are excessive? Tell your bank manager to waive your service charges or you'll take your business elsewhere. Financial institutions hate to lose checking account business because once people move their checking accounts, they tend to move their mortgages, car loans, investments, and other types of business, too.

- When you're shopping around for a checking account, be sure to consider such factors as:

  - Your preferred method of payment (e.g., check, credit card, debit card, telephone banking, Internet banking, or cash)

  - What fees are charged on this type of account and whether or not you will receive a rebate for the fee if you keep your account balance at or above a certain level)

  - The average monthly balance in your checking account

  - How much this balance fluctuates over the course of a month

  - Whether you need to have your checks returned for either tax or recordkeeping reasons

  - How they handle cash advances or overdraft protection. If you have a line of credit on your checking account to cover a check when not enough money is in the account, do they take the next deposit and pay off the credit line in full (the best alternative for you), or do you get billed each month for a minimum amount (a more costly alterative for you)?

FIGURE 4.3
Comparing Bank Charges

	Bank A	Bank B	Bank C
Monthly maintenance fee	_____	_____	_____
Per-check fee	_____	_____	_____
Exceeding minimum number of monthly transactions	_____	_____	_____
Fee for below-minimum balance	_____	_____	_____
Cost of this bank's ATM	_____	_____	_____
Cost of other banks' ATMs	_____	_____	_____
Higher fee if account pays interest	_____	_____	_____
Depositing someone else's bad check	_____	_____	_____
Fee for a bounced check	_____	_____	_____
Stop-payment fee	_____	_____	_____
Fee for copies of checks	_____	_____	_____
Inactivity fee	_____	_____	_____
Certified check fee	_____	_____	_____
Money order fee	_____	_____	_____
Cashier's check fee	_____	_____	_____
Wire-transfer fee	_____	_____	_____
Fee for traveler's checks	_____	_____	_____
Fee to call for balance	_____	_____	_____
Pay-by-phone fee	_____	_____	_____
Overdraft protection	_____	_____	_____
Method for paying overdrafts	_____	_____	_____

- When you're shopping around for a savings account, be sure to consider these factors:

    - What maintenance fees you will be charged and whether or not an additional fee applies if your account balance drops below a certain amount

    - Whether you're allowed to write checks on this account and, if so, what the fee is for writing a check

    - The rate of interest you will be paid on your savings (both before and after compounding)

    - Whether or not interest rates are tiered (i.e., does the interest rate go up once your balance reaches a certain level?)

Credit and Debt

- Pay off any debts that you are carrying, starting with the debts with the highest interest rates. If you're carrying around department store credit card balances and other high-interest debt, get a lower-interest consolidation loan from your financial institution and then retire your department store credit card permanently.

- Make sure that you're getting the best possible deal from your credit card company. Look for a card that offers a low (or no) annual fee and a low interest rate, and that rewards you for your business.

Entertainment

- Rethink your definition of entertainment. It doesn't have to be expensive to be fun. Take your kids to a performance of a local amateur theater troupe, or take up a low-cost hobby as a family, such as hiking.

- Take out a family membership if you're lucky to live near a major attraction such as a children's museum, zoo, or aquarium. Your membership will typically pay for itself after two or three visits.

- Rent videos instead of going to the movies. Hey, you'll be a couple of bucks ahead in the popcorn department alone!

- Trade in your old CDs for new ones at your nearest second-hand music store.

- If you purchase a big-ticket item like a TV set or a VCR, watch the paper for the next few weeks. If you see the item you bought advertised for less money, take a copy of the advertisement back to the store and ask the store to give you the difference. In many cases, they will.

- Purchase electronic games and other pricey electronic gizmos at your local consignment store. Then split the cost with another family and share it back and forth. You'll not only save money, you'll also make it more difficult for your children to develop an electronic games addiction!

> ## Money Talk
> • • • • • • •
>
> "When it comes to entertainment, we look for anything free. We make lots of visits to the local library and park and take advantage of recreation programs run by the city. We spend a lot of time with our kids doing things together that cost little money."
>
> —Leigh, 31, mother of two

- Buy your sports equipment second hand, and sell all the unused sports equipment that you've accumulated in a corner of your garage at the same time.

- Hit the library rather than the bookstore or the magazine stand.

- Make your own wine and beer, either at home or at a commercial "u-brew" operation.

Travel

- Plan to travel out of season. You can expect to save 25 to 50 percent by timing your vacation properly. What's more, you'll beat the crowds. While this is easiest to accomplish before your children start school, you can probably get away with pulling your kids out of school for the odd family trip. Check with your child's teacher before you make your holiday plans so that you won't accidentally hit a week when something particularly special is going on at school.

- Don't assume that you have to hop on a plane to "get away from it all." Sometimes the best vacation destinations can be found in your own backyard.

- Go camping instead of staying in a hotel. You'll spend $25 a night as opposed to $75 or more.

- If you're traveling with kids, stock your car with drinks and snacks before you leave home. That way, you can hit the highway rest stops for bathroom breaks without being forced to pay exorbitant prices for junk food.

- Try to choose a hotel that allows kids to stay for free. Some of the major hotel chains don't charge for kids' meals eaten in the hotel dining room. Failing that, plan to have breakfast and possibly even lunch in your hotel room to save a bit of money.

- If you're traveling by air, you'll get the lowest possible rate if you schedule your trip so that you

Money Talk

"You don't have to stay in the fanciest hotel or eat in five-star restaurants to have a good vacation. There are plenty of places to go and things to see in your own backyard if you just look."

—Cindy, 36, mother of two

leave on a Saturday, Tuesday, or Wednesday and are away over a Saturday. Also, book your flight at least three weeks in advance.

- If you're not in any hurry to get home, volunteer to be bumped if the airline flight is oversold. At a minimum, you'll pick up a voucher for $200 per person, perhaps considerably higher if the airline is particularly eager to get people to volunteer to wait until the next available flight.

Health Care

- If your family isn't covered by a drug plan and your family doctor prescribes an expensive drug, ask him or her if a less expensive generic drug would do the trick.

- Scrutinize your medical insurance options at work. Your employer probably offers several choices— preferred provider, HMO, and/or major medical. You'll want to consider which plan best fits your family's needs and how much of a deductible you can afford to pay.

Show Me the Money!

If your family isn't covered by a dental plan, let your dentist know. Some dentists will reduce their fees for families who are on tight budgets.

- If you live in a community with a dental school, make your appointments there instead. You will pay one-third to one-half of the going rate, and you'll be helping the next generation of dentists to learn the ropes.

Educational Expenses

- If you or your partner are attending college or university on a full-time or part-time basis, find out if work-study programs or scholarships are available to help offset the costs of tuition. Start by contacting the financial aid office at your school, but also be sure to check with your employer or your partner's employer to see if the company will pick up part or all of the cost of your educational expenses.

- Purchase as many textbooks as possible secondhand. If the campus bookstore doesn't sell secondhand books, advertise on bulletin boards or place a small advertisement in the student newspaper. You might also want to check out the growing number of online bookstores that specialize in selling secondhand college and university textbooks.

Insurance

- Don't buy more insurance than you need, but make sure that you buy enough. A good insurance broker will be able to help you to calculate the amount of insurance coverage you need—no more, no less.

- Obtain quotes from more than one company so that you can be sure that you're getting the best possible value for your insurance dollar.

- Consider giving all of your insurance business to one company if they're willing to give you a break on the overall cost.

Child Care Expenses

- Send your child to a co-operative nursery school. Because parents play an active role in running the school, the per-hour rate for child care is considerably less.

- Reduce the number of hours of child care you require. If one parent decides to stay at home full time, there can be significant savings—typically $5,000 to $6,000 per year for each child requiring full-time care.

- If you have more than one child, consider hiring an in-home caregiver rather than sending two or more children to a child care facility. It's often less expensive than paying for out-of-home child care spaces for each of your children, and having someone come into your home is certainly a lot more convenient than having to shuttle your children to a family day care or child care center when you're on your way to work.

Charitable Donations

- Consider contributing to your favorite charity in nonmonetary ways if you find yourself on a tight budget. Volunteers are in chronically short supply, so your offer to help with the next fundraising drive will no doubt be welcome.

In General

- Consider bartering goods and services with others in your community. If you're a great cook, offer to swap bottles of your famous chili sauce for help weeding your perennial garden. If your community has a bartering system (e.g., a local economic trading system, or LETS exchange), consider joining it. You'll have a far greater number of people to trade with than just those in your immediate circle of friends.

- Take advantage of annual sales on particular types of goods. There's no better time to stock up on school supplies than in late August or early September, for example.

As you can see, you can take plenty of steps to reduce the amount of income you require to keep your family in the black. You'll also find lots of other ideas elsewhere in this book.

US, INC.

Some couples decide that the ideal solution to the working versus staying-at-home dilemma is to have one or both parents start a small business. While becoming entrepreneurs is a great idea in theory, the fact remains that not all small businesses turn a profit, and even those that do can take months—even years—to start breaking even.

If you're seriously thinking of launching a small business as a means of supplementing your family's income, do your homework first to make sure that a market actually exists for your product or service. After all, there's no point in spending a small fortune on lawn care tools if your community already has a glut of gardening businesses and you don't have a hope of competing with some of the more established firms.

Once you've determined that there is, in fact, a market for your product or service, you need to write a detailed financial plan for your business. You need to project your revenues and take into account every conceivable expense in order to determine when, if ever, your business will start turning a profit. When you're drafting your plan, make sure to factor in the hidden costs of running a business—things like inventory, equipment, phone bills, and so on. After all, that $20,000 in revenue you're projecting for your first year could disappear in the blink of an eye if you have to buy $10,000 worth of computer equipment and $10,000 worth of inventory to get your business up and running.

After you've looked long and hard at

> ## Money Talk
> • • • • • • •
>
> "When we made the decision that I would not be returning to work after the baby was born, we knew that dollars would be tight. So we took most of my salary during the months before my son was born and stocked up on toilet paper, food staples, laundry detergent, and diapers—anything we figured we'd need. We didn't end up having to buy any of these items until my son was six months old. Planning ahead worked very well for us."
>
> —Jennifer, 26, mother of one

the finances, you need to stop and consider the time and commitment required to make your business successful. You don't want to discover after the fact that the business you launched so that you could stay at home with your kids is requiring 60 hours a week from you! Unfortunately, unless you've experienced entrepreneurship for yourself, you can all too easily underestimate the amount of sweat equity that goes into growing a business. So if you're a novice at this whole self-employment thing, you should definitely talk to other entrepreneurs with similar types of operations to find out how many hours they're putting in each week and use that as a rule of thumb.

You also need to know that your partner is 100 percent behind your decision to launch your own business—especially if some initial scrimping and saving will be required while you pull together the funds to launch and grow your business. Jim, a 37-year-old father of three, gives his spouse, Susan, full credit for doing without "frills" like a clothes dryer and bags of soil for their garden when they were trying to get the business up and running. "Sue has had a tremendous impact on the success of the business. She has made some huge sacrifices to get this thing going," he admits.

> ### "
> ### *Money Talk*
> • • • • • • •
>
> "Ken has worked to 'flatten' out our expenses by running credit balances with a lot of the monthly bills—electricity, water, cable, mortgage, and so on. We're usually paid ahead two or three months so that if he has a lean month in the business, the basics will be covered."
>
> —*Nicole, 28, mother of one*

Entering the ranks of the self-employed is scary enough when you know full well that you can always fall back on your partner's paycheck. If, however, you both decide to leave your jobs elsewhere to start a business together, it can be downright hair raising. If you decide to go this route, you should take steps to create a financial safety net for your family. If you don't give some thought to these issues up front, you could find yourselves facing financial disaster if the business goes through a rough period (e.g., you're sued by a disgruntled customer, you or your partner is permanently or temporarily disabled, or—heaven forbid—one of you is killed in a car accident). This means setting up your business in a manner that will ensure that your personal assets are sheltered, carrying appropriate amounts of life insurance and disability insurance, and getting into the habit of setting aside some money each week so that you'll have enough funds stashed away to buy an umbrella on the next rainy day.

The moral of the story? Self employment is not for the faint of heart. Make sure you take the plunge with both eyes wide open.

We've covered a lot of ground in this chapter, zeroing in on numerous of ways of trimming the fat from your family's budget. In the next chapter, we're going to take things one step further by talking about how you can gain control over your finances by treating money as a tool for achieving your family's dreams.

CHAPTER 5

The Wish List

· ·

Step right up, folks. It's time for a fast-paced game of paycheck roulette. Just give the old roulette wheel a spin, keep your eyes on the little red ball, and find out where this week's paycheck is going to go. It's spinning, spinning, spinning—and it's stopped. The ball has stopped on "car loan." Looks like you'll get to keep that sports utility vehicle on the road for another week or two.

Do you sometimes feel like you're playing paycheck roulette—that there are far more demands on your paycheck than dollars available to meet those demands? If you do, you're not alone. Many parents with young children find themselves short on cash and long on financial obligations.

You don't have to be a rocket scientist to figure out why. I mean, just stop and consider the number of financial balls that you're trying to keep in the air. At this stage in your life, you're probably still paying for your house. You might even have a car loan or two. You've got tons of kid-related expenses to worry about—clothes, shoes, books, toys, sports registration fees, college or university tuition fees, and more—and some sort of emergency is always cropping up to eat away at whatever savings you've managed to squirrel away in the bank. As if that weren't enough to contend with, you're probably suffering from a chronic case of 401(k) guilt syndrome, an all-too-common affliction, which is caused by the failure to max out one's 401(k) contributions year after year.

WHAT'S WRONG WITH THIS PICTURE?

At times you may wonder if you're some sort of financial misfit. You may begin to believe that yours is the only American family that isn't managing to pay off credit card debt, contribute regularly to its 401(k) plans, and still find the necessary funds to dress its children in designer jeans and make annual treks to the Mother of All Family Vacation Spots, Disneyland.

Here's some news that should help to reassure you. Despite what you may have gathered from watching all those glitzy mutual fund advertisements, "having it all" is not the norm. While Americans do have an enviable standard of living, very few of us live in monster homes with three-car garages, and those of us who do manage to take glitzy vacations to high-priced tourist destinations often do so with a little help from the nice people at MasterCard and VISA.

It's funny, isn't it? We spend hours explaining to our kids that what they're seeing on TV isn't real—but then we get caught by the same trap ourselves by falling prey to those slick financial planning ads. Despite what the mutual fund company marketers would have you believe, "real" families—as opposed to those unreasonable facsimiles you'll see on TV—soon learn that financial planning is a matter of making choices and setting priorities, of deciding if that trip to Disneyland is more important to the family than contributing to Junior's college fund. If you can't "have it all"—and frankly that's the case for most of us—you might as well take time to decide what you'd like to have.

TAKING A STEP BACK

Up until this point, we've been focusing mainly on the here and now—how much money you need to bring home each week to cover your day-to-day expenses. While that's very important—after all, you're not going to get very far in saving for that trip to Disneyland if your family can't even afford to buy groceries—budgeting is only a small part of the financial planning puzzle. You need to take a step back and look at the big picture.

Remember back in the late '80s and early '90s how companies spent huge amounts of time and money hiring high-priced consultants to come up with glitzy mission statements and help them to establish corporate goals? That's kind of what financial planning is all about—although without the high-priced help. While you probably won't want to write some nauseating mission statement for your family, you should at least have an idea about where your family's values lie, because your values should play an important role in determining your financial game plan. Here are a few questions to get you thinking.

How important is it to you that:

- One parent leave the workforce to stay at home with the children until they reach a certain age?

- You are able to pay for your child's education when the time comes?

- You get away for a few days each year so that you can spend time together as a family?

- You have funds on hand to spend on recreational activities like hockey, skiing, snowboarding, boating, and so on?

- You have the funds needed to retire early or enjoy a higher-than-average standard of living during your retirement years?

- You are able to get rid of any consumer debt (credit cards, car loans, lines of credit, and so on) that you're carrying right now?

- You pay off your mortgage sooner rather than later?

- You give something back to your community through charitable donations?

You already know from our earlier discussion that couples don't always agree on money, so it's important to find out where your partner's financial priorities lie, too. If you find that you have conflicting priorities, you'll need to figure out a way that the two of you can reach a compromise. If, for example, one partner feels that it's very important to budget for an annual family vacation, while the other partner would prefer to use those funds to pay down the credit card balances, you're going to have some financial wheeling and dealing to do! Fortunately, if you're sufficiently creative and willing to compromise, you should be able to come up with a workable solution. You might, for example, decide to take an inexpensive family vacation so that you will have some funds left to pay off your credit card debts—or you might decide to put all of your spare cash against the credit cards this year and hit Disneyland next year instead.

If you're lucky, there won't be too much to negotiate. You'll discover that you and your partner are basically on the same wavelength when it comes to your financial goals. This was the case for Anne, a 40-year-old mother of three, and her partner, Andreas. "We have a loose financial plan that includes saving money for retirement, saving for our children's education, living comfortably and enjoyably

Money Talk

"It's important not to [set your savings goals] alone. Get your spouse in on the act. And your kids. If they're old enough to read and write, they are old enough to listen and think and contribute; and they may even surprise you with their common sense and logic. Include all members of the family in the discussions and the decisions. Too many misunderstandings about money develop because somebody didn't allow their goals to be known and understood."

—Licensed marriage and family therapist Anne Ziff of Westport, Connecticut now, and being able to afford what gives us pleasure. We agreed on these priorities from day one."

Kristin and Jeff, 30-year-old parents with one child, are also in agreement about their family's financial goals. "Our financial goals are to pay off our mortgage by age 40; to give our children the opportunity to participate in extracurricular activities, take family vacations, and the like; to save for our retirement (between age 55 and 60); and to save for our children's education. Basically, we want it all and we are grappling with how to make it all happen. We recently came to the realization that paying off our house is a big factor in achieving the rest of our goals, so it has become our top financial priority."

Leigh, 31, a mother of two, says that she and her partner, Thomas, 30, have structured their financial lives in order to accommodate their shared desire to have her stay at home to raise their children. "One of the main financial priorities for our family is to make it possible for me to continue to stay home with the kids," she explains. "We also strive to save money for our retirement and our children's education. Money comes out of our account every month for these things, so we don't really have to think about them. There are more things we would like to be able to do right now, but they will just have to wait. We both agree that the most important thing is for me to be at home with the kids."

Some couples, like Fiona, 32, and Christopher, 35, parents of six children, find that a fair bit of negotiating was involved at first. "Initially, as a couple, we needed to refine our priorities, to clearly define where we were going and the steps we would take to get there. This was not always easy as our financial backgrounds were somewhat dissimilar. Lots of discussions, debates, and compromises were required in order for us to come to a meeting of the pocketbooks. It was made easier, however, by knowing that we wanted a rural home, a simple-back-to-basics type of lifestyle, and a way of living that was in harmony with nature. Our priorities at this time are to create alternative energy sources for our home (such as a wood stove, solar power) so that part of our savings can go toward this end. We are also planning on purchasing a large acreage lot within the next five years, and this is a financial savings priority as well."

> ## *Money Talk*
> • • • • • • •
>
> "Right now, our priorities are to pay off our credit cards and bank loan and save up enough to have a downpayment for a house within a year. As for more long-term priorities, we want to save for Isabel's college education and accumulate some substantial retirement savings. But right now, the next two to three years is where most of our focus is. We are just starting to get to the point where we are not living from paycheck to paycheck."
>
> —*Stephanie, 26, mother of one*

Some couples find that their priorities evolve over time. "For the past few years, we have been focused on debt reduction," says David, a 38-year-old father of two. "Our total debt from leftover student loans, furniture purchases, household renovations, car payments, et cetera, seemed to be increasing rather than decreasing. Some of our other priorities, now that we are getting our debt under control, include making retirement savings plan contributions to secure our future, making educational savings plan investments to pay for our children's education, traveling to interesting places, and paying for our children's extracurricular activities, such as karate and swimming."

WALKING THE TALK

Once you've agreed upon your financial priorities and ranked them in order of importance, you're ready to come up with an action plan that will help you to achieve them. While you might be tempted to skip this step because it can be—dare I say it?—a little boring, persevering is extremely important. Bribe yourself with chocolate or do your number crunching over a bottle of wine, but do whatever it takes to come up with a written plan that tells you where you're headed and how you're going to get there.

Your plan doesn't have to rival the *Encyclopedia Britannica* in length or complexity. All you really need to do is to list your financial goals in order of importance, figure out how much money you can afford to set aside each month in order to achieve them, and then spell out what your new financial game plan will mean in terms of your monthly budget. Here's how to tackle this task, step by step:

Show Me the Money!

Thinking of using the services of a financial planner? Be sure to look for someone with the necessary credentials. The Institute of Certified Financial Planners (1-800-282-PLAN), the Financial Planning Association (1-800-945-IAFP), and the National Association of Personal Financial Advisors (1-888-FEE-ONLY) can all provide you with the names of qualified financial planners in your community.

Something else to keep in mind when you're shopping around for a financial planner to work with is how that person will be paid. Some financial planners charge an hourly fee or a flat fee for services rendered. Others make their living from the commissions they receive on the insurance, mutual funds, and annuities they sell. Still others work on a combined fee/commission basis. As a rule of thumb, it's a good idea to find out upfront what percentage of a planner's income comes from fees versus commissions. That way, you'll know when and how that person will be paid, and whether the planner stands to make more money based on the amount of product you buy.

1. List your financial priorities. Being clear about what you're hoping to achieve is important when writing this financial plan. Do you want to pay off your credit card debts, save enough money to retire at age 55, or do something else entirely? Try to be as specific as possible when outlining your goals. The more specifically you can pinpoint your goals, the greater your chances of actually being able to achieve them.

2. Figure out how much money you need to set aside each month to achieve your financial goals. Because you've already analyzed your spending in previous chapters, you should have a pretty good idea about how much extra money you have kicking around, if any. If you don't have any spare cash, you might want to think about cutting back on some of your expenses so that you can set aside money for things that are really important to you—like that annual family getaway or the opportunity to underwrite Junior's Harvard education. Do you need to save $1,000 a month to have a reasonable lifestyle when you retire at age 65, or would $700 a month do the trick? You won't know unless you do the necessary number crunching. A number of useful financial planning tools are available online to take some of the drudgery out of this part of the financial planning process. Check out the tool sections of the major mutual fund companies and you'll find financial planning calculators galore. You'll find our favorite sites listed in the Resources section.

3. Divvy up the funds. If debt reduction is your number one priority—and it's pretty close to the top of the list for most couples with young children—then you may decide to slap every spare cent in your budget against your credit card balance. If, on the other hand, your goals are to

The Bottom Line

* * * * * * *

Marie, 37, and Neil, 38, managed to pull together the downpayment for their first house by putting themselves on a very strict "money diet." They realized that they needed to save $500 a week from the time they made their initial deposit until the time when the deal closed if they were going to have the necessary funds on hand for the deal to go through.

"We had no choice but to be successful," Marie recalls. "There was so much on the line. So we just did it. Before we did anything else with our paychecks each week, we took the $500 lump sum right off the top. Then we put it in a savings account all by itself so we wouldn't accidentally end up spending it on something else. We actually managed to exceed our savings goal a little— enough that we were able to redecorate our kitchen soon after we moved in. That was a nice surprise!"

save for both your children's education and your own retirement, you'll have to figure out how much money you can afford to put into each pot.

4. Adjust your monthly budget accordingly. Having grandiose visions of spending your retirement years on a yacht or of watching each of your magnificent offspring graduate from Ivy League universities is pointless unless you're willing to start working toward these goals today. Make sure that your day-to-day budget reflects your new financial priorities.

Short-Term vs. Long-Term Goals

If the whole idea of setting financial goals is new to you and your partner, you might want to start out by setting a short-term rather than a long-term goal. Short-term goals are goals that you hope to achieve in the next year or two—perhaps putting together the down payment for a new car or setting aside the funds to get the family room recarpeted. Long-term goals, on the other hand, are goals that you likely won't be able to achieve for many years: paying off your mortgage, accumulating the savings you need to retire, and so on. If you're able to follow through on a short-term goal, then you've graduated to the big leagues and may be ready to tackle a medium-term (three to five years) or long-term (ten years or more) goal.

If, on the other hand, you stumble and don't manage to achieve your short-term savings goal, it's important to sit down and do a bit of a savings postmortem. You need to figure out what went wrong and why.

- Was your savings goal too ambitious?

- Were you too disorganized to get your plan off the ground? Something as simple as neglecting to set up an automatic transfer from your checking account to your savings account can make mincemeat out of all your good intentions.

- Did you neglect to factor in life's little curve balls (a broken furnace, leaky roof, or other disaster that may have wreaked havoc on your plans to embark on a serious savings program)?

- Was the payoff (the down payment for the new car) not sufficiently motivating to justify the sacrifices required to meet your goal?

- Was it something that mattered more to your spouse than you, or vice versa?

- Were you guilty of falling prey to the eighth deadly sin—procrastination? That "tomorrow" mentality might have worked well for Scarlett O'Hara, but it won't do a thing for your savings program.

Just a few parting words on the art of saving before we wrap up this chapter—and, trust us, it really is an art.

- Be as specific as possible when you're spelling out your "big picture" financial goals. The more clearly you are able to articulate them today, the greater the likelihood that you'll manage to achieve them over time.

- Recognize the difference between "dreaming" and "planning." A wish list only becomes an action plan when you boil it down into a series of specific, achievable actions (e.g., putting an extra $500 against your car loan each month).

Show Me the Money!

Here's a powerful medium-term goal that can reap huge dividends for your family. Commit to paying for your new car over a three-year period. Then drive your car for another three years and deposit the same monthly payment into your savings account each month. At the end of three years, you'll probably have enough cash on hand to buy your next vehicle. If you can hold out even longer than that, you may even be able to afford a nicer car the next time around.

- Make sure that your financial goals are realistic. That means doing the necessary number crunching up-front rather than discovering a few months down the road that you've set the bar a little too high. Otherwise, you could end up feeling so discouraged that you end up abandoning your goals altogether. You'll find some excellent savings worksheets online at <www.financenter.com>, <www.quicken.com>, and <www.moneycentral.msn.com>, as well as at the Web sites of many of the major mutual fund companies.

- Recognize that your financial goals will evolve over time, but don't make any reckless, spur-of-the-moment decisions. Avoid falling into the all-too-common trap of using money that you've set aside for a medium- or long-term financial goal to pay for something you want right now.

• Don't be afraid to rethink your goals from time to time. As your children grow older, your priorities may change. The week-long family vacation getaway that you enjoyed so much when your child was ten will be less feasible when your child is fifteen and juggling an active social life and a part-time job. As heartbroken as you may be to find out that your fifteen-year-old's definition of torture involves sharing a hotel room with you, there is a bright side to her newfound love of staying at home; you can redirect the funds in the family vacation budget to her college fund without feeling guilty about "depriving" your child of an out-of-state vacation!

Money Talk

• • • • • • •

"Realize that a short-term goal may take priority over your major long-term goal for a year or so. Some unforeseen event can impose a detour on your road map. But if your long-term goal is important, you will get back on the road and keep on toward your planned destination."

—*David W. Bennett, CFP, Total Financial Concepts, Los Angeles CA*

CHAPTER 6

Home Is Where the Mortgage Is

• •

To buy or to rent: that is the question.

Rather than allowing that classic late-third-trimester nesting urge to spur you to put a call into your friendly neighborhood real estate agent, it's important to stop and carefully weigh the pros and cons of home ownership first. Despite what you may have been told by well-meaning friends and relatives, home ownership isn't necessarily for everyone. Here are a few points to consider before you decide whether or not to take the plunge.

- Buying a home isn't always a wise investment. If the real estate market goes down, your house may be worth less than you paid for it—something that can be more than a little demoralizing, to say the least!

- Home ownership tends to tie you down—something that you may or may not be ready for at this point in your life. If you're still hoping to make some significant career moves that might require you to relocate across the country or around the world, then it may not be the best time for you to put down roots in the form of a house and mortgage. Most experts agree that you shouldn't even consider purchasing a house unless you are going to live in it for at least three years—preferably five or more. Your house needs to increase in value by approximately 10 percent to offset the costs associated with buying and selling a home—something to bear in mind if there's even the slightest chance that you could be hit with a set of surprise triplets down the road!

- Home ownership requires a lot of time, energy, and worry. When you rent a home, it's your landlord's problem if your furnace packs it in at 3:00 AM on the coldest day of the year. When you own a home, it's your problem.

- Home ownership can be expensive. Mortgage payments can take a huge bite out of your take-home pay. If you love to travel or you have expensive hobbies and interests that you enjoy (e.g., feeding your children!), you might not be willing to make the financial sacrifices necessary to buy a home.

Facts and Figures
• • • • • •

The first building and loan associations were formed in Philadelphia in 1831. Suddenly, it became possible for people of modest incomes to borrow money to purchase a home.

Of course, the home ownership front isn't all gloom-and-doom. Joining the International Order of Mortgage Holders also brings plenty of advantages.

- You enjoy the satisfaction that comes from knowing that you own a piece of land and the building that sits on it. Home ownership has always been a part of the American dream and, for many people, it's the ultimate symbol of financial security and career achievement—proof that they've "made it."

- You no longer have to worry about handing a rent check over to some sleazy landlord—you know, the kind of landlord who's quick to drop by on rent day, but who is nowhere to be found when the roof starts to leak or the furnace conks out. Granted, the bank that holds your mortgage is kind of like a landlord. But at least the bank doesn't drop by unannounced and hassle you for letting your car drip oil onto the driveway or for playing your music too loudly!

- If you get lucky and purchase a home that increases in value, you could find yourself significantly further ahead financially because of your decision to own rather than rent. Most financial planners agree that home ownership is the best single investment for most people.

- Owning a home is your best way to accumulate capital. Not only is it an investment that puts a roof over your head (a claim that no mutual fund can match!), it's also an asset that can be added to or improved over time.

- Home ownership protects you from inflation. Rent payments can go up and up during periods of high inflation, while mortgage payments either stay the same or increase by a prescribed amount if you have an adjustable rate mortgage.

- Home ownership gives you tax advantages. Uncle Sam indirectly subsidizes some of your home ownership costs by allowing you to deduct the interest you pay on your mortgage and the taxes you pay on your property. Depending on your tax bracket and how much money you end up spending on mortgage interest and property taxes, these deductions could translate into significant tax savings. See the discussion of the tax implications of home ownership elsewhere in this chapter.

In most cases, the decision to buy or rent is an emotional decision, one fueled more by a desire to put down roots than a strict dollars-and-cents analysis of the costs of renting vs. owning. Bottom line? Only you can decide whether you're willing to make the lifestyle sacrifices necessary to scrape together that down payment and to make those monthly payments to the bank year in and year out, because that, in a nutshell, is what home ownership is all about.

Show Me the Money!

Finding it hard to pull together the funds necessary to make a down payment on a home? You can make a penalty-free withdrawal of up to $10,000 from your Individual Retirement Account (IRA) if you're a first-time homebuyer. You may also be able to borrow from your 401(k) account and/or make early withdrawals from your 401(k) account to finance the purchase of a primary residence. Just be forewarned: you're robbing Peter (tomorrow's retirement nest egg) to pay Paul (today's down payment on a home).

Note: There's a bit of red tape associated with this last provision. You have to be able to demonstrate that you're worthy of making such a "hardship withdrawal for an immediate and heavy financial need," and you could be hit with a 10 percent withdrawal penalty and be required to pay income taxes on the amount withdrawn. (Hey, what Uncle Sam giveth, Uncle Sam can taketh away!)

HOW MUCH HOUSE CAN YOU AFFORD?

Once you have decided that you would like to enter the weird and wonderful world of home ownership, your first order of business is to figure out how much house you can afford. After all, there's no point shopping in Cadillac neighborhoods if you're limited to a Chevy price range!

Here are some factors to consider when you're trying to determine how much you can afford to spend on a house.

- *How large a down payment can you afford to make?* Obviously, the more money you can put down, the lower your monthly payments will be.

- *How large a monthly payment can you comfortably afford to make, based on your current income and expenses?* Don't forget to factor in the costs of insurance, utilities, property taxes, and maintenance, as well as all those nasty closing costs that we'll discuss later in this chapter. Also, be sure that you've left yourself enough financial breathing room to be able to sock some money into both your savings account and your emergency fund on a regular basis.

- *How long a mortgage term do you want?* Mortgages can be set up for terms of 15, 20, 25, or 30 years. The shorter the term, the less you spend on interest, but the higher your payments will be.

In addition to deciding how much money you can afford to spend on a home, you need to give some thought to the pros and cons of buying a home in a particular neighborhood.

- How comfortable you will feel in this neighborhood (e.g., whether other families with young children live in the area)

- The quality of the schools (you can save thousands of dollars in private school tuition fees and/or tutoring costs by ensuring that the local public school is up to snuff)

- Whether the schools in this particular neighborhood offer the programs that your family may want, either today or down the road (e.g., an enriched curriculum for gifted children or an after-school childcare program)

- The calibre of the facilities available to families with young children (hospitals, schools, daycare centers, recreation facilities, parks, pediatric walk-in clinics, etc.)

- Whether the street has sidewalks or not, a big factor to consider if your children are still very young and will someday need to master the art of riding a two-wheeler!

- Whether the street is well lit at night, an important consideration if you've got teens who may be cruising the neighborhood after dark

- How well the neighborhood is serviced by public transportation; if no bus route runs through your subdivision, you'll likely be enlisted as chauffeur to shuttle your teenager to and from a McJob

- What moving to this neighborhood will do to your home and auto insurance costs (in general, you can expect to pay more in an urban or suburban setting than if you live way out in the country)

- Whether you're likely to spend more time commuting or running errands than you are right now—something that could increase your automotive expenses considerably

- Whether the utility bills for this house are likely to be larger than what you're paying right now (no surprises here: the local utility company should be able to give you a pretty clear estimate of your projected costs)

- What you can expect to pay for property taxes and what types of services those property taxes do and don't cover (e.g., is garbage collection included in your property taxes, or will you have to pay an extra fee to the company that takes away your trash?)

> ### Show Me the Money!
> • • • • • • •
> Don't forget to ask when the city or town that you'll be moving to last reassessed its property taxes and when it's due to do so again. Since these reassessments can result in hefty tax increases, you'll want to know whether you're likely to find yourself dealing with this particular financial wild card in the immediate future or whether you're off the hook for a while.

Your aim should be to eliminate as many of those last-minute surprises as possible. Nothing is worse, after all, than moving into your new home and immediately discovering that you misjudged the costs of carrying the property or that the house isn't going to meet your family's needs after all.

WHAT TO DO BEFORE YOU CALL YOUR LENDER

There's an art to making your way through the mortgage maze and cutting yourself the best possible deal. Here are seven steps that you should take before you call your lender:

1. Do your homework. Research interest rates, mortgage features, the housing markets, and anything else that might help you to save money on your home or mortgage.

2. Learn how to speak the language—the language of the mortgage industry, that is! If you're not up to speed on terms like amortization and escrow charges and you haven't got a clue about the difference between fixed rate

and variable rate mortgages, perhaps it's time to read through the appropriate sections of this chapter and to consult the glossary at the end of this book.

3. Analyze your financial situation. Make sure you have a clear idea of how much house you can—and can't—realistically afford. You can either ask a potential lender to do some of the number crunching for you or use one of the growing number of mortgage calculators that are available online. (See the Resources section for leads on our favorite online tools.)

4. Consider which type of mortgage will best suit your personality. Are you a gambler who is willing to ride the variable rate rollercoaster—your mortgage rate could climb by as much as 2 percent a year, if interest rates happen to rise—or would you prefer to lock in your mortgage at a fixed rate of interest and a fixed monthly payment for the next 30 years?

5. Prepare to make the best possible case to the lender at the financial institution that you intend to deal with. Anticipate the types of information you'll be asked to provide, and arm yourself with the numbers you'll need to fill out the mortgage application thoroughly and accurately. Nothing shakes a potential lender's confidence more than watching a mortgage applicant underestimate his or her personal debt to the tune of $20,000!

6. Check out your credit report. You don't want to go through the trauma of having your mortgage application turned down because of an error in your file. You might want to flip back to Chapter 3 to get details on how to obtain a copy of your credit report.

7. Tap into the mortgage grapevine. Find out where your friends have their mortgages, how happy they are with their lenders, and whether they were able to negotiate any added bells and whistles (e.g., a cut in the mortgage rate).

Money Talk
• • • • • • •

"Be sure to check out the demographics of the neighborhood. Is it a young neighborhood or is it more 'mature'? You want to make sure that it's a good fit with your stage in life. Be sure to check out the location of schools if you have or are planning to have children. You'll also want to consider such factors as the accessibility to shopping and community resources, and to consider the future growth patterns of the area."
—Kristin, 30, mother of one

HOW THE BANKS DECIDE HOW MUCH TO LEND YOU

It's a little disconcerting to watch some bank employee you've never met in your life punch some numbers into a computer and then tell you how much you can—or can't—borrow. But that's exactly how the mortgage game works these days. The loan officer at your local financial institution will ask you to supply information about your income, current debts, assets, and liabilities. She will feed these numbers into a computer program that will calculate how much money you can afford to borrow. With any luck, you'll be prequalified for a mortgage of some size by the time you walk out the door.

Figuring out why the banks are so big on automated underwriting systems these days isn't difficult. Such systems allow them to process loan applications much more quickly, easily, and—let's admit it—more objectively than in the past. You see, rather than relying on the judgment of the individual loans officer, the automated system evaluates the information that has been keyed in and gives the lender a recommendation about whether or not the loan meets the criteria for approval.

Certain software packages do, however, allow for a bit of human judgment. They refer loans that do not appear to meet the initial criteria for approval to a loans officer, who may decide to collect some additional information from you before making a final decision.

Show Me the Money!
• • • • • • •

Planning to rent out the basement of your new home to bring in some extra cash? While it sounds like a good way to help finance those mortgage payments, renting could be a recipe for disaster. You could end up with the tenant from you-know-where—someone who swears in front of your children and is nowhere to be found on the day the rent is due. As if that weren't bad enough, some jurisdictions prohibit basement apartments. Our advice? Do your homework ahead of time so that you don't get hit with any surprises.

While there's no guarantee that you'll win at mortgage roulette the first time you spin the wheel, you can do plenty to put the odds in your favor. According to Julie Ribeiro, a mortgage officer with National City Mortgage in Trumbull, Connecticut, first-time borrowers can increase the likelihood that their application will be approved if they appear to have a bit of breathing room left in their budget. Bankers don't like to lend money to people who are already buried in debt, Ribeiro explains. "We look at debt-to-income ratios. Mortgage debt, which includes property taxes and homeowner's insurance, should not be higher than 33 percent of total gross household income — higher than it used to be. We also look at total debt (i.e., mortgage debt plus such other monthly debt obligations as car payments). The average now for this ratio is 38 percent."

It's important to keep that magic 38 percent figure in mind when you're determining how much house you can afford. Otherwise, you could find yourself spending so much of your take-home pay on housing-related costs that there won't be much left for anything else—a condition that those in the mortgage business refer to as being "house poor."

WHAT YOUR LENDER WILL WANT TO KNOW

Regardless of which lending institution you approach, it will likely ask you to supply a truckload of information and/or documentation.

- Personal information about your age, marital status, dependents, and your current and previous addresses

- Employment information, including proof of income (W2 forms, copies of your past three years of personal income tax returns, recent pay stubs, or a letter from your employer stating your position and income)

- Details about other sources of income (pension or rental income, for example)

- Copies of the most recent statements from your IRA, 401(k), mutual fund, and brokerage accounts

- Copies of life insurance policies

- Details about your current banking arrangements and copies of your bank statements for the previous three months

- Copies of your most recent credit card statements (or a list of outstanding balances and monthly payments)

- Evidence that you have accumulated the necessary down payment

- A letter from any relative who has given you money, to demonstrate that the money in question was actually a gift and not a loan

- A list of your assets, including property and vehicles

- A list of your liabilities, including credit card balances and car loans, which specifies both the total balance owing and the amount of your monthly payments

- Copies of rent checks written to your landlord during the previous 12 months

- A copy of the property listing

- A copy of the Agreement of Purchase and Sale on a resale home, and possibly a copy of the front and back of the deposit check that you wrote to the vendor

- A set of plans and cost estimates, if you're buying a new home

- A copy of the listing agreement if you're selling the home you own right now, or a copy of the Agreement of Purchase and Sale if the home has already been sold

- A copy of the condominium's financial statements if you're purchasing a condominium

- A certificate demonstrating that the well and septic system are operational (where applicable)

- Fees for a house appraisal, or copy of a recent appraisal report, if one is available

- Permission for the lender to do a credit check on you (and your partner, if applicable)

If you and/or your partner are self-employed, the lender will also ask you to bring along copies of your business financial statements and your income tax returns for the past three years to see how much income you actually manage to take home and how stable your earnings are from year to year.

Facts and Figures

There's a world of difference between prequalifying for a mortgage and being preapproved for a mortgage. Prequalifying means that the lender has estimated your borrowing ability but hasn't required you to go through the lengthy process of formally applying for a mortgage. Consequently, prequalifying is more of a verbal guesstimate than a written agreement to advance you funds the moment you find a house you want to buy.

Preapproval, on the other hand, requires that you actually apply for the mortgage. A loan application can involve upfront fees that may or may not be refundable, but it allows you to lock in a particular interest rate (sometimes for as long as 90 to 120 days), and it guarantees that you'll be eligible to borrow this amount of money, provided that the appraised value of the home comes in on target. Being preapproved for a mortgage allows you to move quickly when you find the house of your dreams. It also gives you a solid figure on which to base your homebuying decisions, rather than simply some loan officer's best guesstimate.

WHEN TO APPLY

You don't have to wait until you're ready to make an offer on a particular property before you apply for a mortgage. In fact, it's a good idea to get prequalified for a mortgage before you start looking, because doing so will allow you to move quickly once you're ready to make an offer.

Don't start packing your bags yet, however. The mortgage isn't actually a done deal until you obtain a satisfactory appraisal on the property and pass a credit check. The bank wants to ensure that neither you nor the property in question are lemons!

The Naked Truth

Show Me the Money!

Want to do some number crunching on your own before you sit down with your mortgage lender? Hit some of the web sites listed in Appendix C. You'll find mortgage calculators that take into account such factors as mortgage principal, interest, closing costs, interest rates, and your tax bracket in calculating the true costs of home ownership.

Just one quick word of caution: resist the temptation to fudge the numbers. If you overestimate your ability to carry a particular size of mortgage, you may need to lower your standard of living.

Before we go any further with our discussion of the ins and outs of homebuying, we think it's important to let you in on one of the financial industry's deepest and darkest secrets. An enormous gulf lies between the amount of money the bank thinks you can afford to borrow and the level of debt you can carry without breaking out into a cold sweat and tossing and turning all night. You don't have to borrow the whole amount that the bank is willing to lend you. In fact, you probably shouldn't. Remember, living in your dream home isn't much fun if you don't have enough money left to buy furniture!

At the root of this buyer-lender disconnect is the fact that the formulas that the banks use to calculate your borrowing ability generally fail to take into account such factors as your financial goals and what type of lifestyle you hope to enjoy. If, for example, you're determined to maximize your 401(k) contributions, you won't have as much money to pour into mortgage payments as someone who's decided that saving for retirement is a low priority at this stage in life. Similarly, if taking a vacation once or twice each year is important to you, you're going to have to knock down your mortgage payments a bit so you'll still have the funds needed to finance those great escapes.

Bottom Line?

You're the only one who can make an educated decision about what you can reasonably afford to borrow. Don't be tempted to download that responsibility to anyone else, especially someone who stands to make money on the transaction!

LEARNING THE LANGUAGE OF LOANS

There's no denying it. You haven't got a hope of making your way through the mortgage maze unless you've got all your mortgage lingo down pat. Here's a crash course in mortgage speak, just in case you've forgotten what some of the more important terms mean.

Money Talk
• • • • • • •

"I have always found that the banks are willing to lend me far more money than I think I should borrow. We have tried to keep our mortgage to less than 75 percent of what the banks would lend us, particularly because we are currently in a period of low interest rates, and if interest rates were to increase significantly, I wouldn't want to be put in a position where I couldn't afford the mortgage payments."

—*David, 38, father of two*

The Types of Mortgages

Let's start by defining the term *mortgage* first. Basically, a mortgage is a secured loan—a pledge of property to a creditor as security for a loan. The mortgagee (or lender) holds the mortgage until the mortgagor (or borrower) repays the debt. The mortgage document spells out the rights and obligations of the lender and the borrower and summarizes the terms of the agreement. This includes the amount of money being lent, the rate of interest being charged, and the repayment schedule that the two parties have agreed upon.

Now let's zero in on the specific types of mortgages. You will find two basic choices on the mortgage menu: conventional fixed-rate mortgages, and variable (or adjustable-rate) mortgages. According to Julie Ribeiro, a mortgage officer with National City mortgage, an adjustable rate mortgage (ARM) is generally your best bet if you think you'll be playing musical houses in the very near future. "ARMs are great for people who don't plan to stay in a house for more than three to five years," she explains. "If people are planning to live in the house for more than five years, a fixed mortgage is usually best."

Conventional fixed-rate mortgages. Conventional fixed-rate mortgages allow you to make a fixed monthly payment at a fixed rate of interest for the life of the mortgage—something that can be as long as 30 years. (Think about it! You could be making the final payment on your mortgage the same week that your baby makes his or her first mortgage payment!) The upside to this type of mortgage is security. You don't have to toss and turn at night if interest rates start climbing because your mortgage rate is locked in permanently. The downside is that you can't take advantage of any drops in rates unless you're willing to refinance your mortgage—something that can cost you a pretty penny in the end.

Variable-rate mortgages (adjustable rate mortgages). Adjustable rate mortgages, on the other hand, are an entirely different animal. With an ARM, your payment is fixed, but your interest rate floats. Consequently, the percentage of your money that goes to cover the principal vs. the interest on the mortgage rises and falls along with the rate. It's an attractive option if interest rates are high when you arrange your mortgage but are expected to fall in the near future.

If you're considering this type of mortgage, keep in mind that the interest rate that you start out with may be unbelievably attractive, but you're not guaranteed to enjoy that kind of rock-bottom rate for the life of your mortgage. Most financial institutions adjust your interest rate once or twice a year to reflect the current market conditions. (They can't boost your interest rate by more than 2 percent in a single year, thanks to government regulations.) While the interest rate on an ARM is typically lower than one on a fixed-rate mortgage, you run the risk that the interest rate will eventually equal or exceed what you would have paid on a fixed-rate mortgage. If this happens, you should immediately get in touch with your financial institution to see if they will keep the payments the same and extend the length of the loan. Obviously, you will end up paying more in interest over the long run, and you could actually end up increasing the size of your debt if the interest you're incurring on the mortgage is greater than the monthly payment you're sending in. (This rather ugly state of affairs is known as negative amortization.)

Of course, if rates hold steady or nosedive, you'll be the one who's laughing all the way to the bank.

Facts and Figures

Worried that your poor credit history will shut you out of the mortgage market entirely? That's unlikely to be the case. According to Julie Ribeiro, a mortgage officer with National City Mortgage, mortgages have been designed to meet the needs of just about anyone—even those with credit problems or no savings history. So don't give up your dream of owning a home just because you've made a few financial faux pas along the way; you'll find plenty of mortgage opportunities out there.

Other Important Mortgage-Related Terms

Here are some other important mortgage-related terms that you'll want to master before you start talking mortgages with your lender.

Amortization. The amount of time it will take you to repay your mortgage. Obviously, the longer you take to repay your mortgage, the lower your payments will be, but the more interest you will pay in the long run. (See Figure 6.1.)

Annual percentage rate (APR). The cost of borrowing, expressed as a yearly rate. The APR includes interest and other charges such as closing fees, and serves as a basis for comparing rates between two lenders.

Cap. A limit on the amount that the interest rate is allowed to climb on an ARM at each adjustment or over the life of the loan. Your lender may also impose a payment cap on you, preventing you from prepaying your entire mortgage at once if you happen to win the lottery.

Closing costs. Fees associated with the buying and selling of property and with setting up the mortgage. These are paid at the time of closing or settlement and may include such things as points, insurance, real estate taxes, and attorneys' fees. Before you reach for your checkbook, try to negotiate the lowest possible fees. You may be able to save thousands of dollars if you're gutsy enough to ask your real estate agent to work for a reduced commission, your attorney to give you a bottom-basement price, and your bank to give you a break on the points front. Unfortunately, not all of the fees you'll be hit with on closing are negotiable; you can hold your breath until you turn blue and the government still won't agree to cut your taxes by one red cent!

Show Me the Money!

If you're looking for a mortgage bargain, you won't have much difficulty finding one in an adjustable rate mortgage. Lenders compete fiercely for mortgage business, so many institutions offer unbelievably low rates in order to land your business.

Of course, the honeymoon period isn't guaranteed to last forever. Market forces could very well drive interest rates sky high, dragging your mortgage payments up along with them.

Escrow account. A special account in which money is held to pay certain expenses, such as taxes and insurance. The down payment for the property is also held in such an account. Escrow funds are paid at the time of closing.

FIGURE 6.1
Payment comparison chart showing the effect of various amortization periods on the costs of a $100,000 mortgage at 10 percent interest

Amortization	Monthly payment	Total payments	Total interest paid	Savings
30 years	$ 877.57	$315,925	$215,925	—
25 years	908.70	272,610	172,610	$ 43,315
15 years	1,074.61	193,429	93,429	122,496

Note: Figures have been rounded. Figures are based on a constant interest rate for the entire amortization period.

Loan origination fee (loan application fee). A fee charged by the lender to cover some of the costs of preparing the various documents associated with the mortgage.

PITI (principal, interest, taxes, and insurance). The four components that may be included in your mortgage payment: mortgage principal, mortgage interest, money for real estate taxes, and insurance.

Points. A charge that is designed to increase the bank's profit on your mortgage and cover closing costs. (See detailed discussion of points elsewhere in this chapter.)

INTEREST ZAPPERS

Looking for ways to minimize the amount of interest you end up paying on your mortgage? Here are some tried-and-true strategies for beating the mortgage lenders at their own game.

- Make the largest down payment you can reasonably afford. It's not rocket science, but it certainly bears repeating: the less money you have to borrow, the less you're going to pay in interest charges.

- Choose the shortest amortization you can live with on your mortgage. You can save a significant amount of money over the long run by increasing your mortgage payment over the short term. (See Figure 6.1.)

- Increase your payment frequency. You can save an extraordinary amount of money by paying your mortgage on a biweekly rather than a monthly basis. Paying more often also happens to be one of the least painful methods of paying off your mortgage early.

- Make additional lump sum payments and/or increase your monthly payments as often as possible. This will drastically reduce the amount of interest you end up paying over the life of your mortgage.

- Consider refinancing if mortgage rates tumble. Even if you have to pick up the costs associated with refinancing (e.g., getting a new appraisal, a new credit report, arranging for title insurance, making your points payment, and so on), refinancing at a lower interest rate may be worthwhile. As a rule of thumb, you'll be ahead if the interest rate on your new mortgage will be at least one percentage point lower than what you're currently paying and if you plan to stay in your home for at least the next five years.

FIGURE 6.2
How Interest Rates Affect Your Mortgage Payment

The following figures are for a $100,000 mortgage amortized over 25 years:

Interest rate (%)	Monthly payment
7.0	$ 665.30
7.5	699.21
8.0	733.76
8.5	768.91
9.0	804.62
9.5	840.85
10.0	877.57
10.5	914.74
11.0	952.32
12.0	1,026.61

ALL IN THE FAMILY

Borrowing money from family members might seem like the ideal solution to your mortgage woes, but it could end up being the biggest financial mistake you ever make. More often than not, there are hidden strings attached to that loan—strings that you might not find out about until it's too late.

Don't follow what we're saying? Let us offer a hypothetical example.

Your parents lend you $50,000 towards the down payment on your first house. You're ecstatic at first, and so are they. After all, few things are more exciting than becoming a homeowner for the very first time—unless, of course, it's becoming the proud parents of a first-time homebuyer!

You no sooner move into your new digs when you decide that you'd like to do a little redecorating. That red plush carpet in the rec room is hideous, to say the least, and you could definitely live without the lime-green fixtures in the downstairs bathroom. Before you know it, you've pumped $15,000 into renovations. You invite the folks over to see the products of your labor, and you're surprised by their lack of enthusiasm. They aren't happy that you've given the Rec Room From Hell a new life, and they're mad that you spent "their" money on something that they see as frivolous and unnecessary. After all, if the circa-1965 orange shag rug in their rec room is good enough for them, why shouldn't the red rug be good enough for you? And besides, if you've got that kind of money to burn, why aren't you offering to pay them back a little sooner? Perhaps it was a mistake for them to lend you this money in the first place . . .

While it's impossible to find statistics on the number of family relationships destroyed by loan-related woes, just judging by the number of couples we know personally who tell horror stories, we'd be willing to wager that the number is fairly significant. If, however, you are determined to ignore our advice and take whatever money your parents or other relatives are ready to throw your way, at least make an effort to do things the right way. Here are a few tips.

- Find out what strings are attached to the money before you agree to take the loan or gift. Will the relatives who are lending you the money expect you to live like paupers until the loan is repaid? Will they expect you to repay them for their generous gift by supporting them in their old age?

- Be clear about how long your parents are willing to lend you the money. Do they want to be paid back in full the next time your mortgage rolls over, or are they willing to lend you the money for a longer period of time?

- Make sure you and your parents agree on a payment schedule. Don't settle for some vague agreement that you will repay the money "when you can afford it." (That day may never come, given the expenses that will likely face you during your first couple of years of home ownership, and you may have some royally ticked off relatives to contend with in the meantime.) Instead, specify the date upon which you will start repaying the loan and how much your payments will be. Then put all of these details in writing.

Show Me the Money!

It definitely pays to shop around when you're in the market for a new mortgage. You could save yourself thousands of dollars in interest and reduce your monthly payments significantly by shaving even a mere quarter-percent off your mortgage rate.

If you give the bulk of your business to a particular financial institution—your checking account and your credit card business, for example—that institution may be willing to offer you a preferential rate on a mortgage. The industry term for this special deal is "relationship pricing." If your financial institution isn't willing to cut you a special deal, then shop around. After all, if they don't value your relationship enough to put their money where their mouth is, why should you?

- Talk about what would happen to the loan in the event that you or your partner were to die unexpectedly. If you died, would your spouse be expected to pay back the loan from the proceeds of your life insurance policy? If your parents died, how would the loan be handled by their estate?

- Figure out how your siblings feel about the arrangement. Are they completely okay with the arrangement, or are they treating this as further proof that Dad always liked you best?

> **Money Talk**
> • • • • • • •
>
> "Start your mortgage with as few years as possible. Everybody just assumed that our first mortgage would be for 25 years, but we really looked at the numbers and decided we could handle the cost of paying it over 20 years instead."
>
> —*Jackie, 31, mother of two*

- Ask yourself if you're taking on more debt than you can handle. It's one thing to take out a $150,000 mortgage on a $200,000 home. It's quite another to take out that same mortgage if you've also got to make payments on a $50,000 loan from Mom and Dad!

- Resist the temptation to lie on your mortgage application. Your bank could pull the rug out from under your home buying dreams if they find out that the gift your parents supposedly gave you is actually a loan.

- Find out whether your parents will expect you to pay interest on the loan or whether they're simply interested in having you pay back the principal. If they intend to charge you interest, find out what interest rate they have in mind and then make sure that it's competitive with the rates being charged by commercial lenders.

- Be prepared to spend some money on legal fees if your parents agree to carry your mortgage for you. An IOU on a scrap of paper simply doesn't cut it when significant sums of money are involved. It's only reasonable for your parents to ask that you draw up a mortgage or promissory note in order to formalize the deal. After all, their life savings are at stake. By going the mortgage route, they ensure that they will be treated as secured creditors in the event that you experience financial meltdown caused by job loss, disability, or some other unforeseen disaster.

- If your parents agree to guarantee (cosign) your mortgage, find out how much of the mortgage they're prepared to guarantee (it can be limited to a specific amount) and how long they're willing to act as guarantors. You should also make sure that they are clear about what they're agreeing to do, just so that misunderstandings don't crop up down the road. In addition to committing to make up any mortgage payments you miss, they're also expressing their willingness to be on the hook for your house insurance and property taxes. Given all that they've done for you, you'd better make a point of getting them something extra special on Mother's Day and Father's Day!

- If your parents are thinking about borrowing money against their own mortgage so that they can lend this money to you, offer to have a mortgage secured against your own home on identical terms to eliminate any risk of their losing their home. After all, you should be prepared to take only so much from relatives—particularly those who are approaching (or well into) their retirement years.

As you can see, you need to think long and hard before you agree to borrow money or accept a substantial gift from relatives. Sure, that interest-free loan may save you money in the short run, but it's no bargain if it ends up costing you your relationship with your family.

FINDING THE HOME THAT'S RIGHT FOR YOU

Now that you've figured out how much money you're willing to borrow and you've settled on the type of mortgage you want, it's time to consider your housing options. Basically, you have two choices: a house on a lot or a condominium.

Show Me the Money!

Purchasing a resale? Hire a home inspector to go over the property with a fine-toothed comb before the deal is finalized. Because you're about to fork over more money than you've probably ever spent on a single item in your entire life, you want to ensure that you're getting top value for your dollar. That means finding out in advance whether the house has any problems with the plumbing or heating systems, the roof, the electrical wiring, or the insulation. You also want to know about any environmental hazards (e.g., a leaky underground oil tank or septic system). You don't necessarily have to walk away from the property if the inspection finds deficiencies, of course, but you can use this information to your advantage in renegotiating the purchase price with the seller.

The best way to track down a reputable home inspector is by getting in touch with the American Society of Home Inspectors (ASHI). You can visit ASHI's web site at <www.ashi.com> or call 800-743-ASHI (800-743-2744).

House and Lot

If you decide to go the house and lot route, the biggest issue that you'll need to tackle is whether you want to go with a new home or a resale. Each scenario has pros and cons. If you purchase a new home, you can feel pretty confident that everything in the house will be in good working order, but you can expect to spend a small fortune on landscaping, decorating, and other unexpected extras. (Hey, those driveways don't pave themselves, you know!) If you decide to go the resale route, you may find that the previous owners have already done the landscaping and decorating work. (Of course, the orange plaid wallpaper that they chose won't necessarily be to your taste!) What's more, you could find yourself scrambling to find the funds to replace a leaky roof, a worn-out furnace, and other big-ticket items.

Show Me the Money!

Thinking of purchasing a home with an underground oil tank? Find out whether the fuel company that services that tank provides tank insurance. Otherwise, you could find yourself on the hook for some heavy-duty cleanup costs in the event that the tank springs a leak—costs that could easily top $30,000. Tank insurance is surprisingly affordable. One homeowner we know got hers for just $120. That's a small price to pay for peace of mind.

Condominiums

The biggest wrinkle you'll encounter in purchasing a condominium (the term used to describe a unit in an apartment or townhouse complex) is the often sticky issue of common costs. As a condominium owner, you are responsible for paying for your share of taxes, utilities, and upkeep costs for the common facilities (e.g., the elevators, recreational areas, entranceways and hallways, and so on). Unfortunately, these charges have a habit of creeping up, so make sure that your budget leaves enough room for these types of increases. You should also be aware of the fact that the condominium association can make extra assessments of common costs (e.g., if the roof needs to be replaced). A condominium association is made up of unit owners, with each condominium unit owner receiving one vote. Even if you vote against the proposed improvements, you're still on the hook for your share of the expenses.

Not all condominiums are designed to meet the needs of families with young children. If there's no playground equipment to be found and your prospective neighbours all have gray hair, you can bet that children aren't particularly welcome in that condominium development.

Regardless of which route you choose to go, it's a good idea to look at properties that are priced somewhat lower than the maximum you can afford. That way, if your real estate agent happens to come across the house of your dreams and it's only a thousand dollars or so over the budget range you've set, you might still be able to afford to buy it. A good rule of thumb is to chop 5 percent off the amount you can afford to spend on a house and then check out properties in that price range. In other words, if you can afford a $200,000 home, start looking in the $190,000 price range instead.

CLOSING COSTS

It's a lesson that many first-time homebuyers learn the hard way: buying a home involves a lot of hidden costs. Typically, these hidden costs add up to somewhere between 2.5 and 3.5 percent of the value of the mortgage.

Here's a list of some of the major types of expenses you can expect to encounter before you walk out of your lawyer's office with the keys to your new house in hand.

- *Mortgage application and processing fees.* You might think your mortgage lender stands to make enough money on your mortgage business without having to charge you a mortgage application and processing fee (to say nothing of a fee for obtaining your credit report from a credit bureau!), but most lenders don't see things that way. They argue that the fee is justified because they could go to all the work of approving you for a mortgage, only to have you take your mortgage business elsewhere. If you're smart, you'll counter that argument by asking them to refund the mortgage fee if you give them your business!

- *Points.* At the time of closing, you may be required to pay *"points"*—a one-time fee imposed by your lender, which typically amounts to approximately 1.5 to 3 percent of your mortgage amount. (Each point that you are required to pay amounts to 1 percent of your mortgage value—e.g., $1,000 on a $100,000 mortgage.) A lender that is charging a higher interest rate on a mortgage is likely to ask for fewer points than one who's giving you a bargain-basement rate.

- *Title charges.* Lenders require title insurance to protect them against claims that someone else owns the property in question. The last thing they want, after all, is for the previous owner's divorced spouse to show up with a moving van and announce that the house is still his or hers!

- *Escrow charges.* A neutral third party holds your money to ensure that the terms of the final sales contract are fulfilled before you get your house and the lender gets your money. For this service, the escrow company charges a fee.

- *Private mortgage insurance.* Your lender will insist that you take out private mortgage insurance (PMI) if your downpayment is less than 20 percent of the cost of the house. The lender is simply protecting its interest in the event that you default. Here's a money-saving tip when it comes to private mortgage insurance: once the equity in your property passes that magic 20 percent threshold, ask your lender to cancel the PMI. You'll save yourself $30 to $100 per month in unnecessary charges.

Show Me the Money!

• • • • • • •

When you use a buyer's broker, your needs are primary. A selling agent accepts listings and is legally obligated to obtain the highest price possible for the seller. A buyer's agent negotiates to obtain the best possible price on your behalf.

It's important to find out if your own agent may have a potential conflict of interest. If the agent is working for both you and the seller (or if the employing agency is representing both you and the seller), there may be no willingness to negotiate the best possible deal for you.

- *Appraisal fee.* Your lender may require that you pay for an appraisal on the home that you are purchasing. They want to ensure that they don't get stuck with a property that is worth less than what you owe them—something that could be financially disastrous for them in the event that you defaulted on your mortgage. While appraisal fees vary across the country, you can expect to pay between $150 and $250 to have a value placed on the house you are purchasing. Of course, if you're smart, you'll try to get your bank to pick up all or a portion of the cost in exchange for the privilege of doing business with you!

- *Survey fee.* Unless the vendor can provide you with a copy of a recent survey that is acceptable to the lender, you should plan to set aside $500 or so to have a new survey prepared. Some lenders are willing to waive the survey requirement if you have title insurance, a type of insurance that protects your investment if a problem arises with the title to your house.

- *Property insurance.* Your lender will want to see proof that you have arranged to have your new house insured—and for good reason. After all, your lender stands to be out a fair whack of cash if your home burns to the ground. You'll find some tips on trimming your house insurance costs later in this chapter.

- *Prepaid taxes or utilities.* You may have to reimburse the seller if certain bills (e.g., oil remaining in oil tank) have been prepaid beyond the closing date. That's why it's important to call the appropriate utility companies to ensure they read your meter on the day of closing.

- *Service charges.* Whether you are buying a new home or a used home, you can expect to spend a small fortune on hook-up charges for such services as phone and cable. You can't do much about these charges, unfortunately, other than simply fork over the necessary cash.

- *Attorneys' fees.* Most purchasers choose to hire an attorney to review the offer to purchase, to search the title of the new property, to draw up mortgage documents, and to tend to closing details. The going rate for a simple attorney-assisted real estate transaction is $500 or more. Obviously, you'll want to try to negotiate the best possible deal for yourself.

- *Moving costs.* You will pay between $50 to $100 an hour for a van with three movers. You can save yourself a bit of cash by recruiting a few able-bodied friends to lend a hand. Just make sure that they're up to the job. The last thing you need is to have someone drop your television set down a flight of stairs!

- *Real estate fees.* Unless you go with a discount real estate broker or sell your home privately, you can expect to pay 6 percent in real estate fees—5 percent if your agent is willing to give you a break on the fee. You won't have to come up with this cash out of your own pocket. These fees are simply built into the selling price of your home. (You'll only pay these costs if you're selling a home at the same time as buying a new one. You won't be on the hook for real estate fees if you're the buyer—at least not directly!)

Show Me the Money!

Don't want to move all that baby stuff and furniture on your own? If you pick the right closing date, you can save yourself hundreds of dollars on the costs of hiring a professional mover. Movers tend to charge 10 to 20 percent more during their busiest periods—the beginning and end of each month and during June, July, and August.

WHAT EVERY HOMEOWNER NEEDS TO KNOW ABOUT PROPERTY INSURANCE

As we noted earlier, your lender will insist that you purchase property insurance on your house or condominium. A homeowners policy such as this is designed to insure your house and its contents against fire and other disasters, to cover your living expenses if you have to live elsewhere while your home is being repaired or rebuilt, and to protect you against lawsuits from individuals who suffer injuries while on your property.

There are limits to what a homeowners policy will cover—something that a lot of people don't realize. Most insurers will only cover the loss of personal property to a value of 50 percent of the total amount for which the home is insured. What's more, they may require you to purchase additional coverage to protect against damage caused by wind, hail, flying objects, and so on. Believe it or not, not all disasters are created equal—at least not in the insurance companies' eyes!

A number of different factors will determine what you pay for property insurance.

- *The location of your home.* A house that is built on the ocean or in an earthquake zone will obviously be more expensive to insure than one in less disaster-prone parts of the country, just as a house in a rural area will cost less to insure than one in a large metropolitan area.

- *The age of your home.* Newer homes are less prone to fires and other disasters than older homes, which may have faulty wiring and plumbing systems.

- *Your home's proximity to fire stations and fire hydrants.* The closer you are to a fire hydrant and a fire station, the lower your premiums will be.

- *Whether or not you have deadbolt locks, smoke detectors, fire extinguishers, and other safety features.* Most insurance companies offer discounts to homeowners who've done what they can to reduce their chances of experiencing a problem.

Show Me the Money!

Most policies limit the amount that they will pay out to the actual cash value of the property that has been stolen or destroyed. You may wish to consider adding a replacement endorsement to your policy to ensure that, rather than giving you a cash payout based on the depreciated value of your goods, your insurance company is responsible for replacing those items.

However, don't assume that your job is over the moment that you line up insurance coverage for your home. Frankly, it's just begun! It's important to review your policy on a regular basis to ensure that it continues to meet your needs. Something as simple as adding an extra room, equipping a home office, or purchasing a lot of high-priced hobby equipment can change your insurance picture considerably. You should also make a point of videotaping the contents of your home at least every couple of years. That way, you'll have an up-to-date record of all its contents—something that could prove invaluable in the event that you have to make a claim.

SELLING YOUR HOUSE

If you plan to sell your home, you'll also want to look for ways to cut costs. Here are a few tips that could save you thousands of dollars.

- If you intend to use the services of a real estate agent, try to negotiate for a reduced commission rate. You're more likely to be successful if you've purchased or sold a home through this agent before or if your house is a high-end property. Many agents are willing to drop the standard 6 percent Multiple Listing Service (MLS) commission down to 5 percent.

- Resist the temptation to play real estate agent unless you know what you're doing. While you might think you're going to save yourself a small fortune by selling your house yourself, you could miss out on making a sale altogether. For one thing, you're an amateur when it comes to establishing a selling price for your home and it's easy to scare off potential buyers if you price your property too high. Unfortunately, there's an even greater problem. As a private seller, you won't be able to list the home in the MLS—the very place that most potential buyers turn for leads on properties for sale.

- Look for a real estate agent who can advise you about how to make your house more marketable. It may be worth your while to invest the time and money into repainting your house to cover up all the crayon marks that were contributed by your budding Picasso, but it might not be worthwhile to go crazy with other types of home decorating projects. According to *Remodeling Magazine,* you can expect to get the best return on your investment if you focus on sprucing up the kitchen and the bathroom. (See Figure 6.3.)

FIGURE 6.3
Which Improvements Pay Back?

Project	Cost	Average Payback
Add a new heating or air conditioning system	$2,000 to $4,500	100% for heating; 75% for air conditioning
Minor kitchen remodeling	$2,000 to $8,500	94% to 102%
Major kitchen remodeling	$9,000 to $25,000	90%
Add bathroom	$5,000 to $12,000	92%
Add a family room	$30,000	86%
Remodel bathroom	$8,500	77%
Add a fireplace	$1,500 to $3,000	75%
Build a deck	$8,000	73%
Remodel home office	$8,000	89%
Replace windows	$6,000	68% to 74%
Build a pool	$10,00 and up	44%
Install or upgrade landscaping	$1,500 to $15,000	30% to 60%
Finish basement	$3,000 to $7,000	15%

Source: HomeAdvisor.com

THE BIGGEST HOMEBUYING MISTAKES— AND HOW TO AVOID THEM

It's one thing to make a financial faux pas when you're shopping for a car. It's quite another to make the same sort of mistake when you're buying a house. After all, a financial error on this scale could haunt you for a very long time.

Here are some of the most common mistakes that homebuyers make and what you can do to avoid them.

- *Getting your heart set on a particular property.* Once you fall in love with a particular property, it's game over. Your ability to think logically goes out the window, and you may find yourself making some very poor decisions. Even if your heart is doing flip-flops at the prospect of owning the property you've just seen and you can already picture yourself doing crafts with your kids in the solarium kitchen, force yourself to put on the brakes before you decide to put in an offer.

- *Mixing up your family's needs with its wants.* It's easy to be seduced by Jacuzzis, French doors, skylights, and other bells and whistles—items that can push the purchase price of a home significantly beyond what you can reasonably afford to pay.

- *Failing to take your family's long-term plans into consideration.* If you plan to add to your family, make sure that you buy a house with a sufficient number of bedrooms. Moving is an expensive proposition, so you don't want to force yourself to do it again in another couple of years' time, just because you lacked the foresight to buy a four-bedroom home.

Show Me the Money!

Give some thought to what you want in a home before you start hitting open houses. Decide which features are must-haves and which ones you could live without. If you don't have a clear idea in your head upfront about what you do and don't need in a house, you run the risk of falling in love with an adorable but impractical house that won't meet your needs as your family grows.

- *Overextending yourself by buying an overly expensive house.* If you borrow the maximum amount of money that the bank is willing to lend you, you could be in for a rude shock. Your budget might not have enough money to pay for anything but the bare essentials. This is fine if you're prepared to be house poor for at least a few years, but it can be the cause of much pain and suffering if you're not anticipating dramatic lifestyle changes.

- *Failing to consider the long-term resale potential of the home.* While you might not have any problem buying a house that backs onto the runway of a major airport, you may have a hard time finding a buyer for the property when you eventually decide to sell.

THE TAX IMPLICATIONS OF HOME OWNERSHIP

Now it's time to turn to an even more taxing subject (groan!)—the tax implications of home ownership. Believe it or not, there's actually plenty of good news on this front. Depending on your tax situation, you could ring up some substantial tax savings, thanks to your mortgage and property tax payments.

As we noted earlier on in this chapter, the interest that you pay to a lender on a mortgage loan is tax deductible. Whether that mortgage is on a place that is used for personal reasons (your home), business (a location for your business), or investment purposes (a property that you have purchased to rent to others), you can claim the mortgage interest as an itemized deduction on Schedule B, Form 1040. However, you will use Schedule E if you own rental property.

> ## Money Talk
> • • • • • •
>
> "Keep your family's long-term financial goals in mind. If you are both currently working but eventually want to have one of you be a stay-at-home parent, make sure you can handle the mortgage on one income."
> —*Susan, 34, mother of two*

Don't make the mistake of assuming that you're going to be able to write off your entire mortgage payment, however. You're only allowed to write off the interest portion of your payment—not the principal repayment. Your lending institution must send you a form each January spelling out the amount of interest and property taxes you paid during the previous year.

Here's the scoop on another mortgage-related income tax deduction that you should know about. If your mortgage requires that you pay points, you may be able to deduct this payment from your taxes. This is a one-time expense. Each point that you are required to pay equals 1 percent of your mortgage ($600 on a $60,000 mortgage, for example). Make sure it is treated as prepaid interest (deductible on your income tax return) rather than as a service fee (not deductible). Obviously, you'll definitely want to find out about this before you agree to give your business to a particular lender. If it turns out that your points are, in fact, tax deductible, it is no longer necessary to pay them with a separate check so that you'll have a record of the transaction. While you're at it, see if your bank will give you a bit of a break on the number of points you're required to pay. Some lenders will do just that in order to land your mortgage business.

Points are a one-time deduction, but mortgage interest and property taxes are treated as annual deductions on your income tax return. Real property taxes, which are imposed on all property owners, pay for roads, schools, and municipal services such as police and fire departments and refuse collection.

Before we wrap up our discussion of the tax implications of home ownership,

> ## Money Talk
> • • • • • •
>
> "Always shop around for the best mortgage rates. You don't have to have all your banking needs met by one institution."
> —*Laura, 30, mother of one*

we have to zero in on a very important topic—what happens when you sell your home.

The Taxpayer's Relief Act of 1997 introduced some significant changes regarding the way that taxes owed on the sale of a primary residence are handled. You can now exclude as much as $250,000 of the selling price of your home if you are a single filer, and $500,000 if you are married. You can do this as often as every two years, provided that the home was your principal residence for two out of the last five years prior to the sale. If you realized profits on any homes sold before May 1997, you must reduce your cost basis on your present home to determine its adjusted basis when figuring the gain on your current home.

Facts and Figures
• • • • • •

Don't throw away records that help to substantiate your home's purchase price and the cost of any improvements. If the IRS audits you, they could ask you to produce these records.

As you can see, there's a lot to consider when you're thinking about buying or selling a home—everything from mortgages to insurance to taxes. Here are the important points to remember.

- Home ownership has both pros and cons. Make sure you carefully weigh both before making the decision to buy. Home ownership isn't necessarily for everyone. Don't let any overzealous real estate agent try to tell you otherwise.

- Owning a home involves a number of hidden costs—expenses that are often difficult to anticipate until you're in the trenches yourself. That's why it's important to do your homework up-front. Make sure you know what you're getting yourself into before you sign on the dotted line.

- Borrowing money from family members may not be the dream solution it appears to be. In fact, it could be the beginning of a very long—and very painful—nightmare.

- Buying a home is a business decision. If you allow your emotions to override your good judgment, you could find yourself paying for your mistakes for years to come. This is definitely one of those situations where you need to think now, act later.

Hello SUV, Goodbye Car

· ·

There's no denying it: owning and operating a vehicle is an expensive proposition. Even if you manage to squeeze your growing family into the most budget-friendly, fuel-efficient, subcompact car you can find, that car's still going to cost you a couple of hundred dollars per month to run. If you succumb to peer pressure and purchase a sports-utility vehicle (the modern day equivalent of the 1975 wood-paneled station wagon), you could find yourself spending considerably more of your after-tax dollars on automotive expenditures.

In this chapter, we'll talk about what it really costs to own and operate a new vehicle, how to save money when you're purchasing a new or used vehicle, how to save money on your financing costs if you require a car loan, and what you can do to reduce the amount of money you spend on automobile insurance.

THE MONEY PIT REVISITED

Think your house is a money pit? Think again. The biggest money pit in your life is likely to be that two-ton hunk of steel that's parked out on your driveway.

While there's no denying that pleasures are associated with car ownership—that new-car smell can be practically intoxicating—a considerable amount of pain

---

Facts and Figures
· · · · · ·

According to the most recent figures from the American Automobile Association, the average cost of owning and operating a car in the United States in 2000 was $5,534.

The average cost per mile for fuel, maintenance, and tires for a car with a driving distance of 15,000 miles is 12.2 cents. Add 1.5 cents if you're driving a two-wheel drive, two-door SUV.

---

is involved, too. Cars are like demanding lovers that take, take, take, and then break your heart. They're expensive to feed. They can be temperamental. And they have a knack for letting you down when you need them most.

The car-worshipping crowd aside, most Americans view car ownership as a necessary evil. Unless you're fortunate enough to live on a bus route or near a commuter train, you may have no choice but to make the commitment to own and operate a car, and what a commitment it is!

Keeping a car on the road can demand a significant chunk of your family's take-home pay. That's why it's important to look for ways to keep your car expenditures as low as possible—a process that should begin the moment you start shopping for a car.

Getting the Best Possible Price on a New or Used Car

New or used. Used or new. You've probably mulled the two options around long enough to give yourself a headache. If you buy a new car, you're less likely to end up stranded on some remote rural road with a baby and a toddler along. On the other hand, if you buy a used car, you just might be able to afford to buy groceries from time to time.

Regardless of which route you decide to go, you'll want to do whatever you can to bring the purchase price down as low as possible. Here are a few tips on getting the best possible deal on a new or used car.

Show Me the Money!
• • • • • • •

Wondering if the used car you're thinking of purchasing has been involved in an accident? Find out the car's vehicle identification number (VIN#), and then give your car insurance company a call. They should be able to look up the vehicle in an insurance industry database and let you know whether any insurance company has had to pick up the tab for accident-related repairs.

Regardless of what your insurance company is able to find out, you'll still need to give the vehicle a thorough examination yourself, of course. The database won't be able to tell you whether or not the owner ended up repairing the damage from any fender benders herself, for example.

- *Do your homework.* Find out what the vehicle you're considering is selling for elsewhere. You can check out other dealers in your area and visit the Web sites of the growing number of companies that sell vehicles online. That way, you'll have plenty of ammunition when you start talking to the salesperson at your local car dealership.

- *Get your financing in place.* If you walk into a car dealership armed with a preapproved car loan, you're sending out a strong signal to the sales staff that you're a serious buyer who's ready to make a deal. That may encourage them to give you their best deal right off the bat rather than putting you through the usual car negotiation torture test.

- *Ignore the sticker price.* In most cases, you should be able to bring down the sticker price on a moderately priced vehicle by at least a few hundred dollars—and sometimes even more. The car-buying gurus suggest that you ask to see a copy of the invoice that the dealer received from the manufacturer, because it more accurately indicates what the dealership actually paid for the car. If the dealer seems reluctant to chop the price, ask for freebies instead. See if you can convince the dealer to throw in a set of car mats, a year's worth of oil changes, and other items that you'd pay for out of your own pocket otherwise.

The Bottom Line

Debra, a 45-year-old mother of three, is every car salesperson's worst nightmare—a smart consumer who's done her homework and who's prepared to shop around for a deal. Here's her modus operandi: "I read *Consumers Report* to find out about the models of vehicles I'm considering. Then, once I know the color, model, and features I want in a car, I start phoning every car dealer over a two-state area. I keep a log of whom I am speaking to, what they say, what price they're quoting me, and whether or not they have the car in stock. When I get to the lowest price, I ask to speak to the sales manager and then confirm the lowest price. I then ask for a fax confirming the vehicle identification number (VIN) and specifying both the price and the equipment. If the dealer isn't prepared to do this, I figure he's not being straight with me. I've purchased four cars this way, and each time I've gotten prices that other dealers said were 'too low to be real.' Best of all, I didn't have to step inside the car dealership until I was ready to drive out with my car!"

- *Be sure you're comparing apples to apples.* If you're comparison shopping between various makes and models, simply comparing sticker prices isn't enough. You also have to consider such factors as what it costs to maintain each type of vehicle, how expensive parts are, and what you can expect to pay for insurance. Don't just take the manufacturer or car dealer's word about the operating costs, however. Make a point of talking to other people who are in the know: friends and family members who own this particular type of car, the mechanic at your local garage, the friendly fellow in the automotive department at your local department store, and so on.

- *Research maintenance costs.* Before you buy a car of a particular make and model, make a pit stop at your local automotive supply store and find out what you're going to pay for oil filters, brake pads, and other frequently replaced parts. Certain makes and models of cars can be extremely expensive to keep on the road. Make sure you know this up front.

- *Time your purchase carefully.* You can save significant amounts of money if you buy your new car on a day when the salesperson you're dealing with is most motivated to make a sale. According to Corey Sandler, author of *The Secrets of the Savvy Consumer,* one of the best days to shop for a new car is December 31—especially if it's snowing! "First of all," he explains, "this is an especially quiet time because of the holiday period. The snowstorm helps cut down on visitors, too. Finally, dealerships routinely create sales contests and quotas and they are almost always tied to the end of the week, the end of the month, or the end of the year." A salesperson who is just one car sale away from landing a big bonus as part of an in-house sales promotion will practically be willing to gift wrap the car for you if it means you'll actually take it! You can crank the pressure up even further if you show up an hour before the dealership closes!

- *Feign a total lack of interest.* You lose a lot of your negotiating ability the moment the salesperson discovers that you've fallen in love with a particular vehicle. That's why it's important to play it cool, even if you know that the SUV you just test drove is definitely the one you want. You can negotiate a far better price if you let the salesperson know that you

Show Me the Money!

Your local car dealer is an independent businessperson who owns all of the vehicles on his lot. He finances his inventory by taking out loans from the manufacturers he deals with. The interest that he pays on those loans is part of his cost of doing business. He can save himself a fair bundle of cash by "moving inventory" near the end of the month to avoid ringing up another month's worth of interest charges. Our advice? Shop around at the beginning of the month, but hold off on making your deal for a few more weeks.

Show Me the Money!

Buy a convertible in the winter when snow is on the ground, and buy an SUV on the hottest day of summer. You'll be able to negotiate a better deal if you make a point of shopping during the "off-season."

are bored by the process of shopping for a car and that you couldn't care less about all of the jazzy features that he or she is determined to tell you about. You will have played your cards right if you manage to give an Academy Award performance—leave the salesperson with the impression that you're prepared to walk if you can't get the price that you want!

- *Don't overdose on options.* While options like sun roofs, power windows, and remote keyless entries are nice to have, they are by no means essential. Before you agree to spend an extra $5,000 to pay for the option package that entitles you to all these flashy extras, stop to consider what else you might be able to do with that $5,000 you're itching to spend— like paying off your credit card balance, contributing to your child's college education fund, or making a hefty contribution to your 401(k). If you're planning to borrow that $5,000, take a moment to consider what you'll actually pay over the life of the loan. Once you put down your calculator, you'll probably decide that rolling down your own window isn't that much of a hardship after all!

Show Me the Money!

Most new car models are introduced in the fall. Dealers don't like to be left with last year's models once the new crop of cars starts to arrive, so you can often cut yourself a pretty good deal on one of last season's "leftovers" if you shop at this time of the year. One important fact to bear in mind: the selection may be somewhat limited. Cars in last season's hottest colors were no doubt snapped up months ago.

- *Forget about trying to keep up with the Joneses.* Don't rush out to buy an SUV just because the family across the street has one. Stop to consider whether you actually need a vehicle this size. Remember: it costs a lot more money to own and operate a full-sized SUV than it does to keep a smaller vehicle on the road.

- *Skip the extras.* Pass on the chance to have the dealer undercoat, rustproof, pinstripe, or otherwise mess with the new vehicle. You'll simply be adding to the purchase price. (If you've got your heart set on having any of these services performed, plan to arrange for these extras after you've bought the car.)

- *Consider your family's long-term needs.* If you've got three children and you intend to have another baby in the next year or two, there's no point in buying a five-person sedan. You would simply have to trade it in—and probably take a painful financial hit as well—when the new baby arrives.

Of course, you can't always anticipate your family's needs in advance since surprises can and do occur. If the stork leaves an unexpected bundle of joy on your porch, you'd just better hope that he drops off the keys to a new minivan, too!

- *Just say no to credit.* It's almost always a bad idea to borrow money for items like cars that depreciate in value over time, and most new cars depreciate a minimum of 20 to 30 percent within their first year. While you might have no choice but to borrow the money if you've got your heart set on a new car—after all, not very many families with young children have an extra $20,000 or so sitting in the bank!—you might be able to swing a cash deal (or, at the very least, borrow less money) if you change your buying strategy and shop around for a preowned vehicle instead.

- *Invest in an inspection.* If you're buying a preowned vehicle, have it inspected by a mechanic you trust. The $50 or so that you pay for a quick checkup could save you thousands of dollars if something turns out to be seriously wrong with the vehicle.

Winning at the Trade-in Game

Buying a car is complicated enough. Buying a new car and trading in your old one at the same time is even more challenging. Here's what to do to ensure that you're receiving top dollar for your vehicle.

Show Me the Money!

Shopping for a used car? Consider buying one that's just come in off a lease. With any luck, the mileage won't be overly high, and the vehicle may be loaded with all kinds of bells and whistles.

If you're lucky, you may be able to arrange to purchase such a vehicle from someone you know who's about to trade in their leased vehicle. You could offer to purchase the car at the preset price specified in the lease agreement, which is typically lower than the market price for that vehicle.

- Invest some money in your vehicle before you trade it in. The money you spend on a tune-up and a bumper-to-bumper cleaning could increase the value of your car by as much as a thousand dollars, especially if a lot of kid-related stains mark your car's interior.

- If you're negotiating a deal with a car dealership, be sure to play your trade-in card very carefully. Automobile dealers are notorious for trying to pull a fast one on you when you're trying to trade in one car and purchase another. They like to blur the two transactions together so that you focus on the balance owing rather than what you're getting for your old car and paying for your new one. It's generally a good idea to keep the fact that you have a car to trade in a secret until you have managed to negotiate the best possible deal on the new vehicle.

- If you're not happy with the pittance that the dealership offers you for your old vehicle—an all-too-likely scenario, unfortunately—then be prepared to go into the automotive sales business yourself. Run a classified advertisement in your local newspaper or in a publication such as the *Auto Trader,* and wait for your phone to start ringing. Your phone is more likely to start ringing if you price your car appropriately. Do some research so that you'll have a realistic idea about what other cars of the same make, age, and condition are selling for, and then price your vehicle accordingly. You can gather this information by checking the classifieds, making the rounds of the used car lots in your town, and/or by hitting some automotive Web sites.

Saving Money on a Car Loan

While the best way to buy a car is by paying cash, that isn't always possible. If you're going to borrow money to pay for a vehicle, be sure to line up the best financing deal possible. Here are a few tips.

- *Tell the dealership to keep its money.* Unless you can take advantage of one of those super-duper deals on dealer financing, it's generally not worth your while to obtain financing from the dealership. Nine times out of ten, you can get a better deal somewhere else. (If a particular car dealership is offering what appears to be a truly extraordinary interest rate, be sure to read the fine print. Often the interest rate only applies for a short period of time, and then you start paying a significantly higher interest rate.)

> ### Facts and Figures
> • • • • • •
>
> Don't expect to get the same loan rate on a used car as you would on a new car. A loan on a used car typically costs 2 to 3 percent more than a loan on a new car.

- *Consider joining a credit union.* They tend to offer bargain basement interest rates on car loans—rates that are often a good percentage point or more lower than what you can get through a bank.

- *Don't get seduced by a low loan payment.* While it's tempting to fixate on the amount of money you have to fork over each month, you should be more concerned with what that loan is going to cost you by the time you finish paying for your car.

- *Reduce the amount of interest you pay.* Put down as much money as possible and then pay off your car loan as soon as possible. The sooner you pay off your car, the more you will save on interest charges. Before you start doubling up on payments, however, be sure to check with your lender to find out if any prepayment penalties apply or whether saving money on interest charges by prepaying the loan early is even possible. Sometimes the lender holds these additional payments, rather than applying them to the outstanding principal.

Show Me the Money!

Don't automatically give your car loan business to the bank that you already deal with. Shop around and find out if you can get a better loan rate elsewhere, and then ask your current financial institution to match that rate. If they say, "Yes," they get your business. If they say, "No," they don't. Either way, you win.

The Hidden Costs of Leasing

Leasing a car is a lot like having a car loan, except for one important difference: you're only paying off a portion of the principal with your monthly payments. Consequently, when the lease expires, money is still owed on the car. At this point, you have to decide whether you would like to purchase the car at the buyout price (the street value of the vehicle at that time, according to the dealer) or give the car back to the dealer and look for a new set of wheels.

Leasing makes more sense for some families than for others. If you and your partner are in the habit of trading in your new car for another vehicle every two years or so, you would probably be further ahead by leasing. If, on the other hand, having the latest-and-greatest vehicle in your driveway isn't all that important to you, then you would definitely get your money's worth out of purchasing rather than leasing a car.

Show Me the Money!

If you have a home equity line of credit that you can use to finance your new vehicle, use it. The interest that you pay on a home equity loan is tax deductible, but the interest that you pay on a standard car loan is not.

If you do decide to proceed with a lease, it's important to go over the lease agreement with a fine-toothed comb so that you'll be absolutely clear about what you're getting into. Here are a few questions you'll want to ask before you sign on the dotted line.

- What is the maximum number of miles you're allowed to drive under the terms of the lease? Make sure it's a realistic figure, or you'll be hit with some hefty mileage charges when the lease comes up for renewal. Most leasing companies will allow you to rack up about 15,000 miles per year without any high-mileage penalties kicking in.

Facts and Figures

Leasing can be a very attractive option if you use your car for business. Uncle Sam allows you to deduct the interest and depreciation charges associated with leasing a car, even though he won't allow you to deduct the interest incurred on a standard car loan.

- What kind of insurance coverage are you required to carry under the terms of the lease? Some leases require that you carry extra comprehensive coverage, which can add to your insurance costs.

- What is the definition of "normal wear and tear"? Are minor scratches a problem, or does the dealer understand that it's next to impossible to keep a vehicle in pristine condition when it's lugging around kids on a daily basis?

- What are your responsibilities with regard to routine maintenance? Do you need to keep detailed records to demonstrate that the car was properly serviced by a reputable garage?

- What would happen if you lost your job and you were no longer able to keep up with your payments? Would you be liable for all remaining payments during the lifetime of the lease?

- What would happen if you decided to move and wanted to end the lease early? What types of penalties would you face?

The Dos and Don'ts of Shopping for Auto Insurance

Regardless of whether you decide to lease or buy your next vehicle, you're going to have to spend some time shopping for auto insurance. If you're lucky, you will have chosen a model of vehicle that's not too expensive to insure, you'll be living in a part of the country where fewer accidents occur, you'll no longer be considered a "young driver" in the eyes of the insurance company, and you will have a clean driving record. All those factors can help to keep your insurance rates down.

Here are a few tips to help you get the maximum bang for your automobile insurance buck once you start shopping around.

Do . . .

- Remember to tell your insurance agent about any special safety and security features that your car has. You may be entitled to a reduction in premiums if your car has security alarms, air bags, antilock brakes, or similar features.

- Save money by choosing the highest possible deductible for both collision (damage to your car that is caused through a collision) and comprehensive coverage (other types of damage to your car). If your car is worth next to nothing, drop the collision coverage.

- Consider carrying uninsured or underinsured motorist liability coverage, even if you've got medical and disability insurance through your employer or a private plan. This type of coverage allows you to collect for lost wages, medical expenses, and any pain and suffer-

Facts and Figures

Auto insurance is a crucial part of your family's financial safety net. Don't even think of getting behind the wheel without it. You need five key types of coverage: liability insurance (to protect you against claims from any people you injure while driving), collision insurance (to pay for the cost of repairing your vehicle and any vehicles you damage if you are the guilty party in an accident), comprehensive insurance (to pay for the cost of repairing your vehicle if some other sort of accident occurs), uninsured and underinsured insurance (to protect you, your passengers, and your vehicle if an uninsured or underinsured driver hits you), and medical payment insurance (to cover any reasonable medical expenses that result from accident-related injuries).

It's a lot to think about, but any good auto insurance agent should be prepared to walk you through your policy to reassure you that all of your bases are covered.

ing you experience as a result of an automobile accident with an uninsured or underinsured motorist. It also applies to passengers in your car who might not otherwise have adequate medical and disability coverage.

Don't . . .

- Don't try to save money in the wrong places. You could end up with bigger money problems than you can imagine if you aren't carrying adequate amounts of bodily injury/property damage liability. Rather than playing insurance roulette and gambling that you won't get sued, ensure that you have enough liability insurance to protect all of the assets you've worked so hard to accumulate. Remember, you don't just stand to lose everything you've managed to accumulate to date, your future earnings could also be garnished if you're on the losing end of a lawsuit.

Facts and Figures

Here's a quick way to estimate the annual depreciation costs on your vehicle. Take the original purchase price and subtract the estimated trade-in value at the time you plan to dispose of the car. (The classified ads are a great source of this type of information.) Then divide this figure by the number of years you own and operate the vehicle. Voilà! You've got an annual depreciation figure to work with.

Operating Costs Revisited

Looking for some ways to reduce the amount of money that you spend on owning and operating a vehicle? Here are a few commonsense tips that could put significant amounts of cash back in your wallet.

- *Use your car less often.* The fact that you own the darned thing doesn't necessarily mean you have to use it each and every time you leave the house. Take your kids for a walk or a bike ride when it's time to mail a letter at the post office or fill a prescription at the drugstore. It's a great way to save money, get fit, and have fun at the same time.

- *Carpool to work.* If you only drive your car every other day, you'll cut your commuting costs in half. You'll also have to cope with rush-hour traffic only half as often—reason enough to find someone else in your neighborhood who's willing to split the driving. If you can't find anyone to carpool with, consider using public transit every other day instead. If you do decide to carpool, make sure your insurance is adequate. A nasty lawsuit will quickly erode any savings you were able to ring up by carpooling!

- *Join a van pool.* Some companies set up van pools for their employees. You simply show up at the designated spot (typically a commuter parking area near the highway), park your vehicle, and then hop in the van with a group of your coworkers, or even employees from another company in the same area.

- *Pass on the designer gasoline.* Pull into any gas station, and you're likely to be faced with at least three choices at the pump: ho-hum gas, good gas, and super-terrific gas. According to some of the experts, premium gasolines are highly overrated and don't justify the added expense. Just stick with regular gas, or whatever fancy name the gas station you're using has chosen to describe its ordinary, everyday gas.

- *Maintain your car properly.* Remember that an ounce of prevention is worth a pound of cure. It's a lot cheaper to maintain your car properly than it is to pay for problems that arise due to poor maintenance. What's more, you'll feel a lot more confident that your car will make it from Point A to Point B without any help from the AAA—reason enough to keep your car well maintained.

> ### Show Me the Money!
>
> Treat your car like an investment. Keep it in good condition. If you can get your vehicle to outlast your car loan by a year or two, you can sock away the money that you'd otherwise be spending in car payments each month and then use that money for the downpayment on your next car. It's the best way to get off the car loan treadmill.

We've covered a lot of territory in this chapter—everything from negotiating the best possible price on a new or used car to shopping around for automobile insurance. Here are the key points to keep in mind.

- Focus on your family's long-term needs when you're shopping for your next new car. A sedan-style car won't do you much good if you're planning to have a large family.

- Be prepared to negotiate the price of whatever new or used vehicle you're considering. If the dealer is reluctant to chop money off the price, see what other types of bells and whistles might be tossed in—everything from free floormats to free oil changes for the life of the car.

- Don't automatically give your automobile loan business to the bank where you have your checking account. Shop around for the best possible rate and terms, and then ask your bank to match the deal.

- Make sure that your vehicle is properly insured. Insurance is no place to cut corners.

CHAPTER 8

Hitting the Books

· ·

While worrying about Junior's university tuition before the child has even mastered the basics of Crawling 101, may seem a little crazy, there's something to be said for setting up an educational savings plan while Junior's still very young. It all has to do with the magic of compound interest; the more time your money has to grow, the more there will be to pay for your child's education when the moment of truth arrives.

WHY JUNIOR NEEDS YOUR HELP

Even if you managed to pay your own way through university, your child will probably not be able to follow in your footsteps. The costs of tuition and other education-related expenses have increased at a rate that has far outpaced the rate of inflation since the early 1980s. Bottom line? No matter how bright or hard-working your child turns out to be, at least a little help from you will likely be needed to pay the way through college.

What It Costs to Send a Kid to College

If you haven't looked at college tuition fees lately, you could be in for a shock. Gone are the days when a kid could finance his education by picking up a part-time job at the local gas station or burger joint. Since 1980, college costs have been increasing by an astounding 6 percent per year. In other words, they've been nearly doubling every ten years!

Ready to hit the panic button? You haven't heard the worst of it yet! The figures we've just quoted you are in today's dollars. If you want to guesstimate what it will cost to send a child to university ten years from now, you have to factor in the effects of inflation. If tuition fees continue to rise at the same rate they've risen over the past twenty years, that $10,909 tuition bill we talked about earlier will have grown to $19,636 by the time your eight-year-old sits down to write a check for the first-year tuition fees. You can do the number crunching for yourself by plugging in an inflation factor of 1.8 for each ten-year period between now and the time when your child will be starting university. In other words, you multiply today's tuition costs by 1.8 in order to obtain the projected cost of a university education in ten years' time.

Next to purchasing a home, your child's university costs will likely be the single greatest expenditure you ever make. While burying your head in the sand and ignoring the problem or the "hope method" may be tempting, (you simply "hope" that your child will end up attending university on a full scholarship!), neither approach is particularly helpful. Nor is blindly assuming that you'll be able to qualify for financial aid. Federal grants simply can't keep up with the rising cost of higher education, and government funds for college grants and loans have been cut time and time again. Like it or not, the buck stops with you.

Facts and Figures

Wondering what these figures mean in actual dollars and cents? Here are the latest College Board figures. During the 1999-2000 school year, the average cost of tuition was $10,909 per year for a public university and $23,651 per year for a private university.

Show Me the Money!

Trying to calculate how much money you'll need to have on hand as each of your kids hits college? You can either work out the numbers for yourself using a calculator, or you can let your computer do some of the work for you. Either hit one of the big financial planning Web sites (see Appendix C for leads on our favorites), or pick up a computer software package that's specifically designed to tackle these types of financial projections.

When to Get Started

It can be hard to find the money to save for your child's education when a million-and-one demands are already being made on your paycheck. After all, our childbearing years tend to be the years when we're carrying around the greatest amount of personal debt. Mortgage payments, car payments, credit card payments—the list goes on and on. (Who knows? You may still be paying off your own student loans!)

FIGURE 8.1
Saving for Your Child's Education

Putting a child through college will cost approximately $250,000 18 years down the road. (This figure assumes four years of college at $15,000 per year, plus inflation.) Here's how much money you'll need to sock away each month to pull together that $250,000 nest egg:

Number of years	How much you need to save each month that you have to make contributions (8% annual return on investment).
18 years	$ 521
12 years	$1,039
8 years	$1,868

If your budget is stretched to the max (as is the case for many couples with young children), you may have to start small when it comes to saving for your child's education. You may even have to postpone your educational savings plans entirely until your family's financial situation is on more solid ground. Unfortunately, you pay a price for putting things off. The longer you wait to start contributing, the less time your principal will have to grow, and the more money you'll have to kick in. (See Figure 8.1.)

" Money Talk
• • • • • •

"I am embarrassed to admit that as conscientious as we are about money, we do not have any savings set aside specifically for education. Our 12-year-old is intelligent, and we are hoping that she will qualify for scholarships and grants, which would pay for at least part of her expenses."

—*Kim, 36, currently expecting her second child*

WAYS TO SAVE FOR YOUR CHILD'S EDUCATION

Once you've decided to take the plunge and start saving for your child's education, you'll need to choose what type of plan you would like to set up for your child: an educational IRA, a state-sponsored college savings plan, a prepaid tuition plan, or some other savings vehicle entirely.

Education IRAs

You've no doubt heard about IRAs. (You'd have to move to a desert island during tax season to escape all the IRA promotions.) You might be less familiar with Education IRAs, however—although they're basically a variation on the same theme.

The Taxpayer Relief Act of 1997 created a brand new type of IRA known as an Education IRA. As of 2000, taxpayers with adjusted gross incomes within certain limits became eligible to contribute $500 annually to an Education IRA for each designated beneficiary. If your adjusted gross income (AGI) is between $95,000 and $110,000 (between $150,000 and $160,000 if you're filing jointly), the $500 limit is reduced; if your AGI is above $110,000 (or more than $160,000 if you're filing jointly), you cannot contribute to anyone's Education IRA.

The Bottom Line
. . . .

Heidi, a 23-year-old single mother of one, has never had much spare cash on hand, but she starting saving for her son's post-secondary education shortly after he was born. "It's a huge priority of mine to be able to put my child through university or to send him to some other type of post-secondary educational institution. Each month, I am putting away a little extra for his future."

- The earnings accumulate in the fund tax free, allowing your child's college fund to grow much more rapidly. According to Vanguard Online, you would be nearly $5,000 ahead at the end of a 19-year period if you used an Education IRA rather than a taxable investment as your savings vehicle. The calculation is based on a $500 annual contribution made to each account at the beginning of each year for 19 years, an 8 percent annual rate of return, the reinvestment of all dividends and capital gains, and a 28 percent income tax rate.

- Contributions can be made to a child's Education IRA, even if that child doesn't have any earned income.

- No taxes need to be paid at the time of withdrawal, provided that the funds are used to pay for higher education programs that qualify under the plan. Qualified expenses include tuition, fees, books, supplies, and room and board as long as the student is attending school on a better than half-time basis.

- Any funds that remain in the Education IRA after you've financed your firstborn's education or when your firstborn turns 30 can be rolled over to another child in the family.

Of course, Education IRAs also have noteworthy drawbacks.

- The amount of money you can contribute to an Education IRA is limited. Some education experts feel that parents who use Education IRAs as their sole savings vehicle will find themselves faced with a shortfall when it comes time to pay for their child's education.

- You can't make contributions to an Education IRA and a state-sponsored tuition program in the same year. Nor can grandparents or others who might wish to make these types of contributions on your child's behalf.

- The money in an Education IRA could be factored into financial aid calculations down the road—something that could make it more difficult for your child to obtain loans or grants.

- You have to pay income tax plus a 10 percent penalty tax on any withdrawals made after the beneficiary turns 30. The same rule applies if you withdraw money to cover non-qualifying expenses.

- You cannot take money from an Education IRA in the same year that you or your child choose to take advantage of a Hope Scholarship Credit or Lifetime Learning Credit.

Section 529 Plans

You've no doubt heard the buzz about Section 529 Plans, which are state-sponsored college savings plans. What you might not realize, however, is that there are actually two basic types of plans.

Show Me the Money!

Can't set up an Education IRA for your child because your income is too high? Here's a tax loophole you need to know about. The Taxpayer Relief Act of 1997 specifies that the *contributor* must meet the income restrictions for contributions, not the child's parents. Consequently, a grandparent or other relative can make the IRA contribution for you if your income is above the specified threshold, but theirs isn't.

1. Prepaid tuition plans in which you buy future tuition credits at today's prices.

2. Tax-deferred savings plans that allow you to postpone payment of any state or federal taxes until funds are actually withdrawn from the plan. These plans are similar to Education IRAs, but instead of being limited to a $500 annual contribution, you can sock away up to $10,000 per year.

Section 529 plans can be set up for the benefit of any child or adult who will attend a public or private college, university, community college, or eligible vocational school in the United States. The tax-deferred plan doesn't restrict students to certain colleges in specific sites as the prepaid tuition plans do. What's more, the plan can be set up by parents, grandparents, or others, regardless of their income level. Annual contributions of up to $10,000 ($20,000, in the case of married couples) can be made without any gift tax consequences. Because the plan is set up in the name of the donor, your child's eligibility for financial aid is less likely to be affected than if you were to go with an Education IRA or other educational savings vehicle. We'll be returning to this important point later in this chapter.

Wondering what this whole gift tax business is all about? Here's what you need to know. You and your partner are each allowed to make a gift of up to $10,000 per year per child without any gift taxes kicking in. Actually, you're allowed to give the money to anyone in the entire world, but we're assuming that at this stage of your life, you'd like to keep that wealth in the immediate family! It's not unusual for wealthy parents and grandparents to take advantage of this opportunity to reduce their taxable estate because the $10,000 gifts that you make do not count against your estate and gift tax exemption. If you intend to set up a Section 529 plan, parents or grandparents can make a combined five-year gift in one year. In other words, they can invest up to $50,000 into a fund that will be used for the child's education. Ideally, the money will be held in the parents' or grandparents' names so that it won't have as large an impact on the financial aid formula.

Of course, no two state-sponsored educational savings plans are alike, so you'll want to shop around before making your final decision. Be sure to ask about management fees and other costs, and find out what types of investments are held in each plan. Also, bear in mind that you have no control over how the money is invested.

Your child can access the funds from a state-sponsored educational savings plan immediately at the start of college. Part of each distribution is nontaxable (the return of the principal), and part is taxable (the earnings on the original principal). Fortunately, these earnings are taxed in your child's hands, so they will likely be taxed

Facts and Figures
• • • • • • •

Make sure you understand how Section 529 Plans work before you set one up for your child. Three helpful sources of information are <www.collegesavingsplan.org>, <www.salliemae.com>, and <www.collegeboard.com>. You can also call the Department of Education (or Department of Higher Education) in the state where you live.

at a lower rate than what you would pay on such earnings—unless, of course, your child is a dot.com millionaire, but if that were the case, college really wouldn't be necessary!

Prepaid Plans

Not only state governments have decided to step into the educational savings arena. Colleges, universities, and banks also offer a variety of vehicles that are designed to help you save for your child's education.

College and university plans. Some colleges and universities offer plans that allow you to prepay your child's tuition fees—the so-called pay now–attend later, or tuition future plans. Rather than paying full price for your child's education down the road, you pay a discounted rate up-front. Basically, the educational institution calculates what it will cost for your child to attend college or university 20 years down the road, estimates what type of return it can expect to earn on your money, and then determines how much it needs to charge you today in order to generate that amount of income over time. If the college isn't able to obtain the return on its investment that it had hoped for, it's stuck making up the shortfall.

That's not to say that the whole venture is risk-free for you, of course. If you purchase one of these plans and then your child decides to go to college elsewhere or (even worse!) decides not to go to college at all, you may lose all but your original investment. In other words, the educational institution gets to keep all of the interest that accrued on your investment. (Ouch!)

Bank plans. Many banks also offer savings plans that are designed to help students and their parents to save for college. Some offer certificates of deposit based on the average tuition rates at certain schools. (In many cases, these certificates are backed with a guarantee that your child's university costs will be covered even if tuition fees shoot sky-high!) These CDs come with maturity dates of anywhere from 1 to 25 years. In most cases, a deposit of $1,000 is required.

Money Talk

● ● ● ● ● ● ●

"I made it through college by working part-time on campus and earning a few scholarships. My husband worked his way through college, too. We want to be able to provide our children with the tuition they need for college, but we expect them to earn some money, too, either through scholarships or grants, or by working part-time. We both found that working during college made us better students because we were paying for our college expenses ourselves. It also helped to have that work experience when it came time to get a 'real' job. Having some experience gave us a little boost over other applicants who didn't have any experience."

—*Cindy, 36, mother of two*

Do-It-Yourself Investing

Up until now, we've talked about some of the formal educational savings plans that are open to students and their parents. There's nothing to stop you from investing your child's educational savings funds on your own, however. No one says you have to opt into one of these plans.

Here are a few pointers to keep in mind before you pick up the phone to call your stock broker.

- Be cautious but not too cautious. While you don't want to gamble your child's whole educational savings nest egg on a single hot stock, it's just as foolish to invest so cautiously that you earn a rock-bottom return on your investment. You may be able to sleep better in the short-run if you go with guaranteed investment products like zero-coupon bonds (bonds that you purchase at a discount and redeem at their full value at term), municipal zero-coupon bonds (the municipal version of the standard zero bond), or baccalaureate bonds (bonds offered by the state to state residents whose children are attending state schools), but you won't enjoy the same gains as you would if you went with equity investments. As the old saying goes, "Nothing ventured, nothing gained."

- Look to the stock market if you're investing for the long term (e.g., if 15 to 18 years are left before your child needs to tap into the college fund). Fast-growing stocks or aggressive mutual funds are the best educational savings vehicles for families that have very young children. You can afford a high level of risk, after all, when you still have plenty of

Show Me the Money!

Don't write off U.S. savings bonds as a means of saving for your child's education. While their rate of return may not be as high as what you could potentially earn by investing in the stock market, the savings bond route has some hidden perks. Not only does the government guarantee the bonds, but the income that they generate is tax-free (if used for tuition and fees) if you and your partner earn less than $83,650; and it is reduced if you and your partner earn between $83,650 and $113,650. (If you earn more than that, none of the income is tax-free.) If you're single, the income is tax-free as long as you make less than $55,750; and reduced if you make between $55,750 and $70,750. (After that, none of the income is tax-free.) Note: All of these figures are based on the 2000 tax year—the most up-to-date information available as this book was going to press. You can find out more about government savings bonds at <www.savingsbonds.gov>.

time on your side. Rather than playing it super-safe, zero in on investments that have tremendous growth potential down the road, even if those stocks aren't reaping tremendous dividends right now. Ideally, you want to pick a fund that offers low fees and up-front charges. See Chapter 10 for more detailed information about the ins and outs of investing.

- Seek out balanced funds and growth funds that invest in both stocks and bonds if you're getting a late start and you've only got ten years to build your child's educational nest egg. These financial vehicles will give you a decent rate of return on your investment while posing very little threat to your principal.

- Once your child reaches age 14, gradually start shifting your money from aggressive, growth-oriented products into more conservative stock and bond funds. You may not make quite the same returns that you made when you were investing in more growth-oriented products, but you'll be assured that your nest egg will be there when your child needs it, regardless of what the market is doing at the time.

- Something else to consider when you're setting up your child's educational savings plan is the tax ramifications for both you and your child. While you may be saving for a noble cause (after all, what could be more noble than paying for your child's education!), the U.S. government isn't about to let you or your child off scot-free when it comes to paying tax on that income.

- Give serious thought to how your child's educational savings nest egg is set up. Don't allow too much money to accumulate in your child's name. Colleges assume that 35 percent of funds in a child's name are available to fund the child's college expenses. On the other hand, they only expect you to fork over 6 percent of your own funds.

- If you allow that money to accumulate outside your retirement account, it will be treated as a household asset—something that could reduce your child's eligibility for financial aid. Bottom line? Saving for your retirement has several

Show Me the Money!

Set up an automatic withdrawal plan with a mutual fund company to save for your child's education. If you invest $100 a month for eighteen years and you make a 10 percent return on your investment each year, you'll have a little over $60,000 sitting in your child's college fund by the time he or she graduates from high school.

bonuses. You'll save on taxes in the year you make such contributions, your earnings will be tax-deferred, and you'll be maximizing your child's chances of qualifying for financial aid.

THE TAX IMPLICATIONS OF SAVING FOR YOUR CHILD'S EDUCATION

Wonder why politicians spend so much time kissing babies? It's because they're so happy to meet the country's newest taxpayers. You see, thanks to the Tax Reform Act of 1986, even the youngest of babes may be tossing some money Uncle Sam's way.

The Tax Reform Act of 1986 took away certain tax advantages that minor children had enjoyed up until that time, introducing what has since become known as the "kiddie tax." While the first $750 of investment income earned by children under the age of 14 isn't taxed, most kids end up paying 15 percent tax on the next $750 they earn. The dot-com millionaire teens, of course, pay much heftier taxes than that, but for the purposes of this discussion, we're talking about average, middle-income kids whose piggy banks aren't exactly stuffed with thousand dollar bills!

It's at this point that things get kind of nasty. If kids earn more than $1,500, their excess earnings are taxed at the same rate that their parents pay, regardless of the income's source.

A Matter of Trust

Some parents and grandparents decide to open up custodial accounts for their children and grandchildren. The theory behind these accounts is great: you (or your child's grandparents) contribute to the plan, and the income the plan generates is taxed in your child's hands. There's just one major pitfall that far too many parents and grandparents choose to ignore: they aren't able to exercise any control over this income once the child in question reaches age 18. If you're lucky, you'll end up with a sensible child who sees the benefits of using his newly acquired fortune to finance university studies.

Facts and Figures

If your child's investments are earning about a 9 percent return each year and that child is under the age of 14, he or she will start paying tax on those investments around the time that the principal creeps above the $5,000 mark. Of course, once your child reaches the age of 14, all earnings and gains will be taxed at the child's own tax rate—a rate that should be less than yours unless, of course, your child happens to be the next Macauley Culkin!

If you're not, you could end up watching your child fritter away what was supposed to be a college nest egg on a flashy new sports car or a trip around the world.

A better alternative to a custodial account is to set up a trust under Section 2503(c) of the 1986 Tax Code. As the trustee of such an account, you maintain complete control over the income and principal until the child reaches age 21. Bottom line? You can provide your child with the funds needed to finance a university education while vetoing plans for that sports car or world cruise.

Delaying the transfer of funds to age 21 has some advantages. Kids tend to do a lot of growing up between 18 and 21, so they're a whole lot less likely to spend the money foolishly if they don't receive their nest egg until they're a little older. (Besides, a whole lot less money will be left in the college fund by that time anyway because they will have been drawing on it during the previous couple of years.) Of course, trusts don't enjoy the same tax advantages as certain other types of investments (the trust pays income taxes at its own rate, and the kiddie tax does not apply), but many parents and grandparents consider higher taxes a small price to pay for the peace of mind they get knowing that the pennies they set aside for their child's education will, in fact, be used for that purpose.

Show Me the Money!
• • • • • • •
Don't overcontribute to the trust that you've set up to fund your child's education. Funds that are not distributed to the child will be taxed at high rates when the trust is wound up.

Tax Breaks Available to Students and Their Families

The federal government recently introduced two new tax credits that every parent with a college-bound student needs to know about, the Hope Scholarship and Lifetime Learning credits. The credits apply to each student in a particular household, but there is a bit of fine print: your income. The credit is phased out for joint filers who have between $80,000 and $100,000 of adjusted gross income and for single filers who have between $40,000 and $50,000 of adjusted gross income.

Here's the scoop on each of these credits.

- *The Hope Scholarship Credit.* This credit applies to certain types of educational expenses that you or your dependent (e.g., your child) incur during the first two years at college. The credit amounts to $1,500 per dependant per year (100 percent of the first $1,000 of expenses and 50 percent of the next $1,000 of expenses). This credit makes it possible for a qualifying student to attend a community college for next to nothing. If you and your partner have an adjusted gross income of $60,000 and you have two children who are attending college on at least a half-time basis, you could be in for some nice tax cuts. If one child attends a community college where the tuition is $2,000 and the other attends a private college where the tuition is $11,000, you could expect to save $3,000 on your taxes, thanks to the Hope Scholarship Credit.

- *The Lifetime Learning Credit.* This credit is targeted at adults who want to go back to school, change careers, or to take a course or two to upgrade their skills; and to college juniors and seniors and graduate and professional degree students. A family will receive a 20 percent tax credit for the first $5,000 of tuition and required fees paid each year through 2002 and for the first $10,000 in 2003. If you've been at home full-time raising children but you decide you want to attend a graduate teaching program at a public university ($3,500), you could see your tax bill chopped by as much as $700, assuming your family has an adjusted gross income of $70,000.

You need to know about a bit more fine print, of course. (We're talking about a government program, after all!) For each qualifying student, you must choose to claim either the Hope Scholarship Credit or the Lifetime Learning Credit. You can't claim both. What's more, you can't take advantage of either of these credits in any year in which you've made a withdrawal from an Education IRA. You can, however, shift your strategy from year to year. You might decide, for example, to use the Hope Credit for the first two years when your child is attending college, but then switch to the Lifetime Learning Credit after that. Also, nothing is stopping you from claiming one type of credit for one child and another type of credit for another child in the same year, because the credits are claimed on a per-student-per-year basis. See IRS Publication 970 for more details.

Show Me the Money!
• • • • • •

You can't claim either the Hope Scholarship Credit or the Lifetime Learning Credit in a year when you have withdrawn funds from an Education IRA. Fortunately, if you're smart, you can find a way around this particular problem. If you expect to qualify for either of these tax credits when your children are in college, opt for a state-sponsored college savings plan rather than an Education IRA. That way, you won't lose out on these valuable tax credits.

PENNIES FROM HEAVEN

In a perfect world, parents would begin contributing to their children's college fund the moment the pregnancy test came back positive. Unfortunately, that's not always possible. Sometimes it's all you can do to keep your head above water financially!

If you find yourself with little or no savings and a child who's about to head off to college, you may have to beat a few bushes to find the necessary funds to pay for your child's education. Here's where—and how—to start looking.

Do Your Homework

One of the first things you should consider is whether or not your child qualifies for financial aid. The term *financial aid* is used to describe scholarships, grants, and loans that are offered to students in financial need.

If your child intends to apply for financial aid, the two of you should plan to meet with the guidance counselor at your child's high school and then do as much research on your own as possible in the hope of identifying possible sources of financial aid. Your public library is one good source of information. The Department of Education Web site <www.ed.gov> is another.

You should also plan to consult with a financial advisor at least a year before your child starts applying for financial aid, so that you can ensure that your family's financial house is in order. Otherwise, you could inadvertently make it next to impossible for your child to qualify for financial aid. This is because the family contribution (the amount of money that the financial aid folks feel that you should be able to chip in to help finance your child's education) is calculated on the basis of your family's income and assets, not just the student's own income and assets.

Show Me the Money!

If you and your partner are divorced and your child is looking for financial aid, it may be in the family's best interests to have the child move in with the parent with the lower income. Of course, if you have remarried, your child's stepfather's income will also be included as money available for the family contribution. In some situations, it may be to your advantage to put your wedding plans on hold until after your children have graduated from college or university.

Grants versus Loans

One of the first things you'll want to determine as you make your way through the financial aid jungle is whether your child is likely to be eligible for grants or loans. Let's quickly run through the lingo. A grant is the closest thing to heaven that a financially strapped student is likely to experience: free money that doesn't have to be repaid. A loan, on the other hand, is just what the name implies—money that has to be paid back.

Grants are intended primarily for genuinely impoverished students—students who have no other way of funding their college or university studies. The largest source of such grants is the Federal Pell Grants program, which pays out a maximum of $3,125 per year to cover college costs for the lowest-income graduates. These grants are tied to income. If your household income goes up, the grant amount is reduced. (A student with a household income of $30,000 to $40,000 could expect to receive approximately a $400 grant.) Other sources of grant money include the Federal Supplemental Educational Opportunity Grants (FSEOGs)—a federally funded program that provides funds to low-income students who can't obtain funds anywhere else—and various state and college grant programs.

> ### Show Me the Money!
> • • • • • •
> If you haven't done so recently, pull out your divorce statement and find out what it has to say about college expenses. If the divorce settlement specifies that the child's father is to contribute $5,000 per year to your child's education, that figure will be factored into your "family contribution" figures, whether your partner actually follows through and makes those payments or not.

Loans, on the other hand, are meant for students who aren't in quite such dire financial straits. Students may be eligible for a Stafford Loan (a loan offered by the U.S. Department of Education), a Perkins Loan (a loan that is awarded to students in financial need by a particular college as part of a financial aid package), or a Parent Loan for Undergraduate Students (a loan that the college arranges on your behalf in order to fund your child's education).

Here's the scoop on these major types of loans.

- *Stafford Loans.* These loans are offered by the U.S. Department of Education. Both subsidized and unsubsidized loans are available. Subsidized loans are reserved for low-income students, while unsubsidized loans are available to all families, regardless of whether or not they meet the government's qualifications for financial aid. When it comes to subsidized loans, first-year students are eligible for up to $2,625 annually; second-year students, for $3,500; third-year and fourth-year students, for $5,500; and graduate students, $8,500 per year. When it comes to unsubsidized loans, first-year students are eligible for up to $2,625 annually ($6,625 if they're independent from their parents); second-year students, for $3,500 ($7,500 if they're independent); third-year and fourth-year students, for $5,500 ($10,500 if they're independent); and graduate students, $8,500 per year ($18,500 if they're independent). The rate charged on these loans is set at 3.1 percent above the 90-day Treasury bill rate, with a cap of 8.25 percent. This means that students don't have to worry about paying more than 8.25 percent on their loans, even if interest rates shoot up. Students can choose either to start making interest payments on their loans immediately (i.e., while they are still in school) or to allow the interest to build up until they start making payments after graduation. Repayment must begin six months after the student leaves school, with the government picking up the interest charges during this six-month period.

- *Perkins Loans.* These loans are made in cases of exceptional financial need. Students can't apply for this type of loan on their own, but a Perkins Loan may be awarded by a particular college or university as part of a financial aid package. The government pays the interest charges on Perkins loans until nine months after graduation, so interest doesn't start to accumulate until after that time.

- *Parent Loans for Undergraduate Students (PLUS).* These loans are offered to parents in all income brackets who are creditworthy and interested in borrowing money to fund their child's education. Parents are entitled to borrow the cost of tuition less the amount of financial aid that their child receives from the school. Repayment periods vary with the loan amount, but the maximum period is ten years. Partial or full prepayment is allowed without penalty. These loans are made each year.

- *Student Loan Marketing Association (Sallie Mae).* Don't forget to contact your local Sallie Mae for other leads on student loans. You may want to seek out a financial institution that specifically works with Sallie Mae, because such banks are generally more willing to allow students to consolidate all of their loans into one, something that makes loan repayment a little less painful. (You can find the address for the Sallie Mae Web site elsewhere in this chapter.)

Home Equity Loans

Here's some good news on the student loan front. About seven years ago, the Federal government stopped expecting parents to tap into their home equity as a means of financing their child's education. This means that you no longer have to make a choice between having a roof over your head or attending Junior's graduation ceremonies. At least that's the theory!

You may still choose to tap into some of this equity for this purpose. In fact, there are some very compelling reasons to use a home equity loan (a line of credit secured by a mortgage on your property).

- Up to $100,000 of the interest on home-equity loans is tax deductible because you're basically taking out another mortgage on your home.

- Rather than borrowing a huge amount of money up-front (as is often the case with other types of student loans), you can simply draw upon the equity in your home as you need it.

- You may be able to make interest-only payments over the duration of the loan, with the principal payment not coming due until long after graduation day.

- You won't be locked into a sky-high interest rate. Current market conditions will determine the amount of interest you pay. Of course, this can turn out to be bad news if interest rates are moving in the wrong direction, but to protect you from such a disaster, most lending institutions limit the amount that interest rates can increase over the course of a given year.

Show Me the Money!

Here's a good reason to encourage your child to repay student loans sooner rather than later. Interest payments that are made on such loans during the first 60 months after payments become due are fully or partially deductible on a tax return!

One of the first financial obligations of many new graduates is repaying their student loans—an obligation that averages out to about $13,500 per student. Student loan interest reductions reduce the burden by allowing the students or their families to take a tax deduction for interest paid in the first 60 months of repayment on student loans. The deduction is available even if an individual does not itemize. The maximum deduction is $2,500 in 2001. The full deduction is allowed if a married couple filing jointly has an adjusted gross income of less than $60,000 and a single filer has an adjusted gross income of less than $40,000. A partial deduction is allowed for married couples who have adjusted gross incomes of between $60,000 and $75,000, and for single filers who have adjusted gross incomes of between $40,000 and $55,000. There is no deduction if your adjusted gross income exceeds these levels.

Borrowing from Your Retirement Savings

More than a few desperate parents have turned to another source of college funds: their own retirement savings nest egg.

On the surface, borrowing from your retirement fund may seem like a good idea. After all, most 401(k) plans permit you to borrow as much as one-half of your balance, up to a maximum of $50,000. Unfortunately, going this route has some major disadvantages. Not only is your interest not tax deductible (as it would be if you took out a home-equity loan, for example), the loan must be repaid within five years. Even worse, if you were to lose your job or quit your job during the life of the loan, the debt would be treated as a distribution from the plan and subjected to a 10 percent penalty for early withdrawal. Add to that the fact that you'll be reducing the amount of money that's available to you upon retirement, and you can see that this is a less-than-attractive option for most people.

As you can see, the secret to coming up with the money you will need to underwrite Junior's education is to start contributing early so that your money will have the maximum length of time to grow. You'll also want to find out as much as you can about tax-sheltered savings programs, scholarships, and bursaries—anything to reduce the costs of sending a child to college. Who knows? If all goes according to plan and you manage to scrape together the necessary funds, maybe Junior will remember to thank you in his speech when he's chosen as class valedictorian!

Show Me the Money!

Thinking of taking out a home equity loan? Don't just hand over your business to your regular financial institution. Shop around for the best possible rate, payback schedule, and fees.

Show Me the Money!

Make a point of keeping on top of financial aid and other tax changes that might affect your child's college fund. Don't wait until your child is a high school senior to discover that the rules of the game have changed for the worse. Stay on top of those changes as they occur and readjust your financial game plan accordingly.

CHAPTER 9

Surviving the First Year

There's no denying it. Starting a family is expensive. There are so many different demands on your paycheck, you may wonder how you're ever going to afford everything that Junior needs.

Here's a bit of good news if you've started to panic about whether you are, in fact, financially ready to become a parent. Despite what the salesperson on the floor of the high priced baby boutique would have you believe, that bundle of joy doesn't have to cost you a bundle—not if you're smart about it.

"So many parents fall into the 'cute and new trap'," says Laura, a 22-year-old mother of one. "Secondhand is just as good as new because babies grow out of things—including equipment—so quickly that items often are barely used."

Babies also don't need nearly as much stuff as we think they do, adds Fiona, a 32-year-old mother of six. "Getting down to the basics of a baby's world, all the baby really needs is his mother. Her arms to hold and comfort him, her breasts to nourish him, and her presence to teach him love, security, and trust."

DON'T SHOP TILL YOU DROP

Take a walk through the baby department of any major retail store and you'll be stunned by the sheer variety of products that are being pitched to parents. In addition to cribs, change tables, strollers, car seats, playpens, baby swings, and all the other big ticket items, you'll find hundreds of other items vying for your attention and a share of your baby equipment budget. Some of them are definitely worth picking up, like those quilted pads that help prevent your baby's head from flopping sideways when in a car seat. Then there are those products that you and your baby can definitely live without—like baby-wipe warmers!

The trick, of course, is to figure out what you need—and what you don't need—before you've worn the numbers off your credit card. Here's a crash course in Baby Equipment 101 for parents-to-be who are looking for ways to avoid overspending.

Facts and Figures

Babies are big business for baby equipment manufacturers. The U.S. juvenile products industry racks up $3.7 billion in sales each year.

- *Don't shop too early.* Shopping for baby should be a third trimester activity, not something you start doing the moment the pregnancy test comes back positive! The more time you spend shopping, the more you're going to spend.

- *Don't overlook baby gifts.* You're going to receive an extraordinary number of baby gifts. Even casual acquaintances—neighbors you've only spoken to once and relatives you haven't heard from in years— will show up on your doorstep bearing parcels full of wonderful things. There's a method in their madness, of course. They know that if they show up with a gift in hand, you'll feel obligated to let them gawk at the new arrival. If you stick to buying just the essentials before baby arrives, you won't be faced with returning all kinds of items that you don't really need—or watching your best friend's face drop when she discovers that you already have a baby monitor.

Show Me the Money!

Looking for a way to save a significant amount of money on all the items you'll need for your new baby? Form a purchasing co-op with other members of your childbirth class and use your combined buying power to negotiate the best possible deal with local retailers on cribs, car seats, strollers, and so on.

- *Don't overbuy.* Despite what some of the baby stores would like to convince you of, all your baby really needs during his first weeks of life are a car seat, a safe place to sleep (a crib, cradle, or bassinet, for example), a baby carrier (a sling or a Snugli, for example), some baby clothes, and some diapers. If you've got some extra money in your budget, you might also want to pick up a few extra bells and whistles, like a stroller, a baby swing, a baby monitor, and a rocking chair for you and baby to enjoy. These last few items aren't essentials, but they're certainly nice to have.

- *Don't clutter your baby's room with unnecessary furniture.* A dresser is nice to have, but it certainly isn't essential. You might choose to store your baby's clothes in an oversized plastic storage container tucked under your baby's bed. The same goes with the change table. You might find it easier to change a wiggly baby by tossing a waterproof pad on your own bed than by trying to discourage doing backflips off a tiny wooden platform!

- *Watch out for items that pretend to be essentials but are anything but.* Does it make sense to buy a high-priced garbage can for your child's room, just because it matches the wallpaper?

- *Test drive items whenever possible.* Before you spend $90 on an Exersaucer (an amazing contraption that allows baby to play in an upright position as soon as baby can support her head) or a Jolly Jumper (that ever-popular baby contraption that turns your wriggling six-month-old into a human yo-yo), make sure that your baby is actually going to use it. Babies have distinct preferences from a very young age. Some want nothing more than to be tucked into a Snugli and strapped to your chest; others view it as the baby world equivalent of a straitjacket. Before you fork over the big bucks for any of these items, see if you can borrow a friend's to find out if it meets with your baby's approval. Who knows, maybe the friend might even give you the item!

- *Encourage others to be practical.* If your coworkers are planning to buy you a baby gift and they ask what you need, suggest that they pool their funds and buy you something practical like a car seat or a stroller.

- *Purchase the base model of a product.* A more expensive model may have features you will never need. A crib with a double drop railing is about $75 more expensive than one with a single drop railing, for example.

> ## Money Talk
> • • • • • • •
>
> "You don't have to carry a diaper bag with Mickey on it. Any bag or knapsack will do. Just get a diaper pad, some diapers, and you're off!"
>
> —*Anne, 40, mother of three*

- *Research maintenance costs.* Check out the cost and availability of replacement parts for strollers and other types of baby equipment before you decide which brand to purchase. Some brands are extremely expensive to repair—assuming replacement parts are available at all.

YOUR BABY'S WARDROBE

- You can spend as much or as little as you'd like on your baby's wardrobe. How much you decide to spend will be determined by how often you're prepared to do laundry and how important it is to you that your baby has a closet full of brand-name garments. Your baby couldn't care less what she's wearing as long as it's warm, dry, and free of itchy lace and scratchy tags.

- Buy only what you need. Babies need clothes, but they don't need dozens of outfits. If you're prepared to do laundry every day or every other day, you should be able to get by with having six outfits in the smaller sizes—perhaps even fewer if baby isn't prone to leaky diapers. If you're expecting twins, you will need approximately one-and-a-half times as much clothing, rather than twice as much, as you would need if you were having one baby.

> ## Money Talk
> • • • • • • •
>
> "Give your baby the chance to test-drive a baby swing before you actually buy one. Two of my three kids hated that swing! Every baby is different, and you won't know until they're born what stuff they'll love and what stuff they'll hate."
> —*Johnna, 35, mother of three*

- Don't buy too many outfits in the newborn size, but do plan to have at least one outfit in this size on hand. More than one mom's been sure that she was carrying an 11-pound baby, only to watch a six pounder make a grand entrance!

- Don't even think about buying a sleeper that doesn't have crotch snaps. It will be such a pain to use that you'll never want to be bothered putting it on your baby. (Why there are sleepers like this in the first place is one of life's greatest mysteries.)

- Look for sleepers that are designed to grow with your baby, like the Snugabye brand that have adjustable ankle cuffs.

- Consider using cloth diapers or non-brand-name disposables. While cloth diapers are the environmentally friendly alternative, they aren't for everyone, so if you do decide to go with disposables, try a few generic brands. If you find that they don't work as well as any of the brand diapers, then you might want to use the expensive diapers at night when you want your baby to stay dry (and asleep!) as long as possible, and the less expensive generic brands during the day when it's not such a hassle to change a diaper every couple of hours.

FIGURE 9.1
The No-Frills Baby Layette

You should plan to have these items on hand before your baby arrives. The following chart indicates how much you can expect to spend if you're purchasing each of these items new. If you plan to borrow certain items from friends and relatives or to pick some of them up secondhand, you can expect to spend significantly less.

6 newborn nighties @ $8 each	$48
6 undershirts with snaps @ $7 each	42
3 sleepers @ $9 each	27
2 baby towel-and-washcloth sets @ $9 each	18
3 sets of fitted crib sheets @ $9	27
12 extra-large receiving blankets @ $9 each	108
3 pairs of socks @ $3 each	9
1 sweater (depending on the season)	15
2 cotton hats @ $6 each	12
1 snowsuit or bunting bag (depending on the season)	40
4 large bibs @ $4 each	16
Total	$362

- Rather than stocking up on baby wipes, try making your own by filling a squirt bottle with a mixture of liquid baby soap and water and then spraying the liquid on some inexpensive washcloths. If you've absolutely got your heart set on using the disposable baby wipes, make them go further by cutting the wipes in half. One family we know swears that an electric knife cuts through the wipes like magic!

- Look for alternatives to the big brand names. If you've got the financial means and it's important to you that your child looks as cute as the babies in the Baby Gap or Osh Kosh ads, then go for it. If, however, you think it's ridiculous to spend $40 on a pair of overalls that your baby will only be able to wear for a few weeks, then you might want to look for good-quality generic brands instead.

- Stick to unisex colors and styles if you're planning to have more than one child. Your daughter might look cute in that frilly pink rosebud bonnet, but her future baby brother may not be able to carry off the look with quite the same style.

- Only buy clothing as you need it. That way, if someone decides to lend you her child's baby clothes, you won't have already spent a small fortune on clothing that you didn't really need.

- Be careful when you're picking up end-of-season clothes. While you might think that your chubby cheeked six-month-old will be wearing a size 2 snowsuit by this time next year, it's hard to predict what size she'll actually be at that time. That $30 bargain could end up being a $30 waste of money.

Show Me the Money!

Expecting more than one baby? Be sure to phone around until you find a baby store that offers a discount to parents of multiples. You're going to need nearly twice as much gear as parents with a single baby: the least the retailers can do is give you a bit of a break at the cash register!

FROM HERE TO MATERNITY

Your baby-to-be isn't the only one who needs a wardrobe. Expectant mothers need clothes, too. Here are some tips on putting together a budget-friendly maternity wardrobe.

- Look for bargains and freebies. Get hand-me-downs from friends and relatives, shop consignment stores, and make a point of hitting the sales racks. Used maternity clothes are often in nearly new condition because they're worn for such a short period of time.

- Hit the sewing machine. If you know how to operate a sewing machine, consider whipping up a few simple jumpers and skirts. You'll save yourself a small fortune, and you won't have to worry about showing up at prenatal classes wearing the same navy blue jumper as half the other women!

- Purchase one or two items at a time rather than buying your entire wardrobe up front. Not only is it hard to predict how much your belly will blossom, it's also a nice pick-me-up to treat yourself to a new outfit during the interminably long third trimester.

- Don't spend a lot of money on maternity underwear until you're sure you're actually going to need it. A lot of women get away with wearing bikini underwear while they're pregnant.

- If you need to switch to a larger bra size while you're pregnant, buy nursing bras rather than regular bras. That way, if you plan to breastfeed your baby, you won't have to go out and buy yourself another set of bras.

- Try to shop somewhere other than the maternity stores. You can save yourself a fortune by avoiding anything with the "maternity" label. Try the plus-sized section of your local department store or shop at a plus-sized women's clothing retailer.

- Think mix and match. Look for high-quality items that can be mixed and matched to create the maximum number of outfits.

- If your husband is at least a few sizes larger than you, try raiding his side of the closet for sweaters, sweatshirts, and other oversized casual clothing.

- If you need a dress for a formal occasion, rent it rather than buying it. You'll save one-half to two-thirds of the cost.

SHOPPING SECONDHAND

While you can save yourself a lot of money by shopping secondhand, you have to know what you're buying. It's been proven time and time again that all kinds of dangerous baby items—items that have been off the market for years, in many cases—are readily available at garage sales.

It's not just garage sales that pose a risk to your child's safety, of course. If you find a car seat advertised on the bulletin board at your grocery store or in your local newspaper, you've got to exercise similar caution.

Here are a few of the items that you should definitely avoid when you're shopping secondhand.

- *Humidifiers, bottle-warmers, and other small appliances.* The problem with purchasing these items secondhand is that you have no idea how old the appliance is, whether it has been used properly or misused, and whether it meets current safety standards.

- *Second-hand cribs.* The problem with purchasing a secondhand crib is that you may have a hard time determining whether it complies with current safety standards. Be careful buying any used crib—even if a crib is new enough to conform with safety standards, it may have been damaged through misuse.

- *Older playpens.* It's unbelievable how long certain types of baby equipment remain in use, and playpens are a prime example. You'll still find some prehistoric playpens kicking around at garage sales. Unless you're certain that a playpen is reasonably new and that it is in good working order (i.e., it won't collapse while your child is in it), just say no to the bargain.

- *Older baby gates.* Accordian-style baby gates with diamond-shaped openings and large Vs at the top have been off the market for nearly a decade, but you'll still find them at garage sales. Avoid them at all costs because they present a strangulation hazard.

- *Car seats.* It's generally a bad idea to purchase a secondhand car seat. You can never be 100 percent sure that the car seat hasn't been involved in a car accident. Even a minor fender-bender can make a car seat unsafe. If you're certain that the car seat hasn't been involved in an accident, you still need to think twice about the purchase. Pass on the chance to buy a car seat that is more than a couple of years old or that is missing its installation instructions.

Show Me the Money!
• • • • • • •

Looking for a good source of secondhand children's clothing? Contact your local Parents of Twins Club and find out if they have an annual garage sale.

You can reduce the risks of shopping secondhand by dealing with a reputable secondhand children's store. In most cases, the owners of these stores make a point of rejecting items that are unsafe. That's not to say that you won't find any unsafe items, but you certainly put the odds in your favor. Regardless of where you shop, you should be prepared to ask the following questions when you're shopping secondhand.

- Who manufactured this product, and when was it made?

- What is the model number?

- Where is the instruction manual?

- How many families have used it?

- Has it ever been repaired?

- Are any of the parts missing? If so, are they essential to the functioning of the product?

- Does the product conform to current safety standards?

YOUR BABY'S ROOM

Every parent has visions of the perfect baby's room, but is it really necessary to spend $2,000 decorating and equipping a nursery for a tiny newborn infant who won't even care? If you'd like to create a beautiful nursery for your baby without depleting your bank account, keep the following tips in mind.

- Let your artistic talents shine. Sandra, a 37-year-old mother of four, used an overhead projector to project outlines of cartoon characters on her baby's wall. She traced the images and painted the cartoon characters in various colors using mistinted paint that she picked up from her local paint store at bargain-basement prices. "All it cost was our time and the cost of the paint," she recalls. Maureen, a 27-year-old mother of one, came up with a low-cost decorating idea of her own. "We painted the walls yellow and red and I decoupaged some pictures from some Curious George wrapping paper. It looked fabulous and cost next to nothing!"

- Dress up the walls with a wallpaper border. If you're not exactly the Martha Stewart type but you can't afford to wallpaper the room, combine painted walls with a wallpaper border at either hip or ceiling height. It'll wear better at ceiling height, but your baby will be able to enjoy the border more if you hang it roughly two-thirds of the way down the wall.

- If you decide to spring for wallpaper, invest in the good stuff—a high-quality scrubbable vinyl—and choose a pattern that won't look too babyish in a few years' time. Pastel ducks may look cute now, but just try to convince your five-year-old boy that ducks are where it's at when he has his heart set on race cars or superheroes!

Show Me the Money!
• • • • • • •

Here's a fun and inexpensive way to decorate your baby's room. Invite friends and relatives to come over and dip their hands into a bucket of paint and then make handprints on the wall. They can sign their names underneath.

- The flooring you choose needs to be similarly durable. Stain-resistant carpet and hardwood floors are worth every penny when you consider the types of abuse the floor is likely to encounter during your baby's first few years. If you've already got wall-to-wall carpet in the nursery and you're concerned that it might not weather your child's babyhood particularly well, an inexpensive area rug might be a good investment.

- Pass on the designer bedding. Babies don't care if they're sleeping on Mickey Mouse sheets or under a Winnie the Pooh comforter. Why should you?

THE REST OF THE STORY

Up until now, we've been focussing on the baby portion of your budget. As hefty as these expenses can be, they're insignificant compared to some of the other big-ticket items in your budget: housing, transportation costs, food, and so on. If you're serious about reducing your spending during baby's first year, you'll also have to consider ways to cut costs in these and other areas, too.

How much you decide to cut your costs is something that you and your family will have to decide for yourselves. Some families choose to make far reaching changes to their lifestyle: getting rid of the second car, looking for alternatives to high-priced prepared foods, and so on. Others prefer to make more modest cuts that don't have quite the same impact on their lifestyle. After all, dining out once a month rather than weekly can hardly be categorized as a major lifestyle change!

If you're ready to make some changes so that you'll have more money left in your bank account at the end of the month, you'll find plenty of inspiration elsewhere in this book—in Chapters 4, 6, and 7, among others. Rather than trying to make all of these changes—something that would no doubt drive your family crazy— simply pick and choose the ones that will deliver the maximum gain for the least pain. That, in a nutshell, is what money management is all about.

Show Me the Money!
• • • • • • •

Find out if your community has a toy-lending library. Check with your local family resource center or the children's department of your local library. For as little as $20 per year, your baby could have access to an ever-changing parade of toys.

Be sure to find out if there's a toy library in the town of any out-of-town relatives you plan to visit. Having a toy library available could save you the hassle of dragging your child's ten favorite toys with you on the plane.

Money Talk
• • • • • • •

"I wanted the best for my firstborn and felt I had to buy her everything. I spent a lot of money on her. Now, it's paying off, of course, because I have two twin girls to clothe, but I have to admit that I really got caught up in that 'buy the best of everything for baby' mentality."

—Lisa, 33, mother of three

CHAPTER 10

Death and Taxes

● ●

Death and taxes. This sure sounds like a fun chapter, now doesn't it? Bet you can't wait to start reading it! While you might prefer to skip this chapter entirely rather than face up to the two ugliest truths out there—your mortality and your tax bracket—you owe it to your kids to read on.

You see, once you have dependents, you are responsible for ensuring that they will be taken care of if something happens to you or your partner. That means writing a will, setting up powers of attorney, and ensuring that your estate won't be subject to any more income tax or probate fees than absolutely necessary. This whole process of putting your affairs in order is known as estate planning, and while it's one of the least enjoyable tasks you'll ever have to do as a parent, it's also one of the most important. That's why we've decided to devote an entire chapter to this subject.

WHERE THERE'S A WILL . . .

Sitting down to write a will may not be the most pleasant task in the world, but it's certainly an important one. After all, if you die without a will, you give up the right to choose your estate's beneficiaries, make gifts to close friends, name the executor of your estate, and designate a guardian for your children. To make matters worse, your estate may also end up taking a bigger financial hit than it might otherwise have taken; you'll pay more income tax and higher probate fees.

If you don't make the effort to have a will prepared, you get your particular state's one-size-fits-all will by default. If you're lucky, the will will roughly correspond with your final wishes. If you're not, the assets that you spent a lifetime accumulating may be handed over to relatives you haven't spoken to in years! Even worse, the proceeds from your estate are handed over to your seventeen-year-old son, who immediately puts the house up for sale so that he can spend a small fortune on some flashy sports car.

The Fine Print

Confused about how to proceed? You're certainly in good company. Most Americans have very little understanding about how their affairs will be handled upon their death—what will happen to the estate they worked so hard to build. The situation is all the more difficult if you happen to have a young family— you'll need to give some thought to designating someone to care for your minor children in the event of your death.

To make matters worse, the estate laws vary from state to state. Because covering all the ins and outs of the laws in the various states would quickly transform this book into a multivolume encyclopedia set (something that would no doubt horrify our publisher), we'll simply give you a quick snapshot of how very differently estate matters can be handled by two different states. For the purpose of this exercise, we've chosen Connecticut and California.

Connecticut. If you die in Connecticut, your assets are divied up in the following manner:

- If you are survived by your spouse and any child or children that you had with that spouse, your spouse receives the first $100,000 of your estate, plus one-half of the remainder. Children receive the other half of the remainder.

- If you are survived by your spouse and your children and one or more of those children is not the child of that spouse, your spouse receives one half of your estate. All the children share the other half equally.

- If you are survived by your spouse and your parents, but you don't have any children, your spouse receives the first $100,000 of your estate, while your parents receive the remainder.

- If you are survived by a spouse only (i.e., you don't have any children and your parents are no longer living), then your spouse receives your entire estate.

- If your only survivors are your children, they receive your entire estate. Similarly, if your only survivors are your parents or your brothers and sisters, then they receive your entire estate.

- If you don't have a spouse, children, brothers or sisters, or living parents, then your estate goes to your next of kin. If there are no kin or step-children, then your entire estate goes to the state of Connecticut. (Ouch!)

California. Now let's consider how this estate drama would play out in another part of the country: California. The rules there are slightly different because, unlike Connecticut, California is a community property state. The term *community property* refers to property that is owned jointly by husband and wife. With the exception of gifts or inheritance, all property acquired by either the husband or wife during a marriage is owned equally by both regardless of whose name is on it. The following states are community property states: Idaho, California, Washington, Oregon, Nevada, Arizona, New Mexico, Louisiana, and Texas. Even if you move out of that state, community property continues to be treated as community property.

If you die in California, your estate will be handled as follows:

- If you have any community property, then that property automatically goes to your spouse.

- If your parents are no long living and you haven't got any children, brothers, or sisters to leave your estate to, and any deceased brothers and sisters didn't have any surviving children, then all of your separate property goes to your spouse.

- If you have a child (or in the event that your child is deceased but has a child), then half your estate goes to that child or grandchild and half goes to your spouse.

- If you haven't got any children but you do have parents or brothers and sisters who are still living, then half of your estate goes to them and half goes to your spouse.

- If you leave more than one child, two-thirds of your estate goes to those children and one-third goes to your spouse.

- If you leave one child, but you have one or more deceased children who have their own children, then two-thirds of your estate goes to those children and grandchildren, while one-third of your estate goes to your spouse.

- If you don't have a surviving spouse, then your estate is divided equally amongst your surviving children.

- If you don't leave a spouse or children, then your estate goes to your parents, sisters, brothers, nieces, nephews, and/or next of kin.

As you can see, estate matters are handled quite differently in these two states, but regardless of the specifics, the law is very clear about how your estate will be handled if you die without a will. Don't put your affairs in the hands of some faceless bureaucratic in the state taxation office. Make a point of sitting down with an attorney and writing a will that will meet the needs of your spouse and your children if anything should happen to you.

As a rule of thumb, your will should contain the following types of information:

Show Me the Money!

While you'll find all kinds of do-it-yourself will kits in bookstores and stationery stores, it's generally a good idea to get legal advice—something that will cost you at most a couple of hundred dollars. There's simply too much on the line to cut corners in this important area.

- An introductory paragraph that indicates whose will it is (i.e., your name and your city and state)

- A statement indicating that you wish to revoke all previous wills

- A statement indicating who your executor and alternate executors are

- A statement giving the executors the right to use their discretion in either selling or not selling any of your noncash assets

- A statement giving your executors permission to pay your debts and death-related expenses out of the proceeds of your estate

- A statement giving your executors permission to transfer the balance of your estate to your partner, if he or she survives you for a period of 30 days, or to a trust that shall be established on behalf of your children

- A statement in which you appoint a guardian to care for your children if you and your partner die

- The signatures of two witnesses, neither of whom should be beneficiaries of the will

Choosing an Executor

The next important decision you'll have to grapple with when putting your affairs in order involves choosing the executor for your estate—the person who is responsible for seeing your will through probate and ensuring that your estate is disposed of appropriately. Just a quick reminder in case you dozed off during your high school civics class, the function of probate court is to authorize and oversee the payment of funeral expenses, taxes, and debts that are owed by the person who died. The executor functions as your representative but works under the court's supervision.

Don't make the all-too-common mistake of choosing your brother simply because he's your closest blood relative. Look for someone who is trustworthy, astute at handling money, and a good administrator. That's not to say that your brother might not be the best candidate for the job, of course. Just don't fall into that old trap of assuming that because blood is thicker than water, he's automatically your best bet.

When you're trying to decide who would be your best bet for executor, be sure to keep the responsibilities of the job in mind. We'll get into those responsibilities elsewhere in this chapter when we talk about what's involved in taking a will through probate, but basically your executor is responsible for burying you or disposing of your remains and winding up your estate.

In most cases, it's a good idea to choose a friend or relative whom you trust and who will understand the needs of your will's beneficiaries. If you choose someone who never had children, for example, he or she might have a hard time understanding just how important it is to have the latest and greatest running shoes when you're 14!

If you decide to name a professional (e.g., your accountant, lawyer, or banker) as your executor because no one in your family or your circle of friends seems to have the necessary skills or is willing to assume the responsibility, you should at least plan to choose a trustworthy person to serve as your coexecutor. This friend or relative can keep an eye on the proceedings to ensure that the professional doesn't double-dip (i.e., charge both executor's fees and professional fees for managing your estate), and can also prevent the probate process from becoming derailed, something that could cause temporary hardship for your survivors. Remember, your estate is "just business" to a professional.

Facts and Figures

If you do not have a will, the court—acting on behalf of the state—will appoint an administrator. Once appointed, this administrator will fulfill the duties that would normally be carried out by an executor.

Housekeeping 101

Don't worry. There's no need to panic. This next section of the chapter doesn't have anything to do with playing Martha Stewart. After all, cleanliness and children are pretty much mutually exclusive. When we talk about housekeeping, we're referring to those boring but important details that could make a huge difference in how easily your executor steers your estate through probate.

Believe it or not, one of the biggest favors you could do for your survivors is to put your affairs in order while you're still alive. Something as simple as keeping a list of the professionals you deal with (your lawyer, accountant, insurance broker, stockbroker, and so on) and a record of the location of important documents such as wills, insurance policies, and investment statements can save your family a lot of time and money come probate time. It's also useful to get in the habit of keeping all of your financial records in single place (perhaps a filing cabinet or fire-safe lock box) and to try to keep those records in some semblance of order. That means weeding through them at least once a year to get rid of anything that is obsolete— like statements for bank accounts that you have long since closed. (You don't want your family to have to pay some accountant $150/hour to wade through your bank statements and investment records, now do you?)

An important note for anyone who relies upon their computer for storing estate-related data: always keep a hard copy of this data in your filing cabinet. That way, this information will still be available to your executor in the event of a hard-drive crash or other disaster.

Show Me the Money!

Make sure your survivors know how to track down all your bank accounts. If your bank is unable to track down an inactive bank account's rightful owner, the unclaimed money is eventually transferred to the state. That's reason enough to keep good records, now isn't it?

CHOOSING A GUARDIAN FOR YOUR CHILDREN

If there's one aspect of the whole estate planning process that you're likely to find particularly difficult, this is it. It's painful enough even to consider the possibility that you might not live long enough to watch your child grow up. It's a thousand times worse to have to choose someone else to step into your shoes if something happens to you.

While choosing a guardian is never easy, it's an essential part of the estate planning process. If you were to die without designating a guardian for your children, the state would end up doing it on your behalf—a very scary thought indeed.

Here are a few points to keep in mind as you consider who would—and wouldn't—be a suitable guardian for your children.

- *Childrearing philosophies.* It's a good idea to choose a guardian who shares your childrearing philosophies. That way, you'll know that, should anything happen to you and your partner, your children will be brought up mostly the way you intended to raise them. This issue weighed heavily on Maria's mind and actually led her to rethink her initial choice of a guardian. "We chose my sister as my children's guardian when we first drew up our will," the 31-year-old mother of two recalls. "She and her husband had kids close to my daughter in age, and she and I are a lot alike. However, over time, I began to realize that I didn't agree with a lot of the parenting techniques my sister used. To make matters worse, she had started smoking again, and I didn't want my children to be brought up in a home with smokers. So, we decided to name my brother as the children's legal guardian instead."

> ## Money Talk
> • • • • • • •
> "We really don't have anyone to be guardians for our children. Our siblings are too young or too irresponsible. Our parents are out of the question. We have one best friend who we would actually feel quite comfortable with, but she is single and taking on the responsibility for raising three kids would mean a huge change to her lifestyle. It is a terrible dilemma to be in."
> —*Johnna, 35, mother of three*

- *Age.* While you might be tempted to choose your parents or your partner's parents as guardians, it's best if you can find someone younger to take on this role. In addition to the fact that your parents are likely to predecease you, by sheer virtue of their age, it's important to remember that a world of difference lies between being a grandparent and a parent. Unless your parents or your in-laws have expressed their willingness to become your children's guardians and they are healthy and energetic enough to take on major childrearing responsibilities, you might want to consider appointing someone else.

- *Your child's relationship with this person.* If your son absolutely adores your sister-in-law, then she may be a shoo-in for the position of guardian. If, on the other hand, your child drives her crazy and she has no patience with him, you might want to rethink your decision to appoint her as his guardian.

- *Willingness to accept the job.* Not everyone is willing to act as the guardian for someone else's children. Just as you wouldn't dream of nominating your best friend for political office without discussing it first, you shouldn't name anyone your child's guardian without first having a heart-to-heart talk about it. Don't be surprised if the would-be guardian says no. After all, you're not just asking this person to stay with your kids for the weekend. You're asking him or her to become your child's parent for life.

Choosing a guardian can be painstaking. Cindy, a 36-year-old mother of two learned this when she went through the process a few years ago. "We ended up choosing our sons' legal guardian through a process of elimination," she recalls. "We had a pool of possible candidates (our parents and siblings) and ruled out all but one for various reasons, like their age, their geographical location, their marital status, and whether or not they had children already. (My sister has two children who are roughly the same age as our boys, and we felt that adding two kids to the mix would simply be too much for her.) In the end, we decided to choose my husband's sister. We felt that she did a great job with her children, and as long as her health is good and she remains willing, we'd like her to have our kids if anything should happen to us."

Here's something else to think about when you're struggling with this all-important decision. Sometimes it makes sense to appoint two guardians rather than one. The first guardian could take on the day-to-day childrearing tasks, while the second guardian could be responsible for overseeing the children's trust fund and handling the children's investments. Unless the guardian you have in mind is as caring as Mary Poppins and as financially astute as Warren Buffet, it might make more sense to go this route.

Show Me the Money!
· · · · · ·

You should always name an alternate guardian in your will, just in case your first choice is unable or unwilling to step in. If you happen to name a married couple as your child's guardian, be sure to indicate which member of the couple would continue to be your child's guardian if they were to separate or divorce.

Minimizing Probate Fees

You already know what income tax is. You've had the pleasure of paying it from the day you received your first paycheck. You might be less clear about what probate fees are, however. Basically, probate is the legal process of administering and implementing the directions in a will, and probate fees are the government's charges on the property covered by the will.

The key to reducing probate fees is to arrange your affairs so that you minimize the value of the assets that pass through your estate. This may mean naming your spouse or child as the beneficiary of your retirement accounts and life insurance policies, placing your assets in a trust so that they don't have to pass through your estate at probate time, and possibly holding some of your assets jointly (a topic we'll discuss in greater detail elsewhere in this chapter).

Just for the record, here's what's involved in probating a will.

- The probate process begins when a will is filed with the court and declared valid. At that point, the executor or administrator is asked to post a bond. The size of this bond will vary according to the size of the estate. It is possible to state in your will that you wish to waive this requirement, something that can save your executor or administrator a lot of grief. Your lawyer will be able to advise you about the pros and cons of going this route.

- An inventory of all assets that are owned in your name only is prepared. Your executor will do a lot of the legwork, but outside appraisers may need to assess the value of any real estate holdings, works of art, or collectibles that you own. At this stage in your life, your daughter's Beanie Baby collection may be the closest thing to collectibles that can be found in your home, but who knows, perhaps you're a gambling type who actually believes that toddlers and Royal Doulton figurines can live under the same roof!

- Advertisements are placed in the local newspaper asking that any claims against your estate be made by a particular date. The executor also ensures that any outstanding bills are paid (including those for your medical or funeral expenses) and that state and federal tax returns are filed. If you owe any taxes, they'll also be paid at this time.

- Once all the number crunching has been completed, what's left of your estate will be distributed to your various beneficiaries.

That, in a nutshell, is what probate is all about. Depending on the laws in your particular state, it can take anywhere from nine months to two or three years to probate a will. Obviously, the more complex your estate and the messier your affairs, the longer the entire process will take. Further, if your executor loses enthusiasm for the process midstream—an all-too-common occurrence—things could drag on even longer than that.

Jointly Held Property

Before we wrap up our discussion of probate, let's talk about the advantages and disadvantages of holding some of your key assets jointly with your spouse.

As you've no doubt heard by now, jointly held assets don't have to be dragged through the whole probate process—something that can save your executor a lot of time and aggravation and minimize probate fees. Jointly held assets are, however, included in the value of the taxable estate—something that's important to note if you happen to live in a state which has an inheritance or succession tax. (And you thought that climate was the key consideration to weigh when choosing a place to put down roots!)

Holding property jointly with your spouse does have some definite advantages.

- Such property passes immediately to the survivor, rather than being held up in probate for months—even years—after your death. In the latter situation, the surviving spouse may be left virtually penniless, unless she's able to convince the probate court to make early disbursements from the account so she can handle her day-to-day expenses.

- Holding property jointly ensures an inheritance for a spouse who has few, if any, funds. If, for example, you were to marry someone who has children from a previous marriage, your partner might want to leave the bulk of the assets held to those children. Your partner might want you to have the house, however, so that you can continue living in it or sell it and keep the proceeds. In this case, the solution would be to put the house in both your names.

- Holding property jointly with your spouse eliminates the need for ancillary probate (probate in another state)—a situation that could arise, for example, if you and your spouse acquired an out-of-state vacation property at some point down the road.

- Holding property jointly with your spouse allows for some protection against creditors. Creditors may not be able to seize jointly held property unless the surviving spouse has assumed liability. You'll have to double-check this with your estate planner, however. State laws vary considerably when it comes to this all-important point.

Of course, there's also a downside to having jointly held property. Here are a few points to consider.

- Your bank account could be frozen when your spouse dies. This could prevent you from accessing the funds in your account until after your spouse's will has made it through probate—something that could take months or years. Fortunately, as we noted earlier, you may be able to convince the executor to release some of those funds so that you can cover your day-to-day expenses while the will makes it through the probate process.

- You may find yourself paying more—not less—tax as a result of holding some of your property jointly. If the family money market account is in the surviving partner's name only, it will not be treated as part of the estate; if it's jointly held, however, it will be included in the list of assets that is used to calculate estate taxes.

Show Me the Money!
• • • • • •

Certain types of wills and trusts can be drawn up in a manner that allows property to pass directly to children or grandchildren—something that can help to keep this property out of the IRS's reach. An estate attorney should be consulted to draw up the trust agreements.

- Jointly held property cannot be willed. Neither spouse has a say in how the surviving spouse will dispose of the property in question. Like it or not, the surviving spouse can do what she wants with the property after the other is gone.

- Holding assets, such as bank accounts, jointly involves certain inherent risks. While you probably don't even want to consider the possibility that your spouse could clean out the joint bank account and head off into the sunset with your next door neighbor, there's nothing to stop your spouse from accessing those funds if your account is held jointly.

As you can see, a lot of factors need to be considered in deciding whether or not to hold your assets jointly with your spouse. That's why it's always a good idea to seek out the services of a good estate planner before making these decisions. You'll find some leads on tracking down an estate planner in the Resources in the back of this book.

ESTATE TAX PLANNING

One of the first things you'll want to talk to your estate planner about, of course, is whether or not your estate is likely to be large enough to be taxed by the federal government. Items that may be taxed upon your death include:

- All property you own, including cash, stocks, bonds, real estate, pension and profit-sharing plans

- One-half of all jointly held property

- The proceeds from life insurance policies that you own

- Any business assets you own

(A taxable estate and a probate estate are different, because your taxable estate takes into account your share of all jointly held property, whereas your probate estate doesn't.)

The estate planning front isn't all doom and gloom, however. Estates that fall below certain levels are not subject to federal estate tax. The individual exemption amounts for upcoming years are as follows:

- 2001: $675,000

- 2002: $700,000

- 2004: $850,000

- 2005: $950,000

- 2006 and after: $1,000,000

Writing a Living Will

Something else you should consider is writing a living will. A living will is basically a message from you to members of the medical profession stating that in the event of terminal illness or injury, you do not want your life to be prolonged by artificial life support systems. You can list particular treatments that you would want to have withheld or withdrawn if you found yourself in such a situation. If you want your spouse to be able to make these decisions on your behalf if you can't do so, you should plan to set up a health power of attorney. Your right to prepare a living will is now recognized by law in a number of states.

When you're preparing your living will, you should also think about setting up a durable power of attorney. This would allow your spouse or other appointee to act on your behalf, and to handle financial matters if you were unable to do so. You can limit the scope of the power, if you wish. For example, you might decide to assign power over your checking and savings accounts, but not over your stock portfolio or your home.

Updating Your Will

Think your job is finished the moment you've drafted your will? We hate to disappoint you, but your job is just beginning! You should make a point of reviewing your will at least once every five years—more often than that if your circumstances change. Circumstances in which you would want to immediately write a new will include:

- If you divorce or remarry

- If you become a parent for the first time

- If you change your name, or if anyone mentioned in the will changes their name

- If your executor dies or becomes incapable of performing the duties of executor

- If one of your beneficiaries dies

- If you sell any of the property that you have bequeathed under the terms of your will

Keep a copy of your will with your financial records so that you can pull it out and review it from time to time to make sure that it's still relevant and complete. Remember, out of sight, out of mind . . .

As you can see, a lot is involved in protecting your family and your estate from disaster. You need to write a will and do what you can to minimize the tax

Show Me the Money!

While the surviving spouse receives unlimited property without paying tax—the so-called marital deduction—it's not possible to dodge the IRS indefinitely. The estate tax ultimately will have to be paid upon the death of the surviving spouse. Of course, there may be changes to the estate tax now that there's a new administration; some experts predict that individual exemptions will be increased, though some are hoping that estate taxes will be eliminated.

consequences and probate costs associated with your death. It can be a time-consuming and difficult process, but you owe it to your family to do it right. Here's how to get started.

- Make an appointment with your lawyer to write a will or to review your existing will.

- Start thinking about whom you would like to appoint as your executor and your children's guardian.

- Consider writing a "living will"—a legal document that will speak for you if you become incapacitated and are no longer able to make decisions for yourself or your children.

- Give some thought to estate planning so that you can minimize both your probate fees and estate taxes. You may not be able to take it with you, but you can do your best to keep as much of your estate as possible out of the hands of Uncle Sam! With a new administration in power in Washington, this issue is definitely one of those you'll want to keep tabs on. We could see some radical changes in the ways in which estate taxes are handled in this country.

CHAPTER 11

Hedging Your Bets

In the last chapter, we tackled the ins and outs of estate planning. Now let's zero in on a topic that's equally important but that most Americans find both boring and baffling: life insurance.

As you know, life is full of risk. You could die decades earlier than you anticipate or lose your ability to earn a living as a result of a debilitating accident. The possibilities are endless (to say nothing of hair raising!).

The purpose of insurance is to buy yourself the peace of mind that allows you to sleep each night. When you purchase insurance, you are paying another party—the insurance company—to shoulder some of the risk on your behalf.

Because insurance companies insure millions of people, they can predict with a high degree of accuracy how many deaths or disabilities will occur in a given period, when they will occur, and what they are likely to cost in terms of payouts to the beneficiaries. This knowledge helps them to set rates.

LIFE INSURANCE: WHO NEEDS IT?

Wondering if you're a good candidate for life insurance? The answer is surprisingly simple. If someone is dependent on your income or if your estate is large enough to be subject to federal estate taxes, then the answer is yes.

As you know, the key purpose of life insurance is to protect your dependents—your children, your elderly parents, and anyone else you are responsible for supporting—from your untimely death. Whether you're a stay-at-home parent or a working parent, your family depends on your contributions—paid and un-

FIGURE 11.1
How Much Life Insurance Do You Need?

	You	Your Partner
Liabilities		
Mortgage	___	___
Car loans	___	___
Other debt	___	___
Total liabilities (a)	___	___
Cash needs	___	___
Final expenses (burial, taxes, probate fees, legal fees)	___	___
Your children's education	___	___
Childcare expenses	___	___
Eldercare expenses (important if you're responsible for caring for an aging parent)	___	___
Other cash needs (e.g., emergency fund)	___	___
Total cash needs (b)	___	___
Amount of money required to replace lost income	___	___
Gross annual income required by family (c)	___	___
Gross annual income of partner (if applicable) (d)	___	___
Annual income shortage or surplus (figure c – figure d) (e)	___	___
Assumed rate of return on investment (adjust for inflation, if desired, using Figure 10.3) (f)	___	___
Amount of money needed to make up income shortage (figure e divided by figure f) (g)	___	___
Total amount of money required without factoring in assets (figure b plus figure g) (h)	___	___
Adjustment for family assets		
Cash savings (savings, T-bills, US Savings Bonds, etc.)	___	___
401(k)s, IRAs, other retirement funds	___	___
Stocks, bonds, and mutual funds	___	___
Your house (principal residence only)	___	___
Life insurance (total of all policies: group, personal, mortgage, credit)	___	___
Business assets (if applicable)	___	___
Any pension plan death benefits	___	___
Total amount available (i)	___	___
Total amount required (j)	___	___

Source: Adapted from a life insurance worksheet developed by the Manufacturers Life Insurance Company.

paid—to maintain its current standard of living. Obviously, the younger your children, the more insurance you need to take care of them until they are old enough to support themselves financially.

You may be surprised by the value of your contributions—financial and otherwise. As you work through the calculations in Figure 11.1, you will see just how significant a financial impact your family would face if you died suddenly. Figure 11.2 will give you an idea of the total investment required to replace your contribution to your family's income.

Show Me the Money!

Reluctant to do a lot of number-crunching on your own? Plenty of terrific online tools are available to help you. You'll find them at such Web sites as Quicken.com, Lifeinsurance.net, MSN.com, and Accuquote.com.

Example:

If a couple earns $36,000 a year, a surviving spouse would need a nest egg of $600,000 invested at 6 percent annually to bring in that amount of income. She would need less, of course, if she and her children qualified for Social Security benefits, if she was working, if she received proceeds from another life insurance policy, and/or she had other income-producing assets to draw income from.

Source: Manufacturers Life Insurance Company

In addition to replacing your lost income, your life insurance should be enough to allow your beneficiary (e.g., your spouse or your children) to cover:

- Mortgages, installment loans, and all unpaid debts, including current bills (heat, electricity, credit card bills, etc.)

- The costs of your children's education

- Your final expenses (funeral and burial costs, appraisal fees, final unreimbursed medical expenses, attorneys' and accountants' fees, taxes, probate fees, etc.) As a rule of thumb, you'll need something in the neighborhood of 2 percent to 5 percent of the total value of your estate, plus at least $5,000 in funeral expenses to cover these unpleasantries.

Show Me the Money!

Resist the temptation to buy into a group life insurance plan without taking the time to read all the fine print. If you're in good health, you could end up subsidizing the insurance costs of other less healthy members of the group. What's more, if the plan ends up being a money-losing venture for the insurer, they could choose to cancel it, which would leave you scrambling to find a new insurer—or left with no insurance at all!

FIGURE 11.2
Money Required to Provide Various Levels of Monthly Income at Various Interest Rates

Annual Income	Monthly Income	Total Investment Required Interest Rate			
		4%	6%	8%	10%
$12,000	$1,000	$ 300,000	$ 200,000	$150,000	$120,000
15,000	1,250	375,000	250,000	187,500	150,000
18,000	1,500	450,000	300,000	225,000	180,000
21,000	1,750	525,000	350,000	262,500	210,000
24,000	2,000	600,000	400,000	300,000	240,000
27,000	2,250	675,000	450,000	337,500	270,000
30,000	2,500	750,000	500,000	375,000	300,000
33,000	2,750	825,000	550,000	412,500	330,000
36,000	3,000	900,000	600,000	450,000	360,000
39,000	3,250	975,000	650,000	487,500	390,000
42,000	3,500	1,050,000	700,000	525,000	420,000
45,000	3,750	1,125,000	750,000	562,500	450,000
48,000	4,000	1,200,000	800,000	600,000	480,000
51,000	4,250	1,275,000	850,000	637,500	510,000
54,000	4,500	1,350,000	900,000	675,000	540,000
57,000	4,750	1,425,000	950,000	712,500	570,000
60,000	5,000	1,500,000	1,000,000	750,000	600,000

Note: If you wish to adjust for inflation, simply subtract the projected rate of inflation from the projected rate of return and look up the difference on this table.

As your life changes, so do your insurance needs. Be sure to reevaluate your life insurance needs at least every five years and to factor in inflation and any tax changes that could affect your estate planning. When you review your policy, you should ask yourself whether you've managed to protect yourself against most major types of disasters, which types of risks you need to cover on your own and which you can reasonably hand over to an insurance company, and whether you're paying a fair price for the coverage you're purchasing.

Types of Life Insurance

A dizzying number of life insurance products are on the market today. That said, once you wade through the marketing hype, you're left with five basic types of life insurance:

1. Term

2. Whole life or Straight life

3. Universal

4. Variable life

5. Hybrids

Term insurance. As the name implies, term insurance covers you for a specific period of time. If you choose annual renewable term insurance, your policy will be renewed each year at an increasingly higher premium. (Like it or not, your risk of dying increases each time you blow out those birthday candles!) If you go for level term, your premium remains the same for a period of five, ten, or fifteen years. It's then reevaluated at the end of that term. If you can prove to your insurance company via a medical exam that you're healthier today than you were at the outset of your previous policy, your premiums may even go down. If not, your premiums will move in the opposite direction.

Term insurance is the cheapest form of life insurance that you can buy when you're young, which goes a long way towards explaining its popularity with families with young children. It offers maximum bang for your insurance-buying buck. It's important to understand what you're buying, however. Unlike other types of insurance which can double as forced savings vehicles, term insurance is a "pure" insurance product. It pays off only if you die during the period that is covered by the policy. At the end of

---

Show Me the Money!
· · · · · ·

When you're shopping for term insurance, be sure to look for a policy that can be renewed without your having to pass another physical examination—something that could make it impossible for you to maintain your insurance coverage if you developed a serious, or, ironically, fatal illness. You should also ensure that the term insurance policy has a guaranteed rate and that it contains a clause allowing you to convert the policy to a whole life policy without undergoing a physical examination. Remember, renewability and convertibility are both important features to have if you find yourself faced with health problems in years to come.

that term, you have nothing left. Okay, you still have your life, which is admittedly priceless, but we're talking dollars and cents here!

Whole or straight life insurance. Whole life insurance (or straight life insurance) is basically two products in one: a life insurance policy with a built-in savings vehicle. Over time, the policy builds up cash value (or savings) on a tax-deferred basis.

During the first few years, only a small percentage of each premium is allocated to savings, but your savings gradually build up over time. You can access this cash by borrowing against the value of your policy (you pay the insurance company the amount specified in your policy) or canceling the policy entirely. You may decide to use this cash to help pay for your child's education, to get your family through a financial rough spot, or to meet your other financial needs.

There's just one drawback to borrowing against your life insurance policy: if you die before this "loan" is repaid, the insurance company reduces the amount that it pays to your beneficiary. For example, if you have a $50,000 policy but you've borrowed $12,000 against it, your beneficiary will only receive a $38,000 payout. That's something to think about seriously before you decide to tap into your life insurance nest egg.

Facts and Figures
· · · · · · ·

The amount of your whole life insurance premium is determined by your age and state of health at the time you purchase the policy. That premium does not increase while the policy is in force. Therefore, the younger you are when you buy a whole life policy, the lower your monthly premiums will be.

Universal life. Universal life insurance is a flexible insurance plan that is interest-rate sensitive. The investments that are built into your plan earn interest from a series of fixed-income investments, so the savings that you build up from these investments tends to rise and fall along with the markets.

You can vary your annual premium by adjusting the amount of the death benefit that your beneficiaries would receive, and vice versa. During your lean years (e.g., your early childbearing years), you might decide to put less into your policy than during your so-called gravy years (your peak career years).

Just one quick word of caution to anyone who's thinking of going the universal life route: if you skip a premium, the administrative and death benefit costs will be deducted from the cash value that has built up in the account. The moral of the story? Be sure that you have enough accumulated cash value to cover these premiums, or you could find yourself without life insurance!

Variable life insurance. Variable life insurance is similar to universal life insurance, but in this case, you have greater control over how the savings portion of your insurance policy is invested. Your money can be invested in stocks, bonds, mutual funds, or even zero-coupon bonds. It's up to you. Of course, you don't exactly have unlimited choice on the investment front since you're limited to the products that are offered by the particular company that you're dealing with. Still, this may be an appealing product for you if you're a savvy investor.

Hybrids. Hybrid insurance policies combine features of both term and whole life insurance policies. As their cash value accumulates each year, they increase the amount of whole life protection you receive and decrease the amount of your term coverage. Hybrid policies are more appealing to older people than to couples with young families. They cost more than a traditional term policy but less than a traditional whole life policy.

Term or Whole Life? Which Is Best?

Many first-time insurance buyers find it difficult to chose between term and whole life insurance products. Rather than flipping a coin and hoping that you're making the best decision, it makes sense to consider how much coverage you need right now, how long you're going to need that coverage (e.g., for the next 18 years, until your new baby is self-supporting), and how much you can afford to spend on insurance premiums.

Show Me the Money!
. . . .
Find out if you have life insurance coverage through work. Many companies offer life insurance to their employees at very reasonable rates, with the coverage amounts and premiums typically based on your salary.

While you might be tempted to opt for the whole life option simply because it's a great method of forced saving, ask yourself whether other investment vehicles would allow you to build up your savings more quickly while providing a greater return. Of course, if you suspect that you'd never actually get around to starting your own savings program, you're probably further ahead to go the whole life route. So don't forget to factor in your investment personality!

Taking Care of Business

It's doubly important for you to carry adequate life insurance if you happen to be self-employed. Your business quite possibly could be the largest asset you have. You need life insurance to protect your business in case you die. Such insurance helps to ensure that a business can continue operating if a partner or major shareholder dies. It can provide the money for the surviving partner or partners to purchase the share that was owned by the partner who died, and it can save the survivors from the possible embarrassment of not having enough money to buy out someone who is willed a share of the ownership—possibly the deceased partner's children. As a rule of thumb, you should take out enough insurance to equal your share in the business, and you should draw up a buy-sell agreement with your partners.

Don't make the mistake of assuming that you don't have any need for this type of insurance if your business happens to be a solo operation. In this situation, life insurance can provide your beneficiary with funds to live on while the business is liquidated, something that can save this person—likely your spouse or your child—the stress and headaches of taking over a business that he may be unwilling or unable to run. So do your family a favor and think this one through carefully. Better yet, get some advice from your accountant and your attorney.

Handling Insurance Proceeds

Another issue you'll need to grapple with is how to handle insurance proceeds—the income that your insurance policy generates over time. Basically, you have the choice of receiving your money in one of four different ways:

1. *Lump sum.* You get a check immediately for the full amount of the policy, less any amount that may have been borrowed against the policy. This is a good bet if you are an experienced investor who has at least a reasonable chance of outperforming the insurance company's investments.

2. *Interest only.* The insurance company holds the principal amount but pays you the interest that your investments are earning. Consider this approach if you're unsure of what to do with the proceeds and you need more time to plan your investment strategy.

3. *Fixed installments.* You receive a check for a fixed amount of money at fixed intervals until the money is all used up. The company also pays you interest on the remaining balance it holds during this time. If you decide to go this route, be sure that your policy allows you to withdraw the entire sum at any given time, should you choose to do so.

4. *Fixed period.* The company agrees to pay you the proceeds plus accrued interest over a certain period. The size of each check depends on the

length of time that the proceeds are spread over. Basically, you're buying an annuity, so be sure to do your homework to ensure that you're getting the best possible return on your investment.

Whom Should I Choose as a Beneficiary?

If you are married or living common law, you will probably name your partner as the beneficiary of your life insurance policy and list your children as alternate beneficiaries. It's important to change the beneficiaries on your policy if your life circumstances change (e.g., if you and your partner separate or if your partner dies). Usually, this is simply a matter of filling out an insurance company form. However, if you've purchased a policy with an irrevocably designated beneficiary, you would have to obtain that person's consent to change beneficiaries—something that could prove difficult if you were in the middle of a particularly difficult divorce proceeding.

If you have young children, you might want to consider bypassing your partner altogether by setting up a trust to receive and manage any proceeds from your insurance policy on the children's behalf until they are older. A financial planner can help you to decide if it would be in your best interests to do so.

Whatever you do, don't die without naming a beneficiary on your insurance policy. If this were to happen, releasing the funds to your heirs would be delayed, and what's more, the proceeds of the policy would be considered part of your estate, which would make them subject to probate fees and legal fees. Proceeds from a life insurance policy are considered part of the estate unless someone else owns the policy. This is why parents will often designate a grown child or set up a trust to benefit from the policy, especially if the estate is subject to estate taxes.

Show Me the Money!

Are you separated or divorced? Make sure you have enough life insurance to cover any support payments you are required by law to make. More often than not, your estate will be obligated to continue making those payments after your death.

DISABILITY INSURANCE

Disability insurance is the Rodney Dangerfield of the insurance world: it doesn't get any respect. A surprising number of people go to great lengths to insure themselves against the ultimate disaster—death—but fail to protect themselves and their families against a more likely catastrophe—temporary or permanent disability.

Here are a few hair-raising statistics on the disability insurance front.

- If you are 35, the odds that you will be disabled for at least 90 days before age 65 are more than twice as high as the odds of your dying before reaching retirement age. Worse, the average length of disability for anyone disabled for longer than 90 days is two-and-a-half years.

- One-third of all disabilities are suffered by people under the age of 45. What's more, the majority of disabilities are caused by medical problems or accidents that can't be predicted in advance.

- Being disabled for a single year can wipe out a decade's worth of savings.

- Approximately 43 percent of all loan and property foreclosures are the result of a disability.

While it's tempting to think that Big Brother—the government—will take care of you and your family if you suffer a permanent disability, the amount of support that you would receive from Uncle Sam is minimal to say the least—assuming, of course, that you qualify at all. Believe it or not, a full 70 percent of all disability claims are rejected by Social Security.

Even if you do qualify, it's hardly a get rich quick scheme. Social Security provides limited coverage to workers who become severely disabled before they reach 65. You'll only qualify if you have a physical or mental disability that is so severe that you're unable to work, and if your disability is expected to last—or has already lasted—for at least twelve months or is expected to result in death. What's more, to be eligible, you must be fully insured under Social Security regulations. Assuming your claim is approved (and as we noted above, there's no guarantee that will happen!), you will have to wait for five months before benefits kick in, and the amount that you receive will be what you would normally start to be paid upon retirement at age 65.

As you can see, you don't have to do much number-crunching to figure out that the disability insurance buck pretty much stops with you. If you're the breadwinner in your family, you need to take out enough disability insurance to replace your monthly income if you are injured or become ill and are no longer able to work. It's important to keep in mind that even a partial disability—a broken arm, for example—can pose a serious threat to your income. We'd hate to think what would happen to our income, for example, if we were suddenly unable to type!

Shopping Around for a Policy

When you're shopping around for disability insurance, you'll need to know how long you will require the coverage (e.g., until you're 65 and you can access your retirement savings) and how much income you'll need to replace each year. Then you'll need to get out your magnifying glass and read the fine print on the policy. Here's what to look for.

- *A reasonable definition of disability.* Some policies are so rigid about the definition of disability that making a claim is almost impossible. Look for a policy with an "own-occupation" or "regular-occupation" disability clause. Other types of policies require you to work at any position for which you are reasonably trained rather than staying off work until you're well enough to return to your usual occupation. Obviously, you pay more for own-occupation coverage, but if you're in a reasonably well-paid profession and you'd have to take a big pay cut to switch to any related work, you'd probably be wise to spring for this kind of coverage.

- *Coverage against both accident and illness.* Some policies will only cover one or the other.

- *Noncancellable and guaranteed renewable.* As the terms imply, you want a policy that cannot be cancelled by the insurer either before or at the time of renewal because you are in poor health. Otherwise, you could find yourself losing your coverage at the very time when you need it most.

- *A reasonable term.* Disability insurance can be as short as one year, may continue until you reach age 65, or may last your entire lifetime. Make sure that the policy you're considering meets your coverage needs.

- *Waiting period or elimination period.* To keep your disability premiums as low as possible, look for a policy with a long waiting period (the

Facts and Figures

Short-term disability insurance provides modest benefits for a short time period. The amount you receive is based on your earnings, but the maximum for such policies is generally quite low. The waiting period can be anywhere from 7 to 21 days, and plans can pay out over as few as 13 weeks or as long as 52 weeks.

Long-term disability insurance is designed to cover you over the long haul, providing a certain percentage of your earnings (typically 50 percent to 60 percent of your base salary) for a specified number of years or until you reach age 65. You may have to go through a lengthy waiting period before benefits kick in—sometimes as long as three to six months.

amount of time you have to wait until benefits kick in). Obviously, you'll want to take into account how much savings you have on hand because you'll be using your nest egg to stay afloat.

- A *future income option.* A future income option allows you to buy additional coverage as your income increases, without presenting any evidence of medical insurability. If you develop a serious health problem down the road, this clause could be worth its weight in gold.

- *Residual benefits.* Look for a policy that will provide you with partial benefits if you are able to work part-time but not full-time.

- *Cost-of-living adjustments.* Over time, inflation can erode the amount of your disability insurance payments. That's why it's important to choose a policy that will be adjusted by either a set percentage each year or by the amount of inflation.

MEDICAL INSURANCE

No family finance book would be complete without a discussion of medical insurance. After all, during this period of your life, you're bound to make frequent visits to the doctor's office and the local emergency ward. It's a rare child, after all, who manages to make it through childhood without at least one ear infection, set of stitches, or broken bone.

Medical insurance is designed to protect your family against the medical repercussions of day-to-day illnesses and major medical emergencies. Its purpose is to prevent you from being financially ruined by physicians' fees, prescription charges, and—heaven help you!—hospital bills.

When you're shopping around for medical coverage for your family, it's important to choose a plan that will deliver the maximum coverage for what you can afford to pay. Here's what's being offered on the medical insurance menu these days.

Indemnity Plans

With indemnity plans, you have the opportunity to choose your own doctor and hospital and to pay on a fee-for-service basis. You don't need a referral to see a specialist. Indemnity plans are pretty much the crème de la crème of plans. Unfortunately, they're becoming prohibitively expensive and far less common. Assuming you can find a good indemnity plan, here's what you need to know about piecing together the appropriate coverage.

Basic hospitalization. As the name implies, this is bare-bones coverage designed to cover all or part of your hospital bills, including semiprivate room, food, X-rays, laboratory tests, operating-room fees, and prescription drug charges. The coverage may be limited to a specific number of days during any given period, with waiting periods required between hospitalizations. This type of coverage is offered through private insurance companies as well as the various Blue Cross firms nationwide. Obviously, the better the coverage, the more you pay. Sometimes basic hospitalization is combined with basic surgical and medical insurance. Everyone should have at least this amount of coverage.

Basic surgical and medical expense. This type of insurance covers fees for doctors' visits and various types of surgery. Usually, the insurer establishes a schedule outlining the fees it will pay for various types of operations. If your surgeon charges more than the approved rate, you're required to fork over the difference. This type of coverage is offered through private companies as well as Blue Shield, and once again, you get what you pay for.

Major medical. Major medical insurance picks up where basic hospitalization and medical/surgical policies leave off, covering the big ticket items that are typically above the maximums provided through standard policies. They cover such "frills" as extensive hospitalization, surgery, other doctors' fees, private-duty nursing, home medical care, diagnostic work, therapies, medical devices, and re-

Show Me the Money!
. . . .

You can reduce the costs of your major medical plan by increasing your deductible and asking for a higher stop-loss limit. Obviously, the price for reduced premiums is increased risk.

habilitation. These policies typically include a deductible that the patient must pay before any insurance company benefits kick in. Once you cover the deductible, most policies cover 70 percent to 80 percent of each claim you file. You're required to cover the other costs yourself. At some point, however, if your claim gets large enough, the insurance starts paying 100 percent of all legitimate claims—the so-called stop-loss limit. Some policies don't put any limit on the amount of benefits you're able to draw; others provide fixed or lifetime maximums.

Health Maintenance Organizations (HMOs)

Health maintenance organizations are nonprofit cooperatives that provide medical care to individuals for a fixed fee each month. The HMO owns and operates hospitals and clinics and hires doctors, nurses, and medical technicians. If

FIGURE 11.3
Ten Questions to Ask Your HMO

1. How much choice do I have when I select a primary-care physician? What happens if I decide to see a doctor outside the HMO network?

2. What steps do you take to ensure that your physicians are competent and able to deliver quality service?

3. How are doctors rewarded for keeping costs down? (In other words, is there an incentive for my primary-care physician to see me less often, deny me certain types of tests, or to turn down my request to see a specialist?)

4. Who determines what is medically necessary—my primary-care physician or someone else behind the scenes?

5. How do I go about appealing such a decision, and how long does the appeal process typically take?

6. What percentage of revenue goes towards treating patients?

7. Do you routinely substitute generic drugs for their name-brand counterparts?

8. How do you go about deciding whether or not to send a particular patient to a specialist?

9. Will I receive prompt care in the event of an emergency? Will I be charged if I go to a hospital outside the network?

10. What mechanisms are in place to allow patients like me to provide feedback about your services?

you belong to an HMO, your premium covers nearly all medical expenses, and you are entitled to care through the HMO 24 hours a day, 7 days a week. The key downside to HMOs is the lack of choice. You must select your primary-care physician from the pool of doctors, and your physician will have to authorize any trips to specialists or trips to non-HMO network hospitals. You can find a list of ten questions that you should ask when you're shopping for an HMO in Figure 11.3.

Point of Service Plans (POPs)

Point of service plans are administered by insurance companies or HMOs. You pay extra for the privilege of going to see a doctor outside the network, but this option is open to you. Basically, you get to enjoy the best of both worlds. You get the coordinated care of an HMO plus the freedom to go see a nonmember doctor if you choose.

Preferred Provider Organizations (PPOs)

Preferred Provider Organizations are networks of doctors. They provide discounted care to members of a sponsoring organization, such as an employer or a union. Patients are required to make a small copayment at the time of service—usually $10 or 10 percent of the total charge, although their share of the bill jumps if they choose to see a doctor outside the network.

Medicare

Medicare is national health insurance that covers everyone 65 years of age or older who pays Social Security taxes or who is eligible for Social Security or Railroad Retirement benefits. Medicare is also available to individuals under the age of 65 who are disabled or who have chronic kidney disease.

Medicare coverage is divided into two parts. Part A is free of charge and covers hospital stays, nursing home care, and a certain percentage of after-hospital care. Part B covers physicians' fees and outpatient services at hospitals as well as certain medical services and supplies. Patients are charged a small monthly fee and must pay at least part of the costs. (The plan covers 80 percent of reasonable medical costs—a figure that is often considerably less than the fee that you've been charged.) Part B does not cover eyeglasses, dentistry, prescription drugs, private nursing, nursing home care, treatment in a foreign country, or routine physical examinations. It is truly "no frills" coverage.

Medigap

Medigap coverage is medical insurance that is designed to bridge the gap between your medical bills and the amount that Medicare pays. It is intended for the same group of people who qualify for Medicare—older people and individuals with certain types of debilitating health problems.

As you can see, you can put in plenty of legwork finding appropriate insurance coverage. Here are the most important points to remember.

- Make an appointment with an insurance broker to review your existing life, disability, and medical insurance policies. (If you haven't had them reviewed because you started your family, you're probably woefully underinsured.)

- Decide which type of life insurance would best meet your family's needs at this stage of your life and how much coverage you need. (As we noted earlier in the chapter, term insurance is generally the best bet for families with young children.)

- Don't forget to look into disability insurance as well. Statistics show that you're far more likely to become disabled than to die during your childrearing years.

- Look for a health insurance policy that will deliver maximum bang for your insurance buck, and make sure that the policy is guaranteed renewable and non-cancelable. If there's one time in your life when you need reliable coverage, it's when you've got a house full of children!

Show Me the Money!

Look for a guaranteed renewable and noncancelable health insurance policy. The last thing your family needs is to have your insurance company bail on you the moment you're diagnosed with anything more serious than a head cold!

Who Wants to Be
a Millionaire?

● ●

It's not hard to figure out why *Who Wants to Be a Millionaire?* managed to attract record numbers of viewers in the months following its network debut. Striking it rich is, after all, every bit as much of a part of the American Dream as purchasing a house in the suburbs and having your proverbial 1.4 kids. If a game show promises to let you make that million without actually having to save and invest your own money—well, hey, what's not to like about the show?

Unfortunately, only a handful of people will ever get the chance to make their million courtesy of Regis and company. The rest of us have to settle for making our fortunes the old-fashioned way, by squirreling away bits of cash and then watching our nest eggs grow over time thanks to some (hopefully) prudent investments. Going this route may not be nearly as exciting as testing your wits on national TV, but then again, you don't risk kissing your fortune goodbye just because you can't remember the name of the 20th President of the United States (James A. Garfield, of course).

That's not to say that saving and investing are without their own challenges, particularly when you have a young family that leaves you short on both cash and time. If money is especially tight for you right now, you may find it difficult to find the funds to invest in anything other than diapers and baby clothes! The point of this chapter is not to make you feel guilty if you don't have the funds on hand to embark on a major investment program today, but rather to allow you to start planning for a time when you will be able to start investing. Who knows? Maybe that day will arrive sooner than you think.

SAVING VERSUS INVESTING: WHAT'S THE DIFFERENCE?

The first thing we should do is to define the terms *investing* and *savings* because these terms tend to get used pretty interchangeably when, in fact, they mean radically different things.

Let's start out by defining investing. Basically, investing means putting something of yourself into something that will allow you to achieve something greater. You invest in your career by taking additional courses that will make your skills more marketable. You invest in your kids by spending time with them in the hope that such an investment will reap the ultimate of dividends—a great kid! The same thing applies to money. You choose to invest your money in a particular stock, bond, mutual fund, or other investment vehicle because you believe that your investment will grow or appreciate over time. It's important to note that investing implies looking ahead over the long term—three years, five years, and perhaps even longer.

Saving, on the other hand, means squirreling away bits of cash that will allow you to achieve some short-term and medium-term goals, like setting aside the funds for a vacation or building up your family's emergency fund. (Most money gurus recommend that you have a rather sizeable nest egg—as much as three to six months' income—tucked away to cushion the blow in the event that you or your partner suddenly find yourselves out of work. If you don't have such savings on hand, you might have to borrow to keep your family afloat in the aftermath of a job loss or put your plans for that dream vacation on hold indefinitely.)

Show Me the Money!

Looking for a place for your family's nest egg? You have three basic options: a savings account or money market account at your bank, a money market account with a mutual fund company, or a certificate of deposit.

If you decide to open a savings account or money market account at your bank, make sure that the minimum balance requirements for that account are reasonable. Otherwise, any interest you earn could be offset by service charges. You should also find out how interest is credited (i.e., is it compounded daily, monthly, quarterly, or annually?) Obviously, the more often interest is compounded, the higher the rate of return.

If you decide to open a money market account with a mutual fund company rather than a bank (not a bad idea, frankly, because mutual fund companies tend to be a bit more generous when it comes to interest), make sure you read all the fine print on the agreement. Some accounts put limits on the number of withdrawals you can make over a given time period and the amounts of such withdrawals (a $500 minimum seems to be the norm).

Because it's important to feel confident that your savings will be accessible when and if you need them, you'll want to put this money into a low-risk savings vehicle—perhaps a savings account, a money market account, or a U.S. Treasury bill. You won't get the same type of return that you might get on a bona fide investment, but then again, you won't find yourself pacing the floor at 3:00 AM, wondering whether the family car repair fund has been vaporized thanks to an unexpected downturn in the stock market.

As you can see, there's a world of difference between *investing* and *saving*. Investing requires time and effort and is much more active than saving, which tends to be a rather passive activity. Investing involves taking some risk. You accept this added risk on the assumption that you'll benefit from higher returns than what you could expect to obtain from ordinary savings. If you can't tolerate the anxiety that goes along with investing, or if you're unwilling or unable to invest the time necessary to educate yourself about the various investment vehicles, you'd be wise to stick with your current savings strategy. If, on the other hand, you're willing to tolerate some calculated risks, you're committed to educating yourself about your various investment options, and you're after a higher rate of return than what a savings account can deliver, then perhaps investing is the right choice for you after all.

> ### Show Me the Money! (continued)
> • • • • • • •
>
> If you decide to take out a certificate of deposit at a bank, make sure you commit to a term that you can live with. You'll find yourself facing a hefty penalty if you decide to make an early withdrawal. On the other hand, don't be too gun shy when it comes to settling on the term, because most banks will pay you a higher rate of interest on deposits that are made for a longer period of time (e.g., a one-year term will yield a higher rate than a six-month term).

Your Investment Game Plan

Once you've decided that you're prepared to go the investment route, you need to spend some time pinpointing your investment objectives. After all, if you're not clear about your objectives, you'll have no way of gauging whether or not a particular investment vehicle is the right one for you. (Just as there is no such thing as a one-size-fits-all diaper, there's no such thing as a one-size-fits-all investment opportunity!) Chances are, you have one or more of the following four objectives in mind: to generate some income over the short run, to allow for long-term capital appreciation, to ensure the safety of your principal, and to minimize your taxes.

Your investment time frame and goals will determine the appropriate invest-ment vehicles. Here are some important questions to consider.

- *Income.* How important is it that this investment start generating income right away? If you are counting on it to generate some income to supple-ment your family's other income sources, choose an investment that will bring you regular, predictable income over the short term. These might include government, municipal, or high-grade corporate bonds and income stocks, such as utilities or Real Estate Investment Trusts (REITs) that pay a substantial portion of their earnings in regular dividends.

- *Safety of principal.* If your goal is to protect yourself against any possible loss of principal, you may have to accept a lower rate of return. You can-not expect high yields from such conservative products as money-market accounts, regular savings accounts, U.S. Treasury bills, and certificates of deposit (CDs).

- *Long-term capital growth.* Do you want to put your money into invest-ments that will grow steadily over the long term? Are you after aggressive growth (investments that yield you some quick bucks so that you can sell at a good profit and then repeat the process)? If your goal is to see your investments grow over the long term (the smartest investment strategy for most people, frankly), your best bets are real estate, stock mutual funds, and certain stocks that pay few or no dividends. These types of invest-ments allow your money not only to stay ahead of inflation but also to provide you with financial security in years to come. (Or at least that's the plan!)

- *Minimizing taxes.* Do you need to keep in mind any tax issues when you're mapping out your investment strategy? If your goal is to protect your earnings from taxation—either entirely or to the greatest extent pos-sible—then you'll want to seek out investments that have been designed with this objective in mind. For example, if you want to defer taxes, then make the maximum allowed contributions to your 401(k) and IRA. If you don't want to pay any taxes at all, then opt for tax-free municipal bonds. The higher your tax bracket, the more valuable the tax-free bonds are. If you are in the 33 percent tax bracket, a tax-free yield of 7 percent is equiv-alent to 10.9 percent taxable bond.

Now that you've pinpointed your investment objectives, make your invest-ment decisions accordingly. Bottom line? No matter how appealing a particular investment vehicle may look, don't get on board unless it's taking you where you want to go.

Then determine how much money you can reasonably afford to invest right now. Obviously, you don't want to pour so much money into your family's investment program that you find it difficult to scrape together the funds to pay the grocery bill or to fork over the cash for your daughter's music lessons.

The Basic Rules of Investing

Don't know when—or how—to get your investment program started? You're certainly in good company. Most novice investors find themselves feeling more than a little nervous when they first step up at bat. Here are some tips on getting your feet wet in the weird yet wonderful world of investing.

- *Build your foundation first.* You wouldn't expect your child to be able to talk in sentences before she can even say "Mama." She needs to put a whole bunch of language building blocks in place first. The same thing applies to investing. You're not ready to start worrying about investing until you've got the rest of your financial "foundation" in place first. That means ensuring that you have some savings on hand to cover any curve balls that come your way (everything from job loss to the need for a new furnace), that you've got a game plan in place for saving for your short-term goals (e.g., a family trip or a new vehicle), that you've got both life and disability insurance to protect your earning power, and that you're basically satisfied with the condition of your home (i.e., you won't be tempted to pull money from your investments to cover major changes or improvements).

- *Review your investment objectives.* Better yet, print them out and review them each time you're considering a particular investment! Simply reminding yourself that your risk tolerance is moderate at best and that you've still got decades to make your fortune may be all it takes to "just say no" to that hot dot.com stock.

- *Get a handle on your family's bottom line.* Something as simple as having another little mouth to feed can dramatically affect the amount of money you have to invest—particularly if those additions to the family arrive two or three at a time! It's not enough to do a net-worth statement (a statement of what you're worth, factoring in both assets and liabilities) and a cash-flow analysis (a statement that illustrates how closely the money coming in matches the money going out) when you first start investing, and then figure that your homework is done. You need to work through the numbers at least once a year to ensure that your investment program is still meeting your needs.

- *Keep well informed.* Read the financial pages of your local newspaper and consider subscribing to at least one consumer money magazine. (If you're on a tight budget, you might simply plan to hit the periodicals section of your local library once a month and flip through a month's worth of financial planning magazines, or spend a few hours hitting some financial industry Web sites.) Most important, don't be afraid to ask your broker or financial advisor questions. After all, that's why they're there!

- *Don't allow your heart to rule your portfolio.* If a stock turns out to be a loser, dump it. Never mind the fact that it was the first one you ever purchased or that you're emotionally attached to it for some other reason. If it's not performing, it's time to move on.

- *Don't look for magic or miracles.* You won't find any. Losses will happen as well as gains, no matter how carefully you make your investments. After all, you can't win 'em all.

- *Don't put all your eggs in one basket.* No single type of investment performs well at all times and under all market conditions. The moral of the story? Diversify, diversify, diversify.

- Keep liquidity in mind. Don't invest your entire life savings in investments that will be hard to sell if you need to get your hands on some cash in a hurry. Keep at least a portion of your savings in a reasonably liquid investment that can be dumped at any time without incurring huge losses.

- *Test the water first.* If you have never bought stocks before—and, frankly, that's pretty much the norm for families with young children—then you might want to get a feel for your risk tolerance by purchasing shares in a mutual fund rather than buying individual stocks. (In a mutual fund, you own pieces of a large number of stocks, so you are able to have your investment eggs in a whole lot of baskets.)

- *Don't get sidetracked by bells and whistles.* The industry is always introducing new products that promise to take advantage of the latest (but not necessarily greatest) tax loopholes. Either stick to the more straightforward products, or if you decide to go with one of these unconventional investment products, be prepared to invest the time required to learn about what you're getting yourself into.

- *Be realistic.* Most significant gains take 24 to 30 months, except in strong bull markets. Don't cash in your chips prematurely just because the market has taken a temporary dive. Remember, you're in this for the long haul, and the market will rebound over time. The longer you hold stocks, the lower the risk.

- *Realize that a cost is associated with going the safe route.* According to finance scholars Eugene F. Fama of the University of Chicago and Kenneth R. French of the Massachusetts Institute of Technology, who were quoted in an article in *Business Week,* between 1950 and 1999, stocks outperformed lower-risk securities by 8.3 percent.

THE FEELING IS MUTUAL

It's not hard to figure out why Americans are embroiled in a 20-year love affair with mutual funds. Mutual funds allow you to have your cake and eat it too. A mutual fund pools the investment dollars of many participants and uses that money to purchase a large portfolio that is widely diversified. As a result, the risk is shared among a large number of investors rather than being placed all on the shoulders of any single investor. You also save yourself the time that you would otherwise spend researching individual stocks and bonds—time that you simply may not have at this point in your life. After all, which would you rather be doing: pouring through the financial pages of your local newspaper or tossing around a Frisbee with your kid?

Facts and Figures

Feeling a little overwhelmed by the sheer number of mutual funds to choose from? You have good reason. There are over 8,700 mutual funds in America today, a far cry from the 500 that existed back in 1979.

How Mutual Funds Work

While the term *mutual fund* sounds mysterious, mutual funds actually function in a straightforward fashion. Mutual funds buy securities and then receive dividends and interest from those investments. If a mutual fund sells a particular security at a profit, it usually gives you a capital gains distribution proportional to the number of shares you own in the fund. If shares in the fund increase in value while you own them, you profit when you sell them. Of course, if you have to sell them while the value is down, you end up selling at a loss.

When you purchase a mutual fund, the number of shares you receive depends on the net asset value of the fund on the day you buy. To calculate the fund's net asset value, you divide the total value of all stocks and bonds it holds by the number of outstanding shares in the fund. The fund's net asset value is calculated daily, with its value moving up or down depending on the market price of the number of securities it holds. If, for example, the net asset value is $12.23 on the day you invest $1,000 in a particular fund, you will receive 81.776 shares.

The Types of Mutual Funds

There are two basic types of mutual funds: closed-end funds and open-end funds.

1. *Closed-end funds.* These funds sell a limited number of shares. These shares are traded on a stock exchange just like actual stocks.

2. *Open-end funds.* These funds sell as many shares as investors are willing to buy. They will buy back shares at any time. These shares are not traded on a stock exchange.

The fund of choice for most investors is the open-ended fund, both because of its flexibility (you can buy and sell shares at any time) and because of the sheer number of offerings.

Although thousands of open-end funds are available to choose from, these funds tend to fall into one of 12 different categories:

Show Me the Money!

Here's something important to note if you'll be purchasing mutual funds with your 401(k) money. Because you are in a tax-deferred plan, any capital gains or income that your mutual fund generates will be automatically reinvested in the fund one or more times per year. Anyone who is investing in mutual funds directly (i.e., not through a 401(k) plan) has the option of reinvesting this income or taking a cash payout. When you reinvest the income, you are buying more shares in the fund.

1. *Money-market funds.* These are "cash" or "liquid" funds that invest for high yields, concentrating on treasury bills, certificates of deposit, and commercial paper (short term notes issued by a finance company or large company).

2. *Corporate bond funds* or *income funds.* These aim for a high level of income by investing heavily in corporate bonds, as well as preferred stock and U.S. Treasury bonds.

3. *High yield bond funds.* Because they purchase lower-rated corporate bonds (sometimes called "junk bonds"), they carry more risk (although generally a higher return) than higher-rate bond funds.

4. *Growth funds.* These funds aim for long-range capital growth (as opposed to current dividends) by purchasing the common stocks of established companies.

5. *Aggressive growth funds.* These also focus on capital growth, but they invest in smaller firms and developing industries—slightly riskier investments than those sought out by growth fund managers.

6. *Balanced funds* (*equity/income funds, total return funds,* and *growth-and-income funds* are all similar). With these, the focus is on conserving capital, promoting long-term growth, and providing you with current income by carefully balancing your portfolio between stocks and bonds.

7. *Specialized funds* or *sector funds.* Relatively volatile funds, these concentrate on a particular field such as banking, health care, utilities, or high tech; but they hold a variety of stocks within that field for diversification.

8. *Tax-free* or *mutual bond funds.* These funds provide tax-free income to individuals in high-income tax brackets by investing in municipal and (in some cases) state bonds.

9. *International funds.* These invest in companies in other parts of the world (typically Europe and Asia).

10. *U.S. government income funds.* These funds purchase such government securities as U.S. Treasury bonds and guaranteed mortgage-backed securities (GNMAs), which are backed by the Federal government, and other notes.

11. *Value funds.* Their strategy is to purchase stocks in undervalued companies whose prices are lower than they seem to be worth, who have dropped in value, or who are currently out of favor.

12. *Index funds.* Such funds purchase shares in all of the stocks held by a particular stock market index (e.g., the Standard and Poor's 500 Index, which tracks 500 stocks) and tend to outperform typical mutual fund companies because of their lower management fees.

A quick review of your investment objectives should help you to decide which types of funds are your best bets. Then, once you've zeroed in on a particular type of fund, you can start tracking down the top-performing funds in that category.

Before you make a commitment to purchase any mutual fund, take a good, hard look at the fund's prospectus. Figure out what the fund's objectives are, how well it has managed to meet those objectives over the years, what types of fees it charges for maintaining your account and for carrying out transactions on your behalf, and what procedures you must follow if you wish to buy or sell shares. When you're checking out a particular mutual fund, be sure to look for several key elements.

Facts and Figures
• • • • • • • •

The average annual total return (price change plus dividends investment) for the Standard and Poor's 500 Index during the past three decades:

1970-79:	7.5%
1980-89:	18.2%
1990-99:	19.0%

Note: The average annual total return for the years 1928 to 1999 was 13 percent.

- *A statement of investment objectives.* This statement should reveal exactly what type of fund this is. If it's an aggressive growth fund, for example, you should expect to find the words *maximum capital appreciation* listed somewhere as a fund goal. If, on the other hand, it's a balanced fund, you should expect to see such words as *income, capital growth,* and *stability* woven into the fund description.

- *A per-share table.* This table tells you how much each share of the fund has earned annually (both dividends and capital gains distributions) since the fund's inception or over the past ten years or so. The table will illustrate the fund's performance—erratic or steady—in both an up-market and a down-market, and it likely will include comparisons with the Standard & Poor's 500 or the Dow Jones. Don't fall into the all-too-common trap of taking this record of past performance as some sort of *guarantee* of future success, however. Changes in the market or the fund's management style can quickly erase that golden track record.

- *A fee table.* A fee table clearly indicates whether you must pay a sales commission on purchases (a so-called "load fee") or whether this fund is a "no load" fund, which does not charge you any up-front fees when you buy in. Beware of funds that charge you for "reloading" when they reinvest a distribution on your behalf. These fees can take a huge bite out of your nest egg over time.

Some fees to watch out for when you're making your way through the fee table include:

- *A 12(b)-1 fee.* Up to 1.25 percent per year may be charged to defray the costs of marketing and distributing funds.

- *Redemption fees.* A small fixed charge based on the value of the shares being sold.

- *Contingent deferred sales charges (CDSC).* Hefty fees are imposed to discourage you from holding shares for very short periods.

- *Operating and management fees.* An annual cost is applied to both load and no-load funds, affecting the return you end up receiving on your investment.

> ### Show Me the Money!
> • • • • • • •
> Don't even think of investing your family's emergency savings in a mutual fund that features a Contingent Deferred Sales Charge (CDSC). You could be hit with a 5 percent penalty if you were to sell your shares during the first year, 4 percent the next year, 3 percent the next year, and so on. Just think of the hefty fees you'd pay if you or your partner lost your jobs and you had to withdraw a significant amount of money from the fund right away. Remember: you should keep your emergency savings in a relatively liquid investment.

- *A statement of investment policies and risks.* You have a chance to get inside the fund managers' heads to see what risks they take—and avoid—in order to meet their investment objectives.

- *An explanation of the types of distributions that can be made for that particular fund.* The fund should permit you to take both dividends and capital gains any way you want them—in cash or reinvested.

- *A policy on how to buy and redeem shares.* It should establish the minimum purchase you have to make in order to open an account, as well as the minimum amount for additional purchases, and it should specify whether telephone transfers may be made.

Dollar Cost Averaging

There's no denying it. Dollar cost averaging is an investor's best friend. By buying your mutual fund shares on a weekly or monthly basis, you can ensure that you never buy all your shares at the highest price and never sell them all at the lowest price. If, on the other hand, you decide to make a large, one-time investment, you could very well end up buying high and selling low, just through sheer bad luck. Dollar cost averaging eliminates a lot of the guesswork that can go along with investing. You no longer have to lie awake tossing and turning at 3:00 AM, wondering if now is the right time to buy into a particular fund.

If you are putting money into a 401(k) plan at work, you are already enjoying the benefits of dollar cost averaging. Because your payroll deduction remains the same from week to week, regardless of what the fund price is doing, the per-share price averages out in your favor. Your average cost per share will probably be lower than if you purchased the shares all at once.

If you're not enrolled in an automatic payroll deduction plan, you'll have to discipline yourself to do your own dollar cost averaging. Decide how much you can put into mutual funds each month and then stick to your plan, regardless of what market prices are doing. Even better, arrange to have the amount of your investment transferred from your bank account to your mutual fund account each week or each month. Note: the fund may set a minimum for such a transfer— typically $50 to $250.

Settling Up with Uncle Sam

Until now, we've focused on the positive aspects of investing, watching the money accumulate in your mutual fund account. Now let's talk about a less enjoyable subject, how your growing wealth is handled by the IRS.

As you already know, you're required to pay income taxes on any income that comes your way, be it from employment, interest, dividends, or alimony. Thanks to the Taxpayer Relief Act of 1997, however, you're likely to be taxed at a lower rate on profits from the sale of stocks, mutual funds, real estate, and other assets—the so-called capital gains tax.

The top capital gains tax rate for individual taxpayers has been reduced to 20 percent for investments that have been held for more than a year and one day. For taxpayers in the 15 percent regular tax bracket, the maximum net capital gains tax rate is an even lower 10 percent.

Show Me the Money!
• • • • • • •

Some funds will waive their investment minimums if you agree to set up an automatic investment plan. Because these minimums typically range anywhere from $1,000 to $2,500, automatic investment is a smart way to sneak in the back door with one of these companies if you don't have enough cash on hand to go in the front door!

What's more, you will be able to use capital gain losses up to a maximum of $3,000 per year to reduce your ordinary income—something that can, in turn, reduce the amount of income tax you pay. If, for example, you have $10,000 in gains and $3,000 in losses, you would only pay taxes on the net gain of $7,000. That's good news if you find yourself faced with some hefty investment losses at some point in your investing career.

Also, some noteworthy tax breaks are available to investors with 401(k) and other retirement savings vehicles—a subject we tackle in the following chapter.

SCAM BUSTERS

If it sounds too good to be true, it probably is. Why then are so many Americans conned by smooth-talking investment brokers? Investment scams rob investors of as much as $40 billion dollars each year. And now that more and more Americans are going online, scam artists have come up with gloriously high-tech ways of reeling in suckers hook, line, and sinker.

At the root of the problem is nothing other than old-fashioned greed. An investor's willingness to suspend belief in order to take advantage of what appears to be a once-in-a-lifetime, get-rich-quick scheme. It can be difficult to tell the good guys from the bad guys. All a swindler needs to look successful, after all, is a three-piece suit, a plush office full of flashy furniture (who can tell it was bought on credit?), and a suitably impressive job title.

The best way to deal with investment fraud is to avoid being had in the first place. Here are some questions you should ask before you agree to do business with anyone in the financial industry.

Show Me the Money!

Watch out for any hot stock tips you happen to spot online. Online bulletin boards at investment Web sites can attract unscrupulous individuals. These people post false information that is designed to drive up the price of a stock. Then they make a killing by dumping their shares while the price is still high. (This procedure—known as "pumping and dumping"—is typically done using small-cap stocks.)

- *Where did you get my name?* If you're told that your name was included in "an exclusive list of investors," that could mean anything from the telephone book to a commercial mailing list to a club membership list.

- *Can you send me information?* Ask for a prospectus, brochure, or other written materials explaining the investment opportunity that you're proposing. Getting information in writing will give you the time to investigate things a little more thoroughly. Don't allow yourself to be pressured into making up your mind prematurely. Bona fide investment opportunities don't turn into pumpkins at midnight.

- *What type of risk is involved?* All investments short of U.S. Treasury bonds involve some element of risk. If you get the brush-off when you pose this question, you'll know that the person has something to hide.

- *Can you provide me with references?* Don't just settle for a list of happy clients (they could easily be the names of friends or coconspirators). Insist on bank and broker/dealer references, too. Then take the time to pick up the phone and ask some probing questions.

- *Is this investment being offered or traded on one of the regulated exchanges?* Some bona fide investments are, but others aren't. If the investment isn't being traded on one of the regulated exchanges (something that offers a certain degree of protection to you as a consumer), find out if a regulatory agency is overseeing this company's operations. If the individual you're dealing with claims to have a "private placement exemption" that allows operation without such supervision, then the shares should only be being offered to a limited number of qualified investors—not to hundreds of people.

As you can see, there's plenty to think about before you take the plunge as an investor. Before you prepare to fork over your hard-earned cash, you need to take the time to:

- Be clear about your investment goals and objectives.

- Be realistic about your resources and saving ability, and about the amount of time you have to accumulate the size of the nest egg you want.

Show Me the Money!

Ask friends and family members to pass along the names of their own financial planners, assuming of course that they're happy with the person they're using. (Hey, you might even want to find out the name if they're not. That'll allow you to scratch at least one name off your list of potential prospects!)

Show Me the Money!

Attend as many seminars and luncheons sponsored by financial planning professionals as you can when you're shopping around for a financial planner. That way, you'll get to check out the financial planners from a distance and decide whether or not you like their styles and ways of doing business. Just be aware that such seminars are often thinly veiled sales pitches for insurance or mutual funds, so proceed with caution.

- Be honest about your ability to tolerate risk.

- Identify the types of savings or investment vehicles that are most likely to help you to achieve your financial goals.

- Learn how to decipher a mutual fund prospectus (we covered most of the key elements earlier in this chapter).

- Know how to protect yourself from unscrupulous investment dealers.

Show Me the Money!

You can save yourself a lot of grief by avoiding the following all-too-common investment mistakes: being impatient, having unrealistic expectations, allowing your investment decisions to be influenced by other people (particularly those who haven't a clue about what they're talking about), failing to be clear about your own investment goals or objectives, failing to understand what a particular investment involves (including the risks), failing to diversify your portfolio so that you don't end up with your eggs in too few baskets, failing to review your portfolio and make changes when the situation warrants it, and—last but certainly not least—succumbing to fear and greed.

CHAPTER 13

Life after Children

• •

As hard as it may be to believe right now, the day will come when your children grow up and leave home. Instead of tripping over dinky cars and wiping up juice spills, you could find yourself living a positively Martha Stewartesque lifestyle. (That last bit may be pure fantasy. If you've been a slob all your life, it's unlikely that you're going to morph into a domestic diva just because the LEGO has been packed away for the very last time.)

What we're trying to point out is that the years when you have your children living at home with you are a very short time in your life—generally 20 years or less. (Sure, some adult children return to the nest for short periods of time if they find themselves out of work or in the midst of a messy divorce, but at that point they're more like tenants than children.) That's why it's important to start thinking now about what your life will be like when your children have left the nest and to plan your future accordingly.

Don't make the mistake of automatically assuming that your retirement years will be spent entirely in leisure, however. Many in the financial planning industry are predicting an end to retirement as we know it. They argue that Baby Boomers will continue working, not because they have to but because they want to; that telecommuting will make working past age 65 more attractive for older workers; and that employers will be forced to come up with innovative retirement plans to encourage valuable workers to stick around as long as possible. So while previous generations of workers banked on having a lot of time to travel and visit their children and their grandchildren, retirement may have evolved into a very different type of experience by the time you reach your so-called golden years.

THE NOT-SO-GOLDEN YEARS

That's not to say that you're necessarily doomed to spend your entire life chained to a computer, of course. In fact, you may decide to buck the trend and exit from the workforce sooner rather than later.

It's one thing to dream of travelling and enjoying life during your retirement years, however, and quite another to begin the financial planning process soon enough to make those dreams a reality. If you're serious about wanting to retire early or about maintaining your current lifestyle after you retire, you're going to have to get serious about saving hefty chunks of your income now. Obviously, the sooner you start your savings program, the less you'll have to contribute. (See Figures 13.1 and 13.2.)

Another way to figure out how much money you'll need during your retirement years is to turn to the ever growing number of studies on the amount of income required to maintain a preretirement lifestyle past age 65. Here are a few statistics that are worth considering.

> ## Money Talk
> • • • • • • •
>
> "When we were first married and had no children, saving for retirement was a high priority. However, when the children arrived, our priorities changed. We now have to save for braces, post-secondary education, and so on. We still save for retirement, but not as much as we did before. We will let compound interest work for us for now."
>
> — Leigh, 31, mother of two

- Studies have shown that most people need about 70 to 80 percent of their preretirement income if they hope to maintain their standard of living.

- You can probably get by on as little as 65 percent of your preretirement income if you've consistently saved 15 percent or more of your annual earnings, you are a high-income earner, your house is paid off, and you are hoping for a modest lifestyle upon retirement.

- You will probably need about 75 percent of your preretirement income if you have managed to save a reasonable but not spectacular amount of your annual income, you will have a small amount of personal debt to pay off during your retirement years and/or rent to pay on a house or apartment, and you are hoping to enjoy the same standard of living during your retirement years as you are enjoying today.

- You will need approximately 85 percent of your preretirement income if you have managed to save very little money over the years (less than 5 percent of your annual earnings), you have a significant mortgage pay-

FIGURE 13.1
The Benefits of Contributing Early to an IRA

	The amount of money accumulated by age 65 by someone who contributes $2,000 per year for 10 years, starting at age 25, but then stops contributing	The amount of money accumulated by age 65 by someone who contributes $2,000 per year for 30 years, starting at age 35
IRA value at age 30	$ 12,671	$ 0
IRA value at age 34	31,290	0
IRA value at age 40	45,975	12,671
IRA value at age 45	67,533	31,290
IRA value at age 50	99,258	58,648
IRA value at age 55	145,843	98,845
IRA value at age 60	214,292	157,908
IRA value at age 65	314,886	244,691

Note: The interest rate used in the above calculations is 8 percent.

ment or a sizeable and growing rent payment, and you want or need to maintain your current lifestyle during your retirement years.

If you'd like to do a more detailed calculation to figure out how much money you should be saving today, simply rework the budget that you prepared back in Chapter 2. Some of the major types of expenses that will increase or decrease significantly once you retire include:

- Groceries

- Restaurant expenses

- Clothing

- Laundry and dry cleaning

- Transportation costs

- Travel

- Entertainment

- Hobbies

- Books and magazines

FIGURE 13.2

Annual Savings Needed to Produce a $100,000 401(k)

The calculations in the table below assume an average annual return of 8 percent per year (compounded monthly) and a marginal tax rate of 28 percent.

Number of years left to save	Savings within a tax-deferred account (401(k), IRA)	Savings outside a retirement account (interest taxed immediately)
5	$16,944	$17,948
10	6,805	7,595
15	3,598	4,304
20	2,114	2,725
25	1,300	1,829
30	835	1,270

- Life insurance premiums

- Medical insurance premiums

- Disability insurance premiums

- Car insurance premiums

- Dental bills

Once you've worked out the budget for your retirement years, you'll need to factor in inflation. Fortunately, any good software package or financial planning Web site should allow you to do this bit of number crunching relatively easily and painlessly. You'll find leads on some of our favorite online tools in Appendix C.

Your next step is to compare your projected expenses with your projected income. Tally up the income you expect to

Facts and Figures
••••••

Trying to guesstimate how much your Social Security benefits will be when you retire? Call 800-772-1213 or go to <www.ssa.gov> to request your copy of Form 7004 (a record of your reported earnings).

receive from your 401(k), any private pensions you belong to, any deferred profit-sharing plans you participate in, your investment income, and earnings from any part-time work you intend to do in your retirement years; and then figure out what your after-tax income will be. (See Figure 13.3.) (You may need a little help from your financial planner in order to make your way through this exercise. Few things

FIGURE 13.3
Your Pension Plans

	Self	Spouse
1. Type of plan	_____	_____
Defined benefit	_____	_____
Defined contribution	_____	_____
Profit-sharing	_____	_____
Money purchase	_____	_____
401(k)	_____	_____
Other	_____	_____
2. Your dollar contribution to the plan	_____	_____
3. Vesting	_____	_____
Full and immediate	_____	_____
Gradual	_____	_____
5-year (cliff)	_____	_____
Years to go until vested	_____	_____
4. Years of service to date	_____	_____
5. Benefits	_____	_____
a. Formula for calculating retirement benefits	_____	_____
b. Amount of Social Security offset, if any	_____	_____
c. Can get credit for working beyond normal retirement age?	_____	_____
6. Requirements for early retirement	_____	_____
Number of years of service	_____	_____
Age	_____	_____
Percentage of reduction for each year of early retirement	_____	_____
7. How benefits are paid	_____	_____
Lump sum?	_____	_____
Annuity—payment per month	_____	_____
Joint-and-survivor 50 percent	_____	_____
Joint-and-survivor 75 percent	_____	_____
Joint-and-survivor 100 percent	_____	_____
Life certain	_____	_____
Straight life	_____	_____
Cost-of-living adjustment?	_____	_____

FIGURE 13.3
Your Pension Plans (Continued)

	Self	Spouse
8. Benefits to spouse if employee dies before retirement	_____	_____
9. Other benefits frozen at earlier employers (list) Projected value at retirement	_____ _____	_____ _____
10. Pension money rolled over from previous employers into IRAs How many? Value of each	_____ _____ _____	_____ _____ _____

are as confusing, after all, as a typical pension plan!) The shortfall is the amount that you will need to make up through your own retirement savings.

Unfortunately, what this figure won't tell you—and what we certainly can't tell you—is how you're supposed to accomplish this bit of financial wizardry while you're simultaneously saving for your children's education, paying off your mortgage, and keeping the bill collectors at bay. It may not be possible for you to make serious inroads towards achieving all of these financial goals at the same time, unless you and your partner have a combined income that is significantly higher than average. If, like the majority of parents with young children, you don't fall into that category, then it's a case of playing one priority off against the other and deciding just how much you can reasonably afford to save toward your retirement during this financially challenging period in your life.

WHAT YOU CAN EXPECT TO GET FROM GOVERNMENT COFFERS

If you're expecting to live the high life on the money that you receive from the federal government, you could be in for a rude awakening. Many financial industry experts predict that the Social Security system may not be able to meet its financial obligations to people retiring after 2035. At the root of the problem is good old-fashioned demographics. While three workers are supporting each retiree today, by 2020, only two workers will support each retiree. Obviously, the federal government is going to have to make some changes to the program in order to keep it out of the red—changes that will affect you, for better or for worse, in years to come.

Some changes are already in the works, of course. The retirement age will rise slowly from 65 to 67 over the next two decades. (By 2022, you'll have to be 67 to be eligible for full Social Security benefits.) That means that you can plan on holding down a job a year or two longer than someone retiring today—unless, of course, you accumulate the necessary funds to finance an early retirement.

Show Me the Money!

Here's something important to note if you're planning to work during your so-called retirement years. The government puts a cap on the amount of money you're allowed to earn while you're receiving Social Security benefits. If you exceed this cap, your benefits will be reduced until you reach age 65.

Security, Not Luxury

The maximum Social Security benefit available to individuals retiring today is a little over $18,000 a year. Of course, the amount you actually receive is determined by how much you contributed over the years and when you start to collect benefits. You can start to draw upon those benefits at any point after age 62, but you pay a penalty for that privilege—you'll receive 20 percent less than if you had waited until you reached age 65. Conversely, if you can hold out until you reach age 70, you'll receive even more money.

Here's some good news for parents who stayed at home to raise children. The stay-at-home spouse is entitled to Social Security benefits, even if that spouse never worked outside the home. If the employed spouse starts drawing benefits at age 62, then the stay-at-home spouse is entitled to an additional benefit of 37.5 percent of the amount of money that the employed spouse is receiving. If the employed spouse waits until age 65 before drawing benefits, then the spouse's benefit is pumped up to 50 percent. (Of course, if the stay-at-home spouse worked outside the home before and after the childrearing years, there may have been enough contributions made in Social Security taxes to be entitled to more than that amount.)

How Social Security Works

You don't have to be a rocket scientist to figure out how Social Security works, but most people do find it at least a little confusing. Here are the facts you need to know.

- You start building up Social Security credits the first time any employer withholds Social Security taxes from your paycheck. (Think back—way back. We're talking about the first time you worked a shift at the local burger joint as a teen!) You're not fully insured immediately, however. It takes 40 quarters—10 years—of coverage for you to become entitled to all of the benefits that Social Security provides. Those quarters don't have to be consecutive, though, so you don't have to be worried about having the clock reset to zero if you leave work to have a baby or two.

- The more you earn during your years in the workforce, the more you will receive come retirement time. Someone retiring at age 65 in 2001 could expect to receive benefits up to a maximum of $18,400. The exact amount, of course, will be determined by his or her work history.

- A certain percentage of your pay is withheld each payday until your annual earnings reach a certain threshold. In 2001, the Social Security tax rate is 7.65 percent and it is withheld on all earnings up to $80,400. If your earnings exceed that amount, Social Security takes an additional 1.45 percent of your pay on each dollar above that amount and puts it toward the cost of Medicare.

- You aren't the only one who's responsible for contributing to the Social Security Trust Fund coffers. Your employer is required to match your contributions. If you are self-employed, you are required to pay twice as much as you would if you were on a company payroll, because you have to make up for the lack of matching contributions.

- Social Security benefits will be treated as income. Consequently, depending on your income, you may have to pay income tax on a portion of the benefits you receive. It's important to know this up-front because taxes will affect the amount of money that's left in your budget during your retirement years.

Show Me the Money!
· · · · · · ·

Social Security provides survivors' benefits to your spouse and children in the event of your death. A widow or widower's benefit is paid if your spouse is responsible for taking care of any of your children who are under the age of 16, but the benefit may be reduced or eliminated if earnings were more than a certain amount. The children, however, are entitled to receive their full benefits until they reach age 18 (age 19, if they are still full-time high school students).

The most important thing to remember about Social Security benefits is that they're designed to provide you with a minimum standard of living, not to allow you to continue to live in the lap of luxury (assuming, of course, that you ever managed to end up in that spot in the first place!) If you have consistently earned just above the maximum wage that is taxed by Social Security ($80,400 in 2001, for example), your Social Security benefit at age 62 will only replace about 23 percent of that income—about $17,500. That's a significant drop in lifestyle, to say the least, and the best reason going for starting your retirement savings program early.

CORPORATE PENSION PLANS

While some of us may take them for granted, company pension plans are still a relatively new innovation. Only a handful were in existence at the turn of the last century, and pension plans didn't start becoming the norm until after World War II. Initially, they were designed to meet the needs of office workers rather than blue collar workers, and in the early years, many pension plans were rocked by scandals.

In 1974, Congress decided to put some legislation on the books to regulate the operation of pension plans. It passed the Employee Retirement Income Security Act (ERISA), which set rules about how pensions are funded, who is eligible for them, and how day-to-day operations must be conducted.

Since then, pension plans have evolved considerably. Today, a wide variety of plans exist, including defined benefit plans, defined contribution plans, and voluntary plans.

Defined Benefit Plans

Defined benefit plans specify (or define) in advance the benefit that you will receive down the road. The benefit is usually calculated based on the number of years of service you have given to a particular employer and your salary during the last few years of your employment. Under the law, your employer is required to fund such a plan in advance to ensure that the necessary funds will be on hand when you retire. The amount of money that your employer contributes to the plan is not part of your salary, nor does it show up on your paycheck. It is something separate and distinct, and consequently you are not taxed on the money. What's more, this type of pension plan is federally insured.

Defined benefit plans are, however, quickly going the way of the dodo bird. They're costly for employers to maintain, and—because contributions are made behind the scenes—employees often don't appreciate the extent of the company's generosity in providing such a benefit. At the same time, the majority of new jobs being created in the United States these days are with small companies that don't typically offer defined benefit plans. So if you've got a defined benefit plan at work, consider yourself lucky. They're becoming far less common than they once were.

Defined Contribution Plans

Defined contribution plans (also known as individual account plans) allow the company to contribute a fixed amount to an individual account, which invests a sum of money on an individual's behalf. A growing number of companies are switching from defined benefit account plans to defined contribution plans because they can limit their costs to the fixed annual contribution rather than trying to predict the future value of a benefit that they may not pay for another 40 years down the road. With defined contribution plans, the risk rests with the employee. If the pension plan's investments have performed well over time, you'll be well off come retirement. If they haven't, well, let's just say that the picture isn't nearly so pretty!

Defined contribution plans have two key drawbacks, at least from the employee's perspective. Contributions are limited, and the plan is not insured. Still, blemishes aside, a defined contribution plan is better than no plan at all.

Show Me the Money!

Planning to job hop in the near future? A defined contribution plan could be just what the doctor ordered. It's less costly to change jobs in rapid succession if your retirement savings are accumulating in a defined contribution plan. There may be breaks in your contributions—your new employer may not cover you during your first year on the job—but you should participate in the plan as soon as you can. At the end of the day—40 years, to be exact!—participating in defined contribution plans hosted by a series of different employers will net you just slightly less than if you'd stuck with a single employer the whole time. (Of course, this is only the case if you stick around at each company long enough for your benefits to vest.)

A defined contribution plan can be set up in one of the following ways:

- *As a money purchase plan.* The amount of each year's contribution is set using a predetermined formula—either a fixed dollar amount or a fixed percentage of your pay, and your employer is legally required to make this contribution.

- *As a profit-sharing plan.* The amount of each year's contribution is determined by the size of the company's profits, with your percentage typically being determined in proportion to the size of your paycheck, and your company is under no obligation to make contributions on a regular—or even irregular—basis.

FIGURE 13.4
How Your 401(k) Grows

Assuming that you have 5 percent salary increases and that you invest 6 percent of your salary each year (with your company topping up your contributions by an additional 3 percent), and assuming that your investments earn 8 percent interest (with interest paid quarterly on your contributions and at the end of the year on your company's matching funds), you can expect to accumulate approximately 10 times your current salary over the next 25 years.

401(k) Plan Account Growth

	Current Salary	*Current Salary*
	$ 35,000	$ 50,000
10 years	$ 56,748	$ 81,070
20 years	$214,953	$307,076
25 years	$370,677	$529,538

Source: Hewitt Associates, LLC

Voluntary Plans

Even if the company you work for doesn't want to get into the formal pension plan business, it may decide to offer you the opportunity to participate in one or more types of voluntary pension plans. Basically, by setting up a "voluntary tax-advantaged plan" (either a 401(k) plan, a 403(b) plan, or some other sort of thrift plan), the company is helping you to start saving for your retirement—something you might never actually get around to doing on your own—and saving you income tax at the same time. (The deductions are made on your before-tax income, so you don't have to pay any income tax on these funds until you make withdrawals from your retirement savings plan decades from now.)

Here's what you need to know about each of these three types of plans.

401(k) plans. 401(k) plans are, quite simply, the greatest thing to hit the retirement world since the invention of the condo. In many cases, employers these days are agreeing to match anywhere from 25 to 100 percent of the contribution deducted from your paycheck each week, up to a predetermined maximum. Because you're allowed to sock away up to $10,500 of your own money in a 401(k) plan each year, it doesn't take long for those retirement savings to start building up. (See Figure 13.4.)

Here are just a few important points to note before you dash over to the payroll department to sign up for a 401(k).

- While you don't have to pay any income tax on the amount you contribute from your paycheck and you don't have to report the contributed amount on your income tax return, you do have to pay Social Security taxes on these contributions.

- Some 401(k) plans may allow you to make contributions above the maximum limit, but in this case, these contributions are paid with after-tax dollars.

- The total amount that you and your employer contribute cannot exceed $35,000 per year or 25 percent of your pay, whichever is less. Your employer can't make any contributions to a 401(k) plan unless you're making your own contributions. You might not like it, but those are the rules!

Show Me the Money!
•••••••

Try to contribute as much to your 401(k) plan as your employer is willing to match. Even better, contribute the maximum that the regulations allow. It's the quickest and easiest possible way to save for your retirement. Remember, you can't spend what you don't have. (Or at least that's the theory!)

- All contributions that you make from your paychecks are vested instantly (i.e., no one can take them away from you). The contributions that your employer makes, however, may not all be vested immediately. Typically, the longer you stay with a particular company, the greater the percentage of those contributions will be vested.

- If you and your spouse are both working and you can't both afford to contribute to 401(k) plans—the best plan of attack, for a number of reasons—then you should at least plan to participate in the 401(k) plan with the employer who provides the best matching program.

- If you change jobs, you can roll the vested amount of your 401(k) plan over into an IRA or some other retirement savings plan. This is an important thing to know about, in case you're likely to be changing jobs frequently or taking time out to have children.

- Signing up for a 401(k) plan is simple. You simply let the payroll department know how much money you'd like to have deducted from your pay, fill out the appropriate paperwork, and—voilà!—you're in. The company takes care of all the headaches associated with administering the plan. That said, you'll probably have to make a few important decisions upfront—like where you'd prefer to invest your contributions. Your options may include a fixed or guaranteed investment contract (GIC) fund, which is invested with an insurance company; a balanced fund which, as we noted earlier, is a mutual fund that invests in both stocks and bonds to provide for both stability and growth; and equity fund, a mutual fund that is aimed at growth; or, possibly, company stock.

You also need to make sure that you are committed to investing a reasonable amount. After all, the penalties involved in taking money from your 401(k) before you're 59½ are considerable. You also have to be able to prove to the government that you're experiencing a financial hardship that is "immediate and heavy." This generally means that you need the money to purchase a first-time home; pay medical expenses for yourself, your spouse, or some other dependant; pay college expenses for yourself, your spouse, or a child (a loophole that's about to be sewn up, unfortunately); or prevent eviction or foreclosure on a mortgage. (Whew!) What's more, you will only be permitted to make a withdrawal if you have no other resources—including those of your spouse or your minor children—to draw upon.

Assuming you qualify to make a withdrawal (and, frankly, not everyone does), you are allowed to withdraw the funds you need in anticipation of the expense (i.e., before you actually incur it). You are not allowed to withdraw any more money than what you genuinely need. Upon withdrawal, you are hit with a 10 percent penalty tax—unless you're using the funds to pay medical expenses which exceed more than 7.5 percent of your adjusted gross income.

Not surprisingly, you're only allowed to take out the amount you yourself have contributed, plus any earnings those funds have generated. In other words, you can't get your hands on any of the money that your employer has contributed.

If you are considering making a hardship withdrawal, talk with your benefits administrator at work. That way you'll receive some help in wading through the necessary red tape.

There is, of course, an alternative to making a withdrawal from your 401(k) account: you can borrow from your account. Approximately 65 percent of companies that offer 401(k) plans make such loans available to their employees. Basically, your company establishes a rate of interest for 401(k) loans—typically the rate is tied to the prime rate (the rate that large banks charge for corporate loans). The interest you pay then goes back into your own 401(k) plan, rather than to a lending institution.

While this "be your own banker" plan might sound like a dream scenario, it can quickly turn into a nightmare. Here's why. If you end up changing jobs before the loan has been repaid, you must pay back the entire amount. Otherwise, it will be treated as a taxable distribution, and you'll be hit with both income tax and a 10 percent penalty. The only exception is if you're older than 59½ years of age. It doesn't matter whether you leave your job voluntarily, are handed a pink slip, or are given your walking papers for siphoning funds from the office coffee fund:

the same deal applies. As if that weren't bad enough, by yanking funds from your 401(k), you're depleting your own retirement nest egg. That's why most financial planners will urge you to proceed with caution if you're thinking about borrowing from your own 401(k) plan. Bottom line? It's a very risky venture.

403(b) plans. 403(b) plans are the twin siblings of the 401(k) plan. But unlike 401(k) plans, they apply only to workers in public schools or other nonprofit organizations such as hospitals, government agencies, or religious organizations. As with 401(k) plans, you're limited to contributing $10,500 or 25 percent of your salary, whichever is least.

Company-sponsored thrift plans. Company-sponsored thrift plans are similar to 401(k) plans, except that your contributions are made with after-tax dollars. Your company may agree to match all or part of your contributions. You can typically withdraw your own contributions to these plans without paying any penalty, but you will have to pay a penalty if you withdraw any of the money that your employer has contributed. You will also probably have to pay tax on any interest the money in the account has earned.

Before we wrap up our discussion of corporate pension plans, we've got one more important topic to tackle—the issue of vesting.

As we noted earlier in this chapter, the term *vesting* describes your legal right to receive money from your pension plan, even if you resign or are fired. How much you receive depends on how much you and your employer have invested in your plan and how long you've been with the company.

Whatever you've contributed is vested immediately. The claim you have on your employer's contributions, however, is determined by the type of vesting that your plan offers.

- Cliff vesting means that you get full benefits (your contributions plus your employer's contributions) once you put in five years' service as an employee.

- Partial vesting means that you get 20 percent of your employer's contributions after three years, plus an additional 20 percent during each of the subsequent four years. In other words, you are fully vested after seven years.

> ## Money Talk
> • • • • • • •
>
> "We've been wanting to start saving for our retirement, but our financial situation has yet to make this possible. Living below the poverty line for a year makes you go through everything, including any retirement savings you may have!"
>
> —Samantha, 33, mother of two

If your plan is fully vested and you quit, are fired, or change jobs, then the money in question is yours, no questions asked. The terms of your plan will specify whether you receive the money in one lump sum or whether you must wait until you reach retirement age before being able to access those funds. If your fund isn't fully vested, you'll only be able to get your hands on a portion of the funds.

Be sure to read all the fine print related to vesting in your pension plan. Specifically, there are a few things you'll want to find out.

- What would happen if you were laid off temporarily or took a leave of absence from your job? In most cases, a break of less than one year won't cost you any vesting, but a longer break may require some sort of waiting period —typically a year—before you can get back into the plan. The exception is maternity or paternity leave. When it comes to the issue of vesting, employers tend to treat such absences as if you were continuing to work full-time.

- What would happen if you became disabled before reaching retirement age? Most plans pay full benefits if you become disabled, but the benefits may be tied to your age or your years of service.

- What would happen if you died before reaching retirement age? Defined benefit plans provide a death benefit to your spouse, assuming your contributions are vested prior to your death. The benefit is paid as an annuity, starting on the date when you would have been eligible for early retirement.

Show Me the Money!

Some companies offer more than one type of pension plan (often called hybrid plans). For example, you may be offered the opportunity to participate in a defined benefit plan as well as a defined contribution plan. If you find yourself faced with this choice, it's important to evaluate each plan carefully and make sure you understand how they work. Even if both plans are based on the same vesting schedule, the defined benefit plan will have less to offer you over the long term, because the company will probably chip away at the defined benefit plan (with an eye to future elimination) and make larger contributions to the defined contribution plan.

INDIVIDUAL PENSION PLANS

Don't have access to a company pension plan? Why not opt for an individual pension plan instead? While you'll have to be a little more disciplined about making your contributions—after all, there's no one to siphon your contributions off your paycheck!—and you won't benefit from having an employer make contributions on your behalf, you can still manage to accumulate a sizeable nest egg by the time you reach retirement age.

If you go the individual pension plan route, you have two major options to choose from: an individual retirement account (IRA) or a Roth IRA.

Individual Retirement Accounts (IRAs)

The key advantage of an individual retirement account (IRA) is the fact that you may be able to deduct some of your contributions from your federal income taxes. You'll note that we say "may." As with anything else that involves Uncle Sam, there's some fine print you need to know about.

- If you are not covered by any pension plan, you may make an IRA contribution that is fully tax deductible, regardless of your income.

- If either you or your spouse is not working, the employed spouse can contribute to an IRA established in the other spouse's name. The total amount you are allowed to contribute to both accounts is capped at $4,000, however, and you aren't allowed to put more than $2,000 into any single account.

- Regardless of who makes the contributions, it's the person whose name is on the account who has control of it. This is an important point to keep in mind in the event that you and your partner separate.

- If your adjusted gross income on a joint tax return is $53,000 or less (or $33,000 or less if you are single), then you may deduct the full amount of your IRA contribution, even if you are covered by a pension plan. (If you are self-employed and have set up a Keogh plan, you are considered to be a member of such a plan.)

Show Me the Money!

Here's something that separating spouses need to know. If a divorce should occur, a former spouse who gets alimony but who has no earned income is allowed to use alimony to continue to contribute to an IRA, up to the $2,000 annual contribution limit.

- If your adjusted gross income on a joint return is between $53,000 and $63,000 (or between $33,000 and $43,000 on a single return), that maximum tax-free contribution of $2,000 (or $4,000 for yourself and your spouse) is gradually whittled away (it's decreased by $200 for each additional $1,000 in income).

- Even if you are not eligible to take the income-tax deduction, you may choose to make contributions of up to $2,000 to your IRA, in which case the earnings (the interest your investment generates) will not be taxed until you take the money out. What's more, because your contributions were made in after-tax dollars, you won't have to pay income tax on your contributions when you withdraw from the plan during your retirement years. (If you make non-tax-deductible contributions to an IRA, you must file Form 8606 with your income tax return. This form highlights the total non-tax-deductible contributions you made during the year as well as the value of all of your IRAs as of the end of the year.)

Now that we've covered the "rules" for IRAs, let's talk about how to make them work for you. If you don't have the funds on hand to make your full $2,000 annual contribution—a fact of life for many families with young children—then you should simply aim to put away as much as you can. You may have to skip a year or two or gradually cut back on your contributions if you'll be taking time out of the workforce to start a family, but don't let your contributions slide too much or for too long, or you could see your retirement dreams go up in smoke.

Show Me the Money!

If you change jobs, you may wish to "roll" eligible company pension plan contributions—401(k)s, profit-sharing plans, money purchase plans, defined benefit plans (if paid out in a lump sum), and employee stock ownership plans—into an IRA rollover. All you have to do to arrange for an IRA rollover is to contact the financial institution where your IRA will be established and arrange for your funds to be forwarded directly. If the check is made out to you, your employer is required to withhold 20 percent of your distribution and send it to the IRS as payment for your federal tax bill. What's more, if you're not yet age 59½, you'll be hit with an additional 10 percent tax penalty for making an early withdrawal. If you don't complete the rollover within 60 days, you'll have to pay taxes on the full amount.

Whatever you do, resist the temptation to take the money and run. A study by the Employee Benefit Research Institute revealed that more than half of workers who receive lump sum payments from their pension or tax-deferred savings accounts fail to save or invest that money.

Once you've determined how much money you can afford to invest in an IRA in any given year, start contributing immediately. Don't wait until April 15th—the deadline for opening an IRA. Not only will you spend hours in line at the bank—no fun at all if you've got a crying baby and a wiggly toddler along for the ride!—you'll also lose out on a lot of interest-earning time. When you make an IRA deposit, it starts earning tax-deferred interest immediately, so a contribution made in January of one year earns 15 more months of tax-deferred interest than a contribution made when you file your tax return in April of the following year.

Wondering how much an IRA can add up to over the years? Figure 13.5 spells it out in dollars and cents.

FIGURE 13.5
How Your IRA Grows

The following calculations are based on the assumption that you make annual contributions until age 40, that those contributions earn 8 percent interest (compounded annually), and that you leave your funds on deposit until age 59½.

Starting at age	Amount of Annual IRA Contribution		
	$500	$1000	$2000
25	$75,792	$151,584	$303,167
35	28,224	56,448	112,896
40	15,058	30,117	60,234

Note: The limits outlined above change each year, so be sure to get updated information from your tax planner or the IRS Web site: <www.irs.gov>.

Roth IRAs

Roth IRAs are another option that is likely to be open to you, unless, of course, you and/or your spouse happen to be high-income earners. You see, to qualify for a Roth IRA, your adjusted gross income has to be less than $150,000 (for joint married filers) or $95,000 (for single filers). If your income is between $150,000 and $160,000 (for joint married filers) or $95,000 to $110,000 (for single married filers), then there is a phase out of the contributions.

Show Me the Money!

If your spouse is covered by a company pension plan, but you're not, you may still be able to deduct IRA contributions. The catch? Your adjusted gross income must be $150,000 or less (generally not a problem for families with young children) to get the full deduction.

If you qualify for both plans, you'll have to decide which is the better vehicle for you: a plan that offers you a tax deduction now (a traditional IRA) or one that offers a tax-free withdrawal later rather than a tax deduction today (a Roth IRA). There is no easy answer. You have to consider such factors as your age, your current income, and your expected tax brackets during your working and retirement years. As a rule of thumb, you'll do better with a Roth IRA if you expect to pay a substantially lower rate of tax after retirement than you currently pay.

Withdrawals from a Roth IRA are tax free provided that your contributions remain in the plan for at least five years and you are at least 59½ years of age. If you withdraw your earnings from an account that is less than five years old and prior to your being 59½, you pay ordinary income tax plus an additional penalty tax of 10 percent on the earnings (not the contribution). However, withdrawals without penalty are permitted under three circumstances: the death of the owner, the disability of the owner, and if you purchase a home. You're entitled to withdraw up to $10,000 for the purchase of a first home for yourself, your children, your parents, or your grandchildren. There's a neat little loophole you need to know about, however. The folks at the IRS define a first-time home buyer as anyone who hasn't owned a home for the last two years. Kind of makes you wonder how they'd define a new parent! Note that any penalties are only on the earnings.

PLANS FOR THE SELF-EMPLOYED

If you are fully or partially self-employed, a Keogh Plan is the retirement savings vehicle for you. You are permitted to invest up to 25 percent of your net self-employed income or $30,000 (whichever is less) into your Keogh plan. That contribution is deductible from your net earned income, and your earnings grow tax deferred until you start withdrawing funds from the plan.

Unlike IRAs, Keogh accounts must be opened by December 31st of the current year. You are, however, allowed to keep your initial deposit small and then add some additional funds once you know where you stand taxwise in a few months' time. Here are some other important points to note.

- A Keogh Plan allows for the highest contribution—up to 25 percent of earned income to a maximum of $35,000. Keep in mind that certain types of Keogh plans require a self-employed person to contribute a fixed percentage of their income every year. Whether or not this provision applies to your plan, the plan must be established in the first year before December 31, though contributions can be delayed until April 15th. Annual filings are required by the IRS, whether or not you contribute in a particular year.

- The SEP-IRA contribution is limited to 15 percent of earned income to a maximum of $30,000. These plans are easy to set up and maintain because no annual filings need to be made. Unlike a Keogh plan, you can wait until April 15th to set up a SEP and still get the tax benefit for the prior tax year.

- Simple IRAs are Congress' latest innovation for the self-employed and small business owner. The maximum contribution is $6,500 annually. These plans are easy to set up and administer. You'll find details on Simple IRAs as well as your other options as a self-employed worker at the IRS Web site <www.irs.gov>.

As you can see, you have a number of different options when it comes to saving for retirement. The only truly bad option is to do nothing at all.

When you're 20-something with your first baby on the way, retirement can seem a lifetime away, but the years fly by fast when you're busy caring for your young family. That's why it's important to put your retirement savings plan in place now, even if you'll have to go easy on the contributions over the next couple of years. Here's what to do to get started:

- Make an appointment with your financial planner to establish a comprehensive retirement savings plan. Your planner will take into account your long-term objectives for your retirement years (e.g., working part-time or hopping on planes to visit all of your grandchildren), the number of years you have to accumulate your retirement nest egg, and other relevant factors.

- Educate yourself about the pros and cons of various retirement savings vehicles. Make sure you understand the tax implications of each option, as this can have a huge effect on your savings down the road.

- Don't be afraid to back off on your contributions for a while if your family circumstances warrant it, but don't make the mistake of abandoning your retirement savings plans altogether. You might never catch up on those years of missed contributions.

CHAPTER 14

The Next Generation

Four-year-old Katie may not be old enough to worry about mutual funds and tax breaks, but she's already mastered a concept that many adults have yet to grasp: you can't spend it if you don't have it.

Her mother, Melinda, 33, explains. "Katie decided that she wanted to buy a $30 bean bag chair. We told her that she would have to save half the money. She took the $5 that her Grandma gave her for Easter and earmarked it for her chair. This gave Grandma an opportunity to offer her a job helping with yardwork. After doing a few more jobs and cleaning all the coins out of the couch, she had enough money for her chair. We took her to the store and she bought it."

Three-year-old Timmy may be younger than Katie, but he's also becoming money-wise. His parents Heather, 32, and Gregory, 43, are already teaching him the basics. "Timmy may only be three, but we're trying to teach him the value of money," Heather explains. "When he's buying something, we let him hand the money to the clerk and wait to get his change back. And when he receives any money, we take him to the bank so that he can deposit it."

Melinda and Heather are wise to tackle money issues in such a forthright manner with their kids—to explain what money is for and how to use it effectively. Far too many parents are reluctant to talk about money with their kids. Unfortunately, by saying nothing, they're actually saying a lot. As Elizabeth Lewin and Bernard Ryan, Jr., note in their book *Simple Ways to Help Your Kids Become Dollar Smart* (Walker and Company, 1994), "Money talks . . .and your kids are listening." Lewin and Ryan explain. "We seem to think of the subject of money as taboo. It's like sex. We hesitate to talk to kids about it. We figure they'll learn somehow, somewhere, from somebody. And they do learn, but sometimes all the wrong things. From a very early age, some children learn that money can be used as a weapon—to control others, to tempt, to make someone feel guilty, to reward, to manipulate. They learn that money is to be spent. Or hoarded . . . . That money causes conflict and skirmish and ruckus and battle."

More important than what you say about money, of course, is what you do. If you and your partner regularly get into heated discussions about overdue utility bills, overextended credit limits, and missed car payments, you're giving your child more of a money education than you realize. Unfortunately, the message that you're passing along is that it's okay to miss bill payments, overspend, and live from paycheck to paycheck, as long as you somehow manage to get away with it.

Facts and Figures
• • • • • • •
According to Teenage Research Unlimited of Northbrook, Illinois, U.S. teens spend more than $153 billion each year.

RAISING MONEY-SMART KIDS

You know it's a good idea to teach kids about money. You might be surprised to learn, however, just how early your child's money management education should begin. Most experts agree that kids are able to grasp the concept of money by the time they reach the age of three.

Does this mean that you should have a heart-to-heart talk about the merits of various mutual funds with your pre-schooler? Of course not! What it means is that you should introduce the concept of money and give your child the chance to start handling small amounts on her own. It's important to explain in very simple terms what money is used for and why most of us aren't able to buy everything we want. Your child will probably want to know where the money comes from and how you get it when you need it.

Show Me the Money!
• • • • • •
Make sure that your child understands that credit cards and debit cards are also a form of money. If a child doesn't see any cash changing hands, he might mistakenly conclude that you don't have to pay for items when you have a piece of plastic in your hand. (Hey, many adults make the same mistake!)

As your child gets a little older, be sure to include him or her in family discussions about money—especially those that involve setting financial goals. It's an approach that has worked well for Fiona, 32; Christopher, 35; and their six children. "We spend time talking with the kids about our financial goals and how we plan on achieving them," Fiona explains. "We strive to make these their goals as well so that they are part of the planning process. When they know why we are scrimping in some areas, they are more likely to be dedicated to saving and to come up with far fewer 'wants.' We also take them shopping so that they can see for themselves just how far a dollar doesn't go! Most importantly, we teach them that money is only a means to a far greater end—not an end in itself. Money is not where you want to go, only the means to get there."

Part of teaching your children to manage money is to arm them with the skills they need to become smart consumers. That means explaining how they can choose the cereal box size that offers the best value, demystifying TV commercials by pointing out how much less appetizing the real-life version of a fast food hamburger looks, and how much of a toy's on-air appeal is actually due to special effects.

The key, of course, is to avoid turning a learning opportunity into a minilecture. The messages heard and the lessons learned will be far more powerful if you allow the kids to draw their own conclusions. After all, you only have to buy a superhero figurine once to discover that it doesn't come with all of the neat accessories (or make any of the nifty noises!) that were demonstrated on TV.

Parents should also do what they can to encourage kids to make their own purchasing decisions and to budget for special purchases. This isn't always easy in a society that thrives on instant credit and instant gratification, notes parenting consultant Kathy Lynn. "If our kids are into instant gratification, it's for good reason," she insists. "It comes from not being asked to wait for anything. We need to teach them that if something's really worth having, it's worth waiting for."

Show Me the Money!

If your child is about to blow a month's allowance on a poorly made toy, you might want to offer your opinion—"That toy looks like it might break quite easily."—but that should be the extent of your involvement. If your child decides to go ahead with the purchase anyway and the toy subsequently breaks, resist the temptation to say, "I told you so," or to run out and replace the toy. Instead, demonstrate that you empathize with him and encourage him to return the broken toy to the store where it was purchased or to write a letter of complaint to the manufacturer or local newspaper.

Here are some other practical tips on raising money-smart kids:

- Work "money talk" into everyday life rather than trying to give your child a crash-course in money management every now and again. Even something as simple as shopping for groceries can provide you with the opportunity to teach your kids some important money-management fundamentals. You might point out that you're buying apple juice rather than orange juice this week, because it's being offered at a better price, or explain why the "sale price" on a particular item really isn't such a great deal after all.

- Teach your child to differentiate between needs and wants. Explain that while she may *want* that flashy new skateboard, she certainly doesn't *need* it. (Warning: It can take a little time for this particular concept to sink in!)

- Encourage your child to open a bank account so that his savings can start earning interest. Most banks offer special "kids' accounts" that have low minimum balance requirements and no fees.

- Help your child to learn about the weird and wonderful world of investing. You might want to encourage your child to track the ups and downs of a favorite stock—perhaps Nike, Walt Disney, or McDonald's—by reading the local newspaper or by visiting some financial industry Web sites. You can also have fun predicting whether the latest-and-greatest fast-food products are likely to send McDonald's stock shooting upward or downward.

- Be generous with your praise when your child makes wise financial decisions. Compliment your seven-year-old for saving some allowance, and let your teen know that you're impressed when time is taken to balance the checkbook each month.

- Be forthcoming about your family's financial situation. Children who are included in family money discussions are better equipped for life in the real world and better prepared to weather any financial storms that may come their way. You're not doing them any favors by keeping them out of the loop when money-related problems arise.

- Tap into online resources that are designed to help parents teach kids about money. The American Bankers Association Web site <www.aba.com> is an excellent starting point. You'll also find leads on other great online resources in the Resources section of this book.

Show Me the Money!

See if your mutual fund company publishes any educational materials that are suitable for the next generation of investors. A growing number of companies are putting out publications that have been especially written for kids.

MAKING ALLOWANCES

Should children receive an allowance? Some parents say yes, and others say no.

Lori, 43, the mother of two teenagers, feels that giving her children an allowance helps them to learn how to manage their money. "My children get an allowance and have to live within those financial boundaries. Holding back or giving them less encourages them to look for a job or do extras around the house for spending money. I let them know that they need to work for money if they want nice things."

Lori is the first to admit that the money flowed a little too freely when her children were younger—something she regrets. "Don't buy your children everything they want," she advises. "They begin to think that you are a money tree and, believe me, they don't appreciate it. My children are older and I am continually cutting back on what I give them because there is no thanks and no appreciation. I am hoping that if I hold back long enough, lack of money will motivate them to get part-time jobs."

Leigh, 31, and Thomas, 32, the parents of two young children, also think it's beneficial to give children an allowance. "Our six-year-old gets an allowance of four dollars per week. That may sound like a lot, but out of that she's expected to contribute money to her Sunday school envelope and pay her dues for Girl Scouts. This leaves her with about two dollars a week for spending money. The money she receives isn't tied to household responsibilities. I don't get paid for making my bed!"

Facts and Figures

Who's the boss? A study by Western International Media, a Los Angeles-based market research firm, indicated that 69 percent of American parents admit to giving into their children's whining and pleading for particular types of merchandise. The study found that 33 percent of video purchases and 40 percent of trips to such entertainment facilities as Discovery Zone, Chuck E. Cheese, and miniature golf courses occur because the child requests it. Even worse, an earlier study conducted by the same company found that 46 percent of toys would not have been bought had the child not nagged his or her parents into making the purchase.

Fiona and Christopher take a different approach when it comes to providing their six children with spending money. "We do not give our children an allowance," Fiona explains. "They are expected to help with chores and responsibilities around the house because they live here. We buy their clothes, shoes, coats, etc., and on occasion give them money to blow on treats or whatever else they may want. Even kids need a little 'mad money' once in a while."

If you do decide to go the allowance route, you should plan to review the amount of each child's allowance once each year—perhaps at the beginning or end of the school year—and to move it upward if she is ready to assume responsibility for a wider range of purposes (e.g., junk food, entertainment expenses, clothing, and so on). If your child wants a larger increase than you initially offer, ask her to prove to you that she's ready for the added financial responsibility. If she makes a convincing case, rethink your position. Perhaps she really is ready to move to the front of the class.

Here are some other words of wisdom on the allowance front.

Show Me the Money!

Keep talking to your child about money, even after he or she leaves home for college. Studies have shown that one-fifth of undergrads carry at least four credit cards, so whether it's realized it or not, plenty of money lessons still need to be learned.

- Pay your child his allowance when it's due—not a day or two after the fact. Otherwise, you'll be teaching him that it's okay to be casual when it comes to honoring your financial commitments.

- Stop thinking of your child's allowance as your money. Once you hand it over to her, it's hers to do with as she pleases. By resisting the temptation to make spending decisions for her, you'll be giving her an opportunity to learn the basics of money management firsthand.

- Have one hard-and-fast rule when it comes to allowances: when it's gone, it's gone. You can't expect

Show Me the Money!

A picture is worth a thousand words—especially when it comes to saving money. Your child will be more likely to stick with his goal of saving up for a new bike if he sticks a picture of that new bike on his piggy bank jar or on the cover of his bank book.

your kids to learn how to budget their allowance if they know that you'll fork over another $5 bill any time they ask for it. An advance on the next allowance is an entirely different matter, of course. You may decide to advance your child some funds if he gets a last-minute invitation to go to the circus with a friend. Just make sure that the advance is repaid or that loan will automatically become an unplanned gift! A good way to remind yourself and your child that there's money to be repaid is to place an IOU jar right next to their piggy bank.

- Don't forget to factor in how much money your teenager may be bringing in from a part-time job. Given that the average weekly spending by teenagers in 1999 was $89—an 8.5 percent increase over the previous year—teenagers have considerable spending power, thanks at least in part to their evening and weekend jobs.

As you can see, you've got plenty of important money-management lessons to teach your children over the next 18 years. Here are the key points to remember.

- Start your child's money education as early as possible—ideally by the age of three.

- Walk the talk of fiscal responsibility. When it comes to teaching kids about money, actions speak louder than words.

- Speak openly about your family's financial situation rather than treating money-related issues as some deep, dark secret. Make talking about money part of your day-to-day routines.

- Teach your child to differentiate between needs and wants and to save for special purchases.

- Decide how you're going to handle the allowance issue, and then make sure you've got the cash on hand to settle your debts come allowance day.

> ## Money Talk
> • • • • • • •
>
> "Blessed are the young, for they shall inherit the national debt."
> —*President Herbert Hoover*

CONCLUSION

• •

"Children are poor men's riches."
—English Proverb

We've covered a lot of ground over the last fourteen chapters. We've talked about how having children changes your financial priorities overnight—for better and for worse—and how tough it can be to make your paycheck stretch far enough to cover all the financial demands you face during this joyous but crazy stage of your life.

We'd love to hear your comments on the book—good, bad, and ugly. (Actually, don't bother with the ugly!) You can either write to us care of our publisher at the address below, or you can reach us via email at pageone@kawartha.com.

In the meantime, thanks for joining us on this ride through the weird and wonderful world of family finance.

Ann Douglas and Elizabeth Lewin
Authors, *Family Finance*
c/o Dearborn Trade
155 North Wacker Drive
Chicago, IL 60606-1719

GLOSSARY

• •

Having difficulty decoding your life insurance policy or making sense of your mortgage agreement? You've come to the right place. Below, you'll find concise definitions of key financial terms—something that should help to demystify any document that the financial industry chooses to throw your way. (Well, maybe!)

Adjustable rate mortgage (ARM) A mortgage whose interest rate and monthly payments vary throughout the mortgage period. The interest rate is determined by a formula and depends on current interest rates. (See variable rate mortgage.)

Adjusted Gross Income (AGI) The sum of your taxable income (wages, interest, dividends, capital gains, pension, alimony received) less your allowable adjustments (retirement account contributions, moving expenses, alimony paid).

Administrator The person appointed by the court to represent an estate when no will was provided or the will does not name an executor. This person is sometimes referred to as a personal representative or estate trustee without a will.

Amortization period The number of years it will take to fully repay your mortgage.

Annuity An investment that pays you a fixed amount of money for a specified number of years or for life.

Appraised value An estimate of the market value of a property.

Appreciated or appreciating asset An asset whose value has increased or continues to increase due to a variety of factors, including inflation.

Assets Things you own, including your house, car, or investments.

Asset allocation A proper mix of asset types to provide overall protection against value loss and to increase gain opportunities. Major asset types or classes are stocks, bonds, and cash.

Beneficiary A person who has been chosen to receive income or assets under the terms of a will, trust, or other type of policy or investment.

Bonds A type of investment that is offered by governments and corporations. You lend a sum of money to the issuer for a set amount of time at a fixed rate of interest.

Capital property Assets such as shares, bonds, and real estate that you hold as an investment.

Capital gain or loss The difference between the price you paid for an investment and the price at which you sell it—in other words, the profit or loss you make.

Cash value insurance Life insurance that contains a savings account along with coverage for the life of the insured.

Certificate of Deposit (CD) A specific term loan that you make to your banker. The maturity dates for CDs ranges from a month to several years. Interest is taxable.

Certified Financial Planner (CFP) A financial planner who has met the training and testing requirements of the Institute of Certified Financial Planners.

Closing date The date on which the sale of property becomes final and the new owner takes possession.

COBRA The name of a piece of federal legislation that requires health insurers and employers to continue to offer health benefits, at the employee's expense, for 18 months after coverage would otherwise end when a person leaves a company.

Codicil A written and properly witnessed legal change or amendment to a will.

Collateral mortgage A loan that is backed by a promissory note and the security of a mortgage on a property.

Collateral Assets that are pledged by a borrower as security for repayment of a loan or other debt.

Community property A term that is used to describe the assets and property acquired after marriage that are owned equally by marriage partners.

Compound interest Interest that is paid on interest. This occurs when interest is paid on an investment at periodic intervals and then added to the amount of the investment.

Conditional offer An offer to buy a property if certain conditions are met (for example, a satisfactory appraisal).

Condominium When individuals own apartments in a building or complex, but common areas are shared with other owners.

Consumer price index (CPI) A monthly report on price changes related to the cost of certain consumer goods and services that is used as a common indicator of inflation. The CPI is used to adjust government benefits such as Social Security.

Contribution The amount of money you put into a savings/investment plan.

Conventional mortgage or fixed rate mortgage A mortgage in which the interest rate is locked in or fixed for the full term. Your monthly payments stay the same.

Current yield The annual rate of return on an investment expressed as a percentage.

Current return The annual return on an investment expressed in dollars.

Debt to income ratio The percentage of gross income required to cover monthly payments associated with housing. Most lenders recommend that ratio be no more than 32 percent of your gross monthly income.

Deductible The amount of out-of-pocket expense you will face if you file an insurance claim. If you have $500 deductible on your car insurance policy, you must pay the first $500 out of your own pocket.

Deduction An expense you subtract from your income to lower your taxable income. Itemized deductions include mortgage interest, property taxes, contributions, and medical expenses over 7.5 percent of adjusted gross income.

Dividends Company earnings that are paid out to shareholders. Dividends can be earned on stocks and certain mutual funds.

Domicile A person's fixed place of residence.

Educational IRA An IRA that allows you to save for a child's future tuition. $500 can be put away for each child per year, subject to certain income eligibility requirements.

Effective interest rate The real rate of interest after the effects of compounding are factored in.

Estate trustee without a will See Administrator.

Estate planning The process of planning for the orderly transfer of all your assets to heirs and others in a manner calculated to minimize taxes, expenses, and delays.

Executor The person or institution named in a will to carry out its provisions and instructions. Also known as a personal representative or estate trustee.

Federal National Mortgage Association (Fannie Mae) A privately owned corporation that adds liquidity to the mortgage market by purchasing loans from lenders and selling them to investors. Fannie Mae guarantees the repayment of principal and interest on the loans that it sells.

Financial advisors The team of experts you use to help you make investment decisions. These could include a lawyer, a chartered accountant, a financial planner, a banker, and/or a stockbroker.

Firm offer An offer to buy a particular property, as outlined in the offer to purchase, that has no conditions attached.

Fixed rate mortgage A mortgage for which the rate of interest is fixed for a specific period of time (the term).

401(k) plan A type of retirement savings account offered by many corporations. Contributions (up to a limit) are exempt from federal and state income taxes. Earnings are tax-deferred.

403(b) plan Similar to the 401(k) plan, but for employees of nonprofit organizations.

Foreclosure A legal procedure in which the lender obtains ownership of the property after the borrower has defaulted on payment.

Grantor The person who establishes or creates a trust. Also called a settlor.

Guaranteed investment certificate (GIC) An investment in which you deposit money over a fixed period of time and are paid a set rate of interest.

Guardian A person who is legally responsible for managing the affairs and the care of a minor or incompetent person.

Healthcare power of attorney A document that gives someone authority to make medical or personal-care decisions for the person executing it.

Heir A person who is legally entitled to receive another person's property through inheritance.

Home equity loan A loan against the equity in your home. It is a second mortgage. Interest paid is tax deductible.

Income tax Federal and state tax that is paid on any income you receive.

Income deferral Postponing income until a future year in order to delay paying taxes on it.

Income splitting A financial strategy that involves shifting income from the hands of one family member to another. It can help to reduce your family's overall tax burden.

Individual Retirement Account (IRA) A custodial account into which individuals can contribute up to a maximum of $2,000 per year. Contributions made to this tax-deferred retirement account may or may not be tax deductible.

IRA Rollover Reinvestment of a lump sum distribution from another IRA, 401(k), or corporate pension plan. The rollover must be deposited within 60 days to avoid taxation.

IRA Transfer The direct transfer of assets in a tax-deferred account from one trustee to another. There are no tax consequences because the owner does not take physical possession of the money.

Inheritance tax A tax that is levied on inherited property in some U.S. states. Tax rates typically depend on the relationship of the heir to the deceased.

Interest The money you earn on an investment or pay on a loan.

Intestate Dying without a will.

Investment Something you put your money into in order to make money.

Investment income Money that is earned on investments you make. Investment income includes interest, dividends, and capital gains.

Irrevocable trust A trust that cannot be changed or cancelled. The opposite of a revocable trust.

Joint tenancy with right of survivorship A form of property ownership in which one partner inherits the property in the event of the death of the other.

Keogh Plan A tax-deductible retirement savings plan for the self-employed.

Leverage The use of borrowed money to acquire investment assets.

Liabilities The amount of money you owe to various creditors.

Lien The mortgage lender's legal claim to the borrower's property.

Liquidity Your ability to respond quickly to an immediate need for cash. It usually involves having investments that are easily converted to cash.

Living trust A revocable or irrevocable written agreement into which a living person transfers assets and property along with instructions to a trustee, who then manages them and plans for their future distribution.

Marginal tax rate (tax bracket) The rate of income tax you pay on the last dollar that you earn over the year. You pay less tax on your first dollars of income and more on the last. Many of your investment decisions may be affected by your tax rate.

Maturity date Last day of the term of an investment or loan.

Mortgage life insurance Insurance on the outstanding balance of your mortgage. It guarantees that the lender will be repaid in the event that you die. It is relatively expensive as compared to term life insurance.

Municipal bond A loan that an investor makes to cities, towns, and states for public projects such as building highways, schools, and parks. Municipal bonds are exempt from federal taxes, and if you reside in the state where the bond is issued, the interest is exempt from state taxes as well.

Mutual funds An investment product in which your money is pooled with the money of many other investors. When you invest in a mutual fund, you purchase units of that fund.

Net worth Your total assets less your total liabilities.

Personal representative See Administrator.

Portfolio A collection of investments.

Power of attorney for property A legal document that gives another person full legal authority to handle property-related and/or financial matters. It can be general purpose or a restricted power to deal with financial matters.

Preapproved mortgage Preliminary approval by the lender of the borrower's application for a mortgage to a certain maximum amount and rate.

Prepayment charge A fee that is charged by some lenders when the borrower prepays a mortgage.

Prenuptial agreement A contract agreed to by a couple prior to marriage that defines rights upon death or divorce.

Principal The amount of money that was originally borrowed. It can also mean the amount originally placed in an investment.

Probate court A specialized court in each state that is set up to handle the management of wills, estates of persons dying without a will, and other related functions, such as guardianships.

Profit sharing plan A savings plan offered by companies to their employees in which a part of the profits is funneled into a tax-deferred retirement account.

Refinance To pay in full and discharge a mortgage and then arrange for a new mortgage with the same or a different lender.

Return The income earned and/or capital gain realized on an investment.

Risk The probability of loss in the future.

Roth IRA An IRA which is not tax deductible. All earnings are tax deferred and withdrawals are tax free.

Second mortgage A mortgage that is granted when there is already a mortgage registered against the property.

Security In the case of mortgages, property that is offered in order to back a loan.

Segregated funds A type of mutual fund that provides a guarantee of the capital invested over a period of time.

Separate property Property owned only by one marriage partner that is kept segregated from the couple's family property.

Settlor The person who establishes or creates a trust. Also called a grantor.

SEP-IRA A simplified employee pension individual retirement account. A plan that allows self-employed people to save money on a pre-tax basis. Such a plan is relatively easy to set up.

Standard & Poor's 500 Index An index that measures the performance of 500 large company U.S. Stocks that account for 80 percent of the total market value of all stocks traded in the United States.

Stocks Publicly traded shares in a company.

Tax credits Credits, like the earned income credit or Hope Scholarship credit, that reduce the amount of tax that you have to pay. A tax credit is more valuable than a tax deduction because the credit results in a reduction in tax owed rather than a reduction in taxable income.

Tax bracket The rate of income tax you pay. (See marginal tax rate.)

Tax shelter An investment that features significant tax savings, such as immediate deductions, credits, or income deferral.

Term The length of time a mortgage agreement covers.

Term deposit An investment product in which you deposit a fixed sum of money for a set period of time and are paid interest.

Term insurance Insurance that provides protection for a specific term or time period, with no investment component.

Testamentary trust A trust that is created by the deceased's will. Most wills include this provision for minors' interest.

Total debt to income ratio The percentage of your gross income that is needed to cover monthly payments for housing and all other debts and financing obligations. It should not exceed 38 percent of your gross monthly income.

Treasury bill Short-term government debt that does not pay interest but is sold at discount and matures at its full face value. Longer term loans to the government are Treasury notes (which mature in one to ten years) and Treasury bonds (which mature in more than ten years). The interest on these federal government bonds is not taxed by states but is federally taxable.

Trust agreement A document that sets out instructions for managing the property left in a living trust, including who is to receive each portion of the trust assets.

Trust A written and formal agreement that enables a person or institution to hold property and manage it for the benefit of the beneficiaries.

Trustee The person or institution that is given the authority to manage trust property according to the instructions contained in the trust agreement.

Umbrella coverage Insurance coverage over and above the liability limits of other specific insurance policies.

Underwriting An insurance company's process for evaluating a person's likelihood of filing a claim on a particular type of insurance.

Variable rate mortgage A mortgage with a rate of interest that changes as money market conditions change. The regular payments stay the same for a specific period. However, the amount applied toward the principal changes according to the movement of interest rates. Also referred to as an adjustable rate mortgage.

Seller take-back A mortgage in which the seller of a property provides some or all of the mortgage financing in order to sell the property.

Unified Gift to Minors Act (UGMA) Uniform state laws that allow irrevocable gifts to a minor by eliminating the need for a guardian or trustee.

Will A document that provides for the transfer of your estate to your beneficiaries and that appoints a guardian to care for any minor children.

· ·

DIRECTORY OF ORGANIZATIONS

Banking

Bankrate.com
11811 U.S. Highway 1
North Palm Beach, FL 33408
561-627-7330
webmaster@bankrate.com
<www.bankrate.com>

Credit Counseling Agencies (Not for Profit)

American Consumer Credit Counseling, Inc.
24 Crescent Street
Waltham, MA 02453
800-769-3571
help@consumercredit.com

Consolidated Credit Counseling Services, Inc.
1981 West Oakland Park Boulevard
Fort Lauderdale, FL 33311
800-SAVE-ME-2 (800-728-3632)
email@debtfree.org
<www.debtfree.org>

Consumer Credit Counseling Service
800-338-CCCS (800-338-2227)
(To find the location of the office nearest you.)
<www.credit.org>

National Foundation for Consumer Credit
8611 Second Avenue
Silver Spring, MD 20910
800-388-2227
questions@nfcc.org
<www.nfcc.org>

Credit Bureaus

Equifax, Inc.
P.O. Box 740241
Atlanta, GA 30374
800-685-1111
customer.care@equifax.com
<www.equifax.com>

Experian Information Solutions, Inc.
P.O. Box 2104
Allen, TX 75013
800-682-7654
<www.experian.com>

Trans Union LLC
Consumer Disclosure Center
P.O. Box 390
Springfield PA 19064
316-634-8440

Education

College Board
45 Columbus Avenue
New York NY 10023-6992
212-713-8000
<www.collegeboard.com>

Sallie Mae
11600 Sallie Mae Drive
Reston, VA 20193
800-239-4269
<www.salliemae.com>

Financial Organizations

American Institute of Certified Public Accountants
Personal Financial Planning Division
1211 Avenue of the Americas
New York, NY 10036
800-862-4272
<www.aicpa.org>

Institute of Certified Financial Planners
3801 East Florida Avenue
Suite 708
Denver, CO 80210
800-282-PLAN (800-282-7526)
membership@fpanet.org
<www.icfp.org>
<www.fpanet.org>

National Association of Personal Financial Advisers (NAPFA)
(fee-only planners)
355 West Dundee Road
Buffalo Grove, IL 60089
888-FEE ONLY (888-333-6659)
info@napfa.org

Society of Financial Service Professionals (insurance agents)
270 South Bryn Mawr Avenue
Bryn Mawr, PA 19010-2195
610-526-2500
Custserv@financialpro.org
<www.financialpro.org>

Government and Consumer Agencies

Consumer Federation of America
1424 16th Street
Washington, DC 20036
202-387-6121
<www.consumerfed.org>

Consumer Information Center (CIC)
Pueblo, CO 81009
888-8-PUEBLO (888-878-3256)
catalog.pueblo@gsa.gov
<www.pueblo.gsa.gov

Department of Public Debt
Department of Treasury
Consumer Service
Parkersburg, WV 26106-2186
877-811-SAVE (877-811-7283)
<www.publicdebt.treas.gov>

Federal Deposit Insurance Corporation
550 Seventeenth Street NW
Washington, DC 20429-9990
202-393-8400
Insurance@fdic.gov
<www.fdic.gov>

Federal Trade Commission
CRC-240
Washington, DC 20580
877-FTC-HELP (877-382-4357)

Internal Revenue Service
(Call local office as listed in your phone book.)
<www.irs.gov>

National Association of Security Dealers
1735 K Street NW
Washington, DC 20006-1500
301-596-6500)
<www.nasd.com>

National Endowment for Financial Education
5299 DTC Boulevard, Suite 1300
Englewood, CA 80111-3334
303-741-6333
eas@nefe.org
<www.nefe.org>

Securities and Exchange Commission
450 Fifth Street NW
Washington, DC 20549
800-732-0330
help@sec.gov
<www.sec.gov>

Social Security Administration
6401 Security Boulevard
Room 4-C-5 Annex
Baltimore, MD 21235-6401
<www.ssa.gov>

Insurance

Ameritas Acacia Companies
5900 O Street
P.O. Box 81889
Lincoln, NE 68501-1889

Insurance Information Network
110 Williams Street
New York, NY 10038
212-669-9200
consumer@iii.org
<www.iii.org>

Master Quote of America, Inc.
21 North LaSalle Street
Chicago, IL 60601
800-337-5433
masterquote@masterquote.com
<www.MasterQuote.com>

Quotesmith.com
8205 South Cass Avenue, Suite 102
Darien, IL 60561
800-556-9393
customercare@quotesmith.com
<www.quotesmith.com>

USAA
9800 Fredericksburg Road
San Antonio, TX 78288
800-531-8000
<www.usaa.com>

Investing

American Association of Individual Investors
625 North Michigan Avenue
Chicago, IL 60611
800-428-2244
members@aaii.com
<www.aaii.com>

ICI Investor Awareness Campaign
P.O. Box 27850
Washington, DC 20038-7850

Investment Company Institute (ICI)
1401 H Street
Washington, DC 20005
202-326-5800
<www.ici.org>

Morningstar, Inc.
225 West Wacker Avenue
Chicago, IL 60606
800-735-0700
productsupport@morningstar.com
<www.Morningstar.com>

Mutual Fund Education Alliance
1900 Erie Street, Suite 120
Kansas City, MO 64116
816-471-1454
<www.mfea.com>

Vanguard Group, Inc.
P.O. Box 709
Valley Forge, PA 19482-0709
800-871-3879
online@vanguard.com
<www.vanguard.com>

Real Estate and Mortgages

Fannie Mae Consumer Education Group
3900 Wisconsin Avenue
Washington, DC 20016-2899
800-688-4663
fmfwebmaster@fanniemaefoundation.org

Retirement

American Association of Retired Persons
601 E Street NW
Washington, DC 20049
800-424-3410
member@aarp.org
<www.aarp.org>

WEB SITE DIRECTORY

Banking

<www.bankrate.com>
Provides up-to-date interest rate data as well as general information on credit cards, bank rates, mortgages, and auto loans.

Credit Counseling

<www.consumercredit.com>
The Web site of American Consumer Credit Counseling, Inc. Includes helpful information on debt consolidation and credit counseling.

<www.credit.org>
The Web site of the Consumer Credit Counseling Service. Features numerous articles on a variety of topics related to credit and debt management.

<www.debtfree.org>
The Web site of Consolidated Credit Counseling Services, Inc. Features a debt calculator, a debt quiz, and other tools to help you to decide if you're headed for financial trouble.

<www.nfcc.org>
The Web site of the National Foundation for Credit Counseling. Features budget calculators and information on managing credit and debt.

Credit Bureaus

<www.equifax.com>
The Web site of Equifax, Inc., one of the country's largest credit bureaus. You can order a copy of your own credit report from the site.

<www.experian.com>
The Web site of Experian Consumer Assistance, another major credit bureau. The site features an interesting article on Internet fraud.

<www.tuc.com>
The Web site of Trans Union LLC, another major credit bureau. You can order a copy of your own credit report from the site.

Education

<www.collegeboard.com>
The Web site for the College Board. Features online registration for SAT tests, help with essay preparation, and other topics of interest to students and their parents.

<www.salliemae.com>
The Web site for Sallie Mae. Offers information on loans, grants, and other topics of interest to students and their parents.

<www.savingforcollege.com>
Features information on prepaid tuition plans and includes links to other helpful education-related Web sites.

Financial Planning (General)

<www.financenter.com>
A Web site packed with useful financial calculators.

<www.moneycentral.com>
MSN's money Web site. Topics covered include basic money management, insurance, mortgages, education, retirement, estate planning, market news and data, financial tools, and more.

<www.smartmoney.com>
The online counterpart to *Smart Money* magazine. Packed with useful tools, articles, and other bells and whistles.

<www.quicken.com>
The Web site of the manufacturers of the highly popular Quicken money management software program. Features information on basic money management, insurance, mortgages, education, retirement, estate planning, market news and data, financial tools, and more.

<www.yahoo.com>
Yahoo! is a great starting point for links to sites focusing on such topics as basic money management, insurance, mortgages, education, retirement, estate planning, market news and data, financial tools, and more.

Financial Planning Organizations

<www.aicpa.org>
The Web site of the American Institute of Certified Public Accountants. Includes useful tax-related information.

<www.financialpro.org>
The Web site of the Society of Financial Service Professionals (formerly the American Society of CLU & ChFC), a group representing insurance agents. Includes helpful information on a variety of insurance-related topics.

<www.fpanet.org>
The Web site of the Institute of Certified Financial Planners. Includes useful information about the profession.

<www.napfa.org>
The Web site of the National Association of Personal Financial Advisors (NAPFA), a group representing fee-only planners. Includes helpful tips on hiring a fee-only planner.

Government and Consumer Agencies

<www.consumerfed.org>
The Web site of the Consumer Federation of America. Includes links to various consumer education-related sites.

<www.fdic.gov>
The Web site of the Federal Deposit Insurance Corporation. Features statistics about banking, an educational Web site for kids, and information on banks in your area.

<www.ftc.gov>
The Federal Trade Commission's Web site. Features useful information on topics related to consumer protection.

<www.irs.gov>
The Web site of the Internal Revenue Service. A surprisingly friendly and easy to use site that features every IRS form or publication you could ever want!

<www.nasd.com>
The Web site of the National Association of Security Dealers. Provides market statistics and information about security-related regulations, dispute resolution, and the basics of savings and investing.

<www.nefe.org>
The Web site of the National Endowment for Financial Education. Features information on financial education-related topics for children and teenagers.

<www.publicdebt.treas.gov>
The Web site of the Department of Public Debt. Contains answers to common questions about interest rates, buying and cashing savings bonds, and taxes.

<www.pueblo.gsa.gov>
The Web site of the Consumer Information Center (CIC). Features text versions of hundreds of consumer publications. See the "Money" section for an extensive list of brochures on topics related to money management and retirement planning.

<www.sec.gov>
The Web site of the Securities and Exchange Commission. Features information on investor education and assistance, as well as a mutual fund cost calculator.

<www.ssa.gov>
The Web site of the Social Security Administration. Allows you to request a copy of your personal earnings and benefits estimate.

Insurance

<www.ameritas.com>
The Web site of the Ameritas Acacia Companies—a group of insurance companies. Contains detailed information on the company's products and services.

<www.instantquote.com>
Allows you to compare quotes on life insurance after filling in an online form. Also features a detailed glossary of insurance terms.

<www.iii.org>
The Insurance Information Network's Web site. Contains detailed information on various types of property insurance—home, auto, and so on.

<www.masterquote.com>
Provides quotes on medical, disability, and life insurance.

<www.quotesmith.com>
Allows you to obtain quotes on practically every conceivable type of insurance.

<www.selectquote.com>
Excellent source of information and quotes on life insurance.

<www.ussa.com>
The Web site for USAA, a company that provides insurance coverage to military families. Contains detailed information on USAA products and services.

Investment

<www.aaii.com>
The Web site of the American Association of Individual Investors. Features investment information and useful online tools.

<www.disclosure.com>
Features information from the Securities and Exchange Commission. Allows you to obtain financial statements for certain companies.

<www.ici.org>
The Web site of the Investment Company Institute—a trade association that provides data and educational information on mutual funds.

<www.investoreducation.org>
The Web site of the Alliance for Investor Education—the consumer education association made up of a consortium of financial industry groups and associations, including the American Stock Exchange. Packed with useful information on various aspects of investing.

<www.investoreducation.org>
The Web site of the Alliance for Investor Educator. Contains valuable advice on avoiding investment scams.

<www.marketplayer.com>
A site that promises to provide "real-life financial training to the individual investor who wants to learn how to make money in the market."

<www.mfea.com>
The Web site of the Mutual Fund Education Alliance. Contains useful advice on choosing mutual funds for your portfolio.

<www.money.com>
The Web site of the magazine of the same name. Features articles, columns, tools, and much more.

<www.morningstar.com>
Features investment news, investment tools, and detailed analyses of the investment style and performance of various mutual funds. The "portfolio Xray" feature allows you to analyze your portfolio and identify potential pitfalls in your current investment strategy.

<www.motleyfool.com>
A fun Web site that seeks to arm investors with the facts they need to make informed investment decisions without boring them to death along the way.

<www.schwab.com>
The Charles Schwab Web site. Offers detailed information on the company's products and services, as well as investing in general.

<www.vanguard.com>
Features detailed information on various aspects on investing. (There's even an "online university" on the site.)

Money Web Sites for Children and Teens

<www.2020green.com>
A Web site that's designed to teach kids the basics about the world of finance: borrowing, spending, investing, and more.

<www.allowancenet.com>
An online allowance-tracking system for parents and kids.

<www.kidsbank.com>
A fun site that teaches kids about money. The brainchild of the Sovereign Bank.

<www.mainxchange.com>
Home to a highly popular stock market simulation game.

<www.younginvestor.com/gameroom.shtml>
Features brainteasers, a stock market game, puzzles, and more.

Parenting

<www.babyzone.com>
A parenting Web site that focuses on pregnancy and parenting.

<www.babycenter.com>
A parenting Web site that focuses on pregnancy and the first three years of life.

<www.ctw.org>
The official Web site of the Children's Television Workshop.

<www.family.com>
Disney's official Web site for families.

<www.familyplay.com>
Women.com's parenting Web site.

<www.having-a-baby.com>
Official Web site of parenting author Ann Douglas.

<www.interactiveparent.com>
A network of parenting Web sites.

<www.iparenting.com>
A network of parenting Web sites.

<www.momsonline.com>
The Oprah-affiliated parenting Web site.

<www.parenthoodweb.com>
A health-oriented Web site devoted to pregnancy and parenting.

<www.parentsoup.com>
An iVillage Web site devoted to parenting.

<www.parentsplace.com>
A second iVillage Web site devoted to parenting.

Real Estate and Mortgages

<www.1st-in-mortgage.com>
Features mortgage quotes, a glossary of mortgage terms, a mortgage guide, and more.

<www.1st-mortgage.com>
The AmTrust Mortgage Corporation's Web site. Offers detailed information on mortgages and can help you to track down a mortgage broker in your area.

<www.fanniemae.com>
The Fannie Mae Consumer Education Group's Web site. Allows you to view Fannie Mae property listings and provides detailed information on a variety of mortgage-related topics.

<www.homeadvisor.msn.com>
An excellent source of information on various aspects of home ownership.

<www.realtor.com>
The Web site of the National Association of REALTORS®. Provides detailed information on buying and selling real estate, as well as tools that will allow you to search for a home or a REALTOR® in your area, to calculate your ability to afford a home, and more.

Retirement

<www.aarp.org>
The Web site of the American Association of Retired Persons. Contains useful information on retirement planning.

RECOMMENDED READINGS

Books

Daugherty, Greg, *The Consumer Reports Mutual Fund Book.* Yonkers, New York: Consumer Report Books, 1994.

Douglas, Ann, and John R. Sussman, M.D., *The Unofficial Guide to Having a Baby.* New York: IDG Books, 1999.

Estess, Patricia Schiff, *Money Advice for a Successful Remarriage.* iUniverse.com, 2001.

Lewin, Elizabeth S., *Your Personal Financial Fitness Program,* New York: Facts on File, 1997.

Lewin, Elizabeth S., Ryan, Bernard, Jr., *Simple Ways to Make Your Kids Dollar-Smart,* New York: Walker & Co., 1994.

Morris, Kenneth M., Siegel, Alan M., Morris, Virginia B., *The Wall Street Journal Guide to Planning Your Financial Future.* New York: The Wall Street Journal, Fireside Press, Inc., 1998.

Quinn, Jane Bryant, *Making the Most of Your Money.* New York: Simon & Schuster, 1997.

Reader's Digest Association. *The Complete Book of Money Secrets.* Pleasantville, NY, The Reader's Digest Association, Inc., 1999.

Tyson, Eric, MBA, *Personal Finance for Dummies,* IDG Books Worldwide, Foster City, California, 1999.

Magazines and Online Publications

Bottom Line Personal: A concise, information-packed newsletter on money, credit, investments, and other topics related to family finance. 800-633-9970. There's also an online version of the publication: <www.bottomlinepersonal .com>

Money: An excellent source of information on investing and other personal finance topics. 800-274-5611. Again, there's an online version of the publication: <www.money.com>

Some Articles You Might Want to Track Down

Bodnar, Janet, "What to Tell the Kids," *Kiplinger,* February 2000. 87-92.

LaPlante, Clare, "10 Great Money Moves for the New Millennium, *Your Money,* October/November 1999. 76-80.

Lowry, Katharine, "Teaching Your Kid about Money, *USAA Magazine,* April, 1999. 18-21.

Woolley, Suzanne, Caplin, Joan, Pachetti, Wang, Penelope, Haggin, Lesslie, "4 Goals and Strategies," *Money,* April, 2000. 76-99.

INDEX